Never Hitchhike on the Road Less Travelled

(Bad, bad, bad idea!)

Hilarious travel tips and misadventures on the weird and winding road taken by...

WILLIAM THOMAS

Author of the runaway bestseller
The Dog Rules (Damn Near Everything!)

KEY PORTER BOOKS

National Library of Canada Cataloguing in Publication

Thomas, William J., 1946-
    Never hitchhike on the road less travelled / William J. Thomas.
ISBN 1-55263-477-9
    1. Travel. I. Title.
PN6231.T7T48 2002   910   C2002-903847-2

THE CANADA COUNCIL | LE CONSEIL DES ARTS
FOR THE ARTS | DU CANADA
SINCE 1957 | DEPUIS 1957

ONTARIO ARTS COUNCIL
CONSEIL DES ARTS DE L'ONTARIO

The publisher gratefully acknowledges the support of the Canada Council for the Arts and the Ontario Arts Council for its publishing program.

We acknowledge the financial support of the Government of Canada through the Book Publishing Industry Development Program (BPIDP) for our publishing activities.

Key Porter Books Limited
70 The Esplanade
Toronto, Ontario
Canada M5E 1R2

www.keyporter.com

Design: Jack Steiner
Electronic formatting: Beth Crane, Heidy Lawrance Associates

Printed and bound in Canada

02 03 04 05 06 07 6 5 4 3 2 1

For Monica Rose
—a tourist,
a traveller,
but above all, a real trooper

Two roads diverged into a cloverleaf,
Hitchhiking, I could not travel both.
So I took the one of peace, of relief,
A long, winding road of scrub brush and heath.
Two days later, I'm peeing in the same undergrowth.
Never hitchhike on the road less travelled.
It's a bad, bad, bad idea.

— Sincerest apologies to Robert Frost

Also by William Thomas

The Dog Rules (Damn Near Everything!)
Margaret and Me
Malcolm and Me
Guys — Not Real Bright and Damn Proud of It
Hey! Is That Guy Dead or Is He the Skip?
The Tabloid Zone: Dancing with the Four-Armed Man

Contents

Introduction

Why I Leave the House with Luggage in Hand

> *I'm the type of guy that likes to roam around.*
> —"The Wanderer," Dion and the Belmonts

Everyone has a hero, and mine is Harry Chapin. When I was in my twenties, the songs of Harry Chapin, which were really travelogues of the mind, took me places and introduced me to characters thousands of miles beyond my headphones. Then Harry died, so awfully young, and I began travelling through Europe by backpack rather than round and round on his big black vinyl discs.

For a while, I was a television writer. Coming off the success of scripting the film *Breaking All the Rules: The Story of Trivial Pursuit* for CBC, I began work on a movie about Reuben Ship, a great and unheralded Canadian comedy writer who first got steam-rolled by Joseph McCarthy in the United States and was then hung out to dry by our government and the CBC once he got home to Canada. I did the research and, remembering why I got into writing—you can do it anywhere in the world—I took off to write the script on a quiet beach in the Bahamas.

In 1988 Harbour Island was a little known, lovely sand spit, five minutes by motorboat from the island of Eleuthera. No tourists and few travellers went to Harbour Island because of its inconvenient location.

I eventually rented a simple, weather-beaten cottage that stood on stilts at the top of a footpath that snaked its way through a tropical tangle down to Pink Sands beach. There, over a period of three months, I worked diligently every morning, writing a very bad script. (Travel tip to writers: okay, so you can't do it anywhere in the world.)

But before I found the cottage, just to get the lay of the land, I rented a room at the Sunset Inn, a draughty, ramshackle shell that was already in a state of disrepair on the day of its not-so-grand opening.

One afternoon, I went to a hole-in-the-wall café near Dunmore Town, on the beach between the dock that greets visitors off the boat ferry from Eleuthera and a grungy wharf where the local fishermen unload their tuna and grouper, cleaning and selling it on the spot. As I looked around, Wilmer Gold seemed to materialize out of nowhere, like a shadowy Elmore Leonard character.

I hadn't seen him when I walked into the place, a breezy Bahamian family kitchen with a few tables and chairs and a square hole in the wall through which plates of food were passed in from the cooking hutch outside. He must have been in the washroom, but now he was just there, sitting in the corner, doing a messy job of eating a juicy hamburger, from which the slice of tomato kept trying to escape. I sat down next to him because, although there was another table, the only other chair was beside his.

"Gold," he said, "from Vancouver Island." He offered a bony, spotted hand.

"Thomas . . . from Wainfleet," I countered, and setting a Styrofoam cup of thick coffee on the table, I shook his hand.

"Oh, it doesn't matter," he said, doing battle once more with his burger. He dismissed Wainfleet with such an air of casualness, I could only assume he'd been there.

There followed a silence that was awkward, but apparently only on my part.

"So how you doing?" I asked.

"What?" And he turned an ear to me that contained a turn-of-the-century hearing aid, the size of which was such that I'm certain it picked up ship-to-shore transmissions and radio talk shows from Miami.

I said, "I said, 'how are you doing?'"

"Oh," he said, with that same sort of ambivalent air, "I never know." And with that, he went back at the hamburger as the tomato hit the tabletop.

Gold was a timeworn vision of jauntiness and spunk. Gold was old. He wore a baby-blue leisure suit over a blazing blue Hawaiian shirt, white sneakers, and a white-brimmed gold hat. A leather-encased Rolleiflex camera dangled loosely from his neck. His white moustache was closely clipped, and his white hair neatly combed back under the brim of his hat. His eyes danced brightly when he talked, languishing softly in liquid pools when he didn't. He was slightly stooped, so that even when he spoke in the negative, he seemed to be bobbing a bit, nodding in agreement.

"Where you coming from?" I asked, and then repeated the question after a second showing of the hearing aid, a piece surely destined for the Smithsonian.

"Over there," he yelled, like I was the deaf one, and pointed across the bay to the island of Eleuthera, a three-dollar water taxi away.

The hamburger and the hearing aid slowed the current of our conversation to the point that I got up and left, and I doubted that he noticed. But then, as I passed the open window, I heard him say: "Carry on, now. Carry on."

Later that day, I discovered that Gold and I were renting adjacent rooms at the Sunset Inn; the walls being so thin, we were technically roommates.

Out on the porch that evening, he brought me a book he'd written entitled *Logging As It Was*, published in 1983. He was very proud of this book, and had every reason to be. It was a superbly photographed history of the logging industry on Vancouver Island. A professional photographer all his life, he had taken most of the pictures.

Sitting directly across from me, where he could read my lips and I his eyes, he told me his life story. Born on a farm in Alberta, he moved with his family to "that godforsaken place called Edmonton," and then on to the red fir logging town of Youbou, British Columbia. He still lived in the log house he helped build on Cowichan Lake. His photographs have appeared in magazines such as *Look*, *Life*, *Time*, and *Maclean's*. The T. Eaton Company once crisscrossed Canada with an exhibition of Gold's life work.

As he talked, he fondly fingered the 250-page chronicle, the crowning achievement of his life. He travels with great passion, and has selectively photographed all seven continents. His wife died six years ago, but he still travels, and passionately, but alone.

He'd come to Eleuthera on the overnight mail freighter out of Nassau. I'd heard of this treacherous tub, but nobody I'd met on the island had the nerve to take it. In a few days, when the moment moved him, he'd take a boat over to Spanish Wells, and then: "Oh . . . I never know."

Gold tramped around the world for two and three months every winter, cheaply and sporadically, listening to the waves and the whims of his soul for destination and direction. He had worked the shutter of his Rolleiflex from the Coral Sea to Kathmandu, pausing long enough to live a little of the local life and record it on film. He'd had an American tourist stagger into his tent in Kenya, covered in blood, speared for having taken a photograph of a Masai warrior without permission. He'd seen sacred bulls eating out of food stalls in the markets of Calcutta, while all around them people went without. A few years before, he had been robbed by two thugs on a desolate side street in Samoa.

"I trust everybody," he said. "Yes . . . yes, it does get me into trouble sometimes, but that's the way I am."

At the bar that night, I asked Gold two questions: if he would tell me his age and if he wanted a drink. He said no to both questions. As I slowly reduced a glass of Scotch to a mere mound of crushed ice, I pushed the issue of age.

"Guess," he said, and his eyes brightened to the challenge. "No," he said, nodding, to the year 1904, my first venture at his year of birth. I thought I'd insulted him, so I started guessing higher. "No," he said, "wrong way." Then I went down from 1904 until he stopped me at 1893.

Good god, the man was ninety-five years of age. Gold was not old; he was an authentic antique! But a fine and functional antique, indeed.

We fell silent as we watched the Calgary Olympics coverage on a bad black-and-white Bahamian television, as Jim McKay went on about "going for the gold" and "catching the brass ring," in the process making modern-day millionaire heroes out of teenagers with good muscle memory.

All the while, I stood beside a man who, at ninety-five years of age, still had the courage and tenacity to venture out in the world alone, so as to know it a little better. And maybe himself, as well.

Jack London once said something about preferring to die in a fiery collision, as a meteorite speeding through space, than to turn slowly into dust from disuse. Jack London would be proud of Ol' Gold.

Later that night, when I went to borrow a razor blade from Gold, a mickey of Dewar's fell out of his suitcase. Now I, too, was proud of Ol' Gold. Ninety-five and a nipper!

And that's when I knew that when I grew up I wanted to be as good as Gold—old but still curious, slowed but not stopped, made vulnerable by age but still vital. Looking at Gold, I knew that no matter what your age, when you walk the paths of a foreign land, your mind is never more open. And tolerance follows you home.

Travelling—lightly and far afield, with an alert, inquisitive air—turns the time you spend back at home into special moments of respite. Travel keeps home life from becoming routine and mundane. Travel turns your house into a hospice, a base camp for rest and relaxation. It's a most natural contradiction: the only thing I enjoy as much as getting away is getting back home again.

Your home is truly the castle you return to, after a personal campaign of exploration. In Gold I'd met a true crusader. A role model with a leather-beaten Rolleiflex camera hanging around his neck, a talisman of the true traveller he was.

I travel, therefore I am . . . alive, and moving, and miles away. Wilmer Gold, I'm glad I met you. I will carry on, now. I will.

A child on a farm sees a plane fly by overhead and dreams of a faraway place. A traveler on the plane sees the farmhouse and dreams of home.
—Carl Burns

Part One

Early Bohemian Tramping

A tourist is often a guest;
a traveller is always on a quest.

Holland: Where the Beer Is Frothy and the Cash Is Cold

When you're tramping across countries and through big cities for extended periods of time, two resources need renewing: money and tranquility. In October 1973 Breda, a small medieval city at the bottom of the Netherlands, provided both.

I had taken a ferry from Harwich, England, to the Hook of Holland, and the crossing was so unusually violent my stomach hurt for days from vomiting. A horrible thing, seasickness. I sat for hours in the crowded cafeteria trying to convince myself I was not ill, as my sinking dizziness did an awkward dance with the erratic spasms of the ship. Then I bolted for the aft deck and exploded over the side. Only when I finished did I notice three more passengers at the rail, all trying to look nonchalant while tossing their breakfast overboard. I will spare you the details, but a bit of travel advice: if you must get into the queue to spew, the front of the line, upwind, is by far the best position. (I'm sure that little man with the white hanky hates me to this day!)

Rotterdam was overwhelming; its massive industrial piers and oil refineries dwarfing any character or soul the city might have. Amsterdam was schizophrenic: incredible art and obnoxious riff-raff in the streets, elegant gable canal houses and hookers posing for window shoppers. And the canals—romantic by night, filthy by day.

Like most young travellers, I stayed in a tiny room in a ginger-bread, clapboard hotel where the stairs were so narrow that

Cultural Misunderstanding

Scandinavian vacuum cleaner manufacturer Electrolux obviously didn't consult their American dealers before they ran a national magazine ad campaign with the slogan: "Nothing sucks like an Electrolux!"

anything larger than a backpack had to be pulleyed up from the street by rope. These hotels were hippie havens; the breakfast omelettes were fabulous, but I had a lot of trouble convincing the chef to leave the magic mushrooms out of mine.

Once the dishes were done, the restaurant area turned into an all-day impromptu music festival, marked by a blue haze of hash smoke that wafted well into the night. I spent all my nights in that creaky structure staring at the ceiling, certain that somebody would doze off while smoking dope and I'd have to rappel down the pulley and rope system in order to live.

So when I hitchhiked down the middle of Holland towards Belgium and discovered Breda, I was looking for rest and, although I didn't know it yet, the replenishment of resources.

Warning to hitchhikers travelling in Holland: the Dutch are friendly, and they will stop and give you a ride, but after a few miles that crossbar becomes, quite literally, a big pain in the ass.

Some places just feel right, and Breda, quiet and comfortable with castles, parks, and flower gardens, seemed like the Europe I'd set out to find. In my small hotel near the train station, everybody took breakfast in the downstairs bar, with complimentary beer served by a huge red-haired barmaid named Elsa.

In the evenings the place filled with locals, and the game at the bar was to tell, I'm guessing, dirty jokes to Elsa until she laughed so hard the floor shook. When Elsa laughed, her pigtails wigged straight out, and the roar that filled the room sounded like somebody was tickling the Jolly Green Giant. Any story that didn't make the glasses on the shelf rattle was just not a very good joke.

Elsa poured bowl-shaped glasses of the best beer I'd ever tasted: Oranjeboom Beer. She pulled a hard tap, as they say, with the foam spilling over into a stainless steel bowl. She used a wooden spatula to scoop the head off your glass, and once everybody had been served, Elsa drank the bowl of sudsy beer . . . and all at once, to a rousing round of cheers. Elsa never got drunk; she got a buzz-on at breakfast and then nurtured it for the rest of the day.

It was in this bizarre and beery atmosphere that patriotic fervour reared its ugly head. And thank God. Normally, in this part of the world, frantic nationalism is frowned upon. Many towns are still uncovering unexploded bombs as powerful reminders. But when the Dutch get their hands on a hero, the flag-waving that follows is of almost American proportions.

On October 20, 1973, Rudi Lubbers was the Dutch hero du jour. A hardworking heavyweight, Lubbers had punched his way to championship of the Netherlands and then Europe. And on this night all of Holland would turn on their television sets to watch Lubbers fight the greatest boxer that ever lived: Muhammad Ali. Ali had just beaten Ken Norton to get a rematch with Joe Frazier. Lubbers was just a bit of fun in between. For Ali it was a light workout, and the heavy bag was stuffed with money. For Lubbers and his compatriots it was the greatest fight in the history of the sport in Holland. Live from Jakarta, the fight was all the Dutch could talk about for the entire week.

I used to be a boxing buff before the sport allowed ear eating and, along with every other sports fan of the day, I knew what Ali would do to Rudi Lubbers. Every other sports fan except, of course, the ones in Holland. When I mentioned to a couple of guys at the bar that my sympathies went out to the Rudi Lubbers family, I was soundly shouted down. The argument got a little heated until one guy slammed his fist down on the bar and it was full of cash.

Normally I prefer to rise to the occasion and not the bait, but a little voice in the back of my head said, "They started it, stupid." So I went upstairs and counted my money. On the budget I was maintaining, I could last another six months in Europe. If I doubled my money, I could stay a year. I set aside enough for two more months of travel, kissed my open plane ticket home for good luck, and reasoned that the worst that could happen was I'd surprise my mother at Christmas.

I went back to the bar and took the loud guy's bet, along with everybody else's. Elsa, laughing and quaffing, put the pile of cash and traveller's cheques in the fridge.

It was a weird night of television. Every time a news break came on, Nixon had fired another attorney general for being involved with something the president abhorred—ethics. The Dutch understood all this politics about as well as I understood the announcer.

The fight was not pleasant for Rudi and me. The worse he got beat up, the nastier the looks got towards the Canadian in the corner. What few punches the Dutchman landed triggered incredible applause. Then Ali would hit him with a calculated flurry of jabs, and all eyes at the bar would shift from the television set to the fridge. Ali was kind to Lubbers, out-pointing him by something like 40 to 2 and letting him stay on his feet for the full twelve rounds. By the late rounds, it looked like Ali would let Lubbers live. Whether the large and exuberant boys at the bar would grant this upstart Canadian a similar reprieve was somewhat in doubt.

In the end, the bettors were actually fairly gracious in defeat. (It helped that I bought rounds, of course, until the bar closed.) Each man alone had not lost a whole lot, but together, their losses stretched my travels for months beyond my previous means. I checked out early the next morning with a mittful of cold cash, fresh from the fridge.

Everybody knows of Muhammad Ali, and few sports fans remember Rudi Lubbers. But Rudi Lubbers was very good to me.

Oh Sure, I Was Once a French Chef

Andorra in the '70s was a tiny but breathtaking mountainous country of grassy meadows and icy lakes. Its capital, and only city, Andorra la Vella, was and is the highest in Europe, at one thousand metres. Andorra remains, technically, the last feuded protectorate in the world. Sitting high in the rugged Pyrenees, a co-principality governed by both Spain and France, Andorra is a cheap date. To this day, the governance agreement dictates that in even-numbered years the Spanish bishop receives 12 francs, plus six hams, six chickens, and six rounds of cheese. On the odd years the French prince receives a cash tribute of 960 pesetas. While the bishop gets fat, the prince gets screwed; but, hey, a deal's a deal.

Then, Andorra was slow and quiet, all rushing rivers and grassy pastures, stone houses and narrow wooded paths with herds of shaggy wild horses trotting through villages. Once in a while, the skinned carcass of a large animal would startle you as it disappeared under a wooden bridge, jettisoned from the tanning factory upstream. At some point, though, as in many principalities, numbered bank accounts begat the condos, and duty-free shopping brought highways congested by bargain hunters. Where once it was a kingdom of wild flowers and quaint villages, Andorra is now known as "The Supermarket in the Sky."

But back when I first visited in 1973, it was a haven for adventurous skiers with little money, the poor man's Alps.

When I banged on the door of the Hotel Andorra le Vielle to ask for a room, an old and odd man answered the door and spoke to me in a language that sounded French, utilized some Spanish words, but could only be called gibberish. It was just after lunch, and he was dead drunk. He mumbled something about being

DO NOT PASS

Savvy Traveller

A Paris hotel quoted TV producer and hotelier Merv Griffin a price of $90 per suit to do his dry cleaning. Annoyed, Griffin donated the garments to a local mission thrift shop. After waiting for the suits to be cleaned and set out for sale, he bought them back at $2 apiece.

closed, but then offered me a seat when he saw me wrestling the pack off my back. Unsteadily, he disappeared through the door behind a tiny booth that was the front desk.

I sat there for a very long time, thinking he was fixing me a room. I had read all of Frommer's section on Andorra when I heard snoring coming from down the hall. I tiptoed through the door to see the old man passed out on a cot in a dark room with the door open. He was wearing a silly white nightcap with a tassel.

Naturally I took the room at the far end of the hall, where there was less noise.

In the morning the old man looked quite rested and almost suave, an aging silver-haired Parisian, exhausted after another season of running this inn alone (his wife having left him because of his "little problem"). The skiers were all gone and the hotel was closed, he said, as diplomatically as possible. I was welcome to fix myself something in the kitchen before I left.

He brewed coffee at the bar, and I went through the swinging doors of the simple little restaurant to the kitchen, where I made two chicken salad sandwiches. He seemed amused that I thought to make him something to eat, so he opened a bottle of red wine, and we had lunch. The wine fired his spirits, and pretty soon his hands were flying around like those of a mad concert conductor, and his speech became louder and more difficult to follow.

The second bottle of wine he drank himself, and the coffee he brought to the table had so much brandy in it I thought he might accidentally set himself on fire with the sparks from his Galois cigarette. By the time I packed and left, he was face down on the table, asleep. I was unable to find the key to lock the door behind me.

I walked all over town for hours, but the small hotels were closed for the season, and the bigger ones were too expensive. Finding myself back in front of the Hotel Andorra le Vielle, I tested the door. It was still open. I went in, dropped my pack, and went into the kitchen, where the hotel keeper was still hunched over the table. I slammed my hand down on the bar to see if he was dead. He woke up, looked around, slowly focused in on me, and then launched into some tirade about his ex-wife. It was as if I'd never left. So I stayed.

I cleared the dishes, he opened a bottle of red wine, and I went into the kitchen and made spaghetti Bolognese. I managed to get three glasses of wine out of the next three bottles. He passed out on the table again, I did the dishes and went to bed.

On the second day, two backpacking couples arrived at the hotel, and I put them in rooms next to mine. When I introduced them to our host, I found out his name was Serge. It was great. Every morning Serge would be sober and would tell us that the hotel was unfortunately closed. Then I'd make lunch for six, and he'd pass out after a rousing but sad recounting of his life story. After the two couples and I went into the hills for the afternoon, we'd return to the hotel in early evening and wake up Serge. Then I'd make dinner, and we'd party until the innkeeper blacked out. While the others did the dishes, I would walk Serge down to his room. Then we'd all have brandy and go to bed. In the middle of the night, I was occasionally wakened by Serge shouting or sometimes crying in his sleep.

And that became our routine for about a week. It was like this weird commune of travellers, fuelled by wine and led by a man nobody understood. It prepared me for life under Jean Chrétien.

Tourists Too Stupid to Travel

One of the first questions American tourists ask upon crossing the border into Canada is: "Where are the Indians?" Answer: Cleveland.

The hotel kitchen was well stocked and roomy, and I went from spaghetti to roast chicken to stuffed trout to a small leg of lamb done on a rotisserie oven. But by week's end I was running out of recipes. I wanted to see Barcelona and make my way down to Málaga before it got too hot in the south of Spain.

I told Serge I was leaving. The two couples had checked out the day before. The old man didn't say anything, just shuffled around pretending to make coffee. But by the time I'd packed, changed my bed, and placed a small pile of money behind the bar (which he tried to refuse with a wave of his hand), his thirty-year-old daughter, a shopkeeper across town, had shown up. In English, she told me I could stay as long as I wanted. Her father enjoyed my cooking, she said.

I think he liked it because it was soft. He used it as a pillow.

It was an awkward goodbye. I walked south out of town towards the highway to Barcelona, trying not to notice the construction cranes that signalled the end of a once serene mountain city.

"A French chef!" I thought this would look great on my resumé. As long as the interviewer was intoxicated, and nobody followed up by calling Serge.

The Straight Tower of Pisa

Just as Cleveland is known as "The Mistake by the Lake," the name Pisa is recognized worldwide as a big error in engineering.

Pisa, of course, is famous for its leaning tower, but also leads the world in tackiness. For an entire mile before you get to the tower, both sides of the road are lined with junk shops selling every imaginable cheap souvenir featuring the tower, the Pope, and Christ. No doubt by now they're hawking "Jean Paul II, the Bobblehead."

When structural engineers determined the tower on the Campo del Miracoli was tilting too much, about four metres off-kilter, measuring from top to bottom, they undertook an extensive project to fortify the structure so it would continue to lean at its present angle, but no more. It was a big job, and they closed the tower to tourists for five years. In the spring of 1996, when I visited the spot, it was all fenced off, but you could still pose in front of it so that it looked like the tower was about to fall on top of your head. Which is what everybody was doing when an American woman noticed the construction site and said, "Hey, honey, what are they doing to the tower?"

To which the brightly dressed man next to her replied, "Oh, didn't you hear? They're gonna straighten it up."

Americans abroad. Who needs comedy clubs in Europe when American tourists are so free with their opinions?

The Straight Tower of Pisa—what a unique attraction that'll be.

Cutting It in Burgundy

Streets flooded. Please advise.
—Robert Benchley, in a telegram to a friend after arriving in Venice

Confucius said a journey of a thousand miles begins with a single step, but mine began with two white lies.

In 1978 I had a real job and was hating every minute of it. And each time I threatened to quit they gave me a bigger car. My (former) wife said go, just go and do what you really want to do. We both knew that was writing. So, with nothing published other than a letter to the editor, I telephoned the *Wine Press* magazine in Toronto and told them I was a writer.

"That's great," said the editor, bored.

"And I want to go to Burgundy and work the great *vendange* and write a feature for your magazine," I said.

"That's great," he said, with more enthusiasm, but it may have been towards his lunch. He was chewing while he talked to me.

"So you'll send me to France, and we'll get things done," I said, going for the closer. The job I'd just quit was in sales.

"No, no," he chortled. I wasn't sure if he was laughing or choking on food. "No, I'm not sending you anywhere. But if you do the piece, mail it back to me and I'll have a look."

I'm sure he brushed off a dozen wannabe writers a week with this kind of apathy but not me. My status of writer now validated by an editor, I had a purpose and a plan. I called a man by the name of Michel Troubetzkoy at the French Trade Commission in Toronto.

"Yes, Monsieur Troubetzkoy," I said. "I'm a writer, and I have an assignment to go to Burgundy and do a travel feature on the *vendange*."

"Ziss is wonderful," he said. His excitement was real.

"Great," I said, "so I'll need a return ticket Toronto to Paris and . . ."

Cultural Misunderstanding

In 1963, the world watched the most beloved president of the United States, John F. Kennedy, use four historic words to define the line between East and West. That line, the Berlin Wall, was a massive barrier of concrete, barbed wire, and armed guards separating dictatorship from democracy. When Kennedy declared "Ich bin ein Berliner," he intended to tell Germany and the world that, as long as the Berlin Wall protected the western sector, he was, in spirit, one of them. A Berliner. And the free world went mad in their applause for this handsome and courageous leader and his personal assurance of their safety.

One problem: if you put "ein" before "Berliner" it no longer means "citizen of Berlin." "Ein Berliner" is actually a kind of soft turnover filled with jam.

So, as a tolerant and open-minded traveller, please forgive those guys way in the back in that plaza in West Berlin that day who, instead of applauding, turned to one another in disbelief and said, "Kennedy's a jelly donut?"

"No, no, I'm sorry but I cannot help you there. But if you go, here's the name of a winemaker in Beaune who will hire you."

And so began my quest for great wines and an honest living.

Toronto to Paris—who was I kidding? My wife dropped me off at the Peace Bridge at Fort Erie at 7:00 a.m. on a beautiful September day, and I hitchhiked to New York City. I arrived by 5:00 p.m. The trip was a breeze, except for the state trooper who picked me up on the throughway, only to scold me and drop me at the next exit, where it was legal to hitchhike. Just as I was about to get out, some lunatic in a souped-up station wagon blew by the clearly marked cop cruiser, and after a harrowing chase I got a dozen more miles down the road. And quickly, too.

Freddy Laker was in business then, and after I bought my $99 ticket at his Manhattan office, I boarded the shuttle out to Kennedy and from there flew Laker Airways to London. After a few days in London, I took the tube down to the last stop on the southern line, Elephant & Castle, and hitchhiked to Dover. I had planned, after crossing the English Channel, to take a train from Calais to Paris, but as it happened French railway workers were on strike, so I hitched that stretch, too.

I rode all the way to Paris with a batty English couple in a beat-up Bentley. They put me in the back seat between their ten-year-old twins, a boy and a girl, who were constantly trying to kill each other. After I took a couple of game pieces in the head and the girl poured pop on my backpack, the father, watching it all in the rear-view mirror, said, "It's quite all right, you can strike them if you like."

From Paris down to Lyons I was scrunched in the back of a Morris Mini with all the camping gear of a Swiss couple headed for Spain. The exhaust was so hot I burned the bottom of my right foot, and for the last hundred kilometres I assumed a kind of yoga position, holding my feet in my hands above the heat.

Arriving in Beaune, France, on October 2, 1978, I became one of many *vendangeurs*—workers of the fields—during this festive harvesting of the burgundy crop.

With Michel Troubetzkoy's encouraging words "Eeet wheel be fun" echoing in my ears, I plunged straight into the opening day of the *vendange*. Having been issued a school-bus-yellow raincoat and rubber boots too narrow for even a French foot, I rode in the back of the bus to the Clos des Mouches, a vineyard several kilometres southeast of Beaune. There, with a hundred or so other workers of all ages, I awaited the instruction of Jacques Lillien, the vineyard manager.

"Jackie," a large, jovial man with ruddy skin the colour of the local wine, was a fitting image for a field boss. He strode slowly through the masses, designating who would be cutters and who would be carriers for the day. I immediately decided to be a cutter. While I could see that cutting was going to be continuous, backbreaking labour, I knew I could handle the small pails the cutters filled as they crept along the rows with their pruning shears. And by volunteering to cut and pick, I would avoid the other alternative: carrying on one shoulder the huge thirty-five-kilogram cases filled from the pails to trucks usually parked fields away.

Very pleased with my quick thinking, I stood up as Jackie approached and, making cutting motions with my hands, I indicated my preference. Ignoring my hands, and noting my six-foot frame, he screamed "*Porter!*" and it was done. I was beat. It was sort of like having always wanted to be first-string quarter-back and at the opening practice the coach makes you second-string centre. I quickly looked over at the cases. They had gotten bigger.

I love the European system of no system at all. A North American would lay everything out precisely with charts, average times, numbered rows, etc. But the *vendange* is pleasant chaos. Cutters start down rows that other cutters are already occupying; carriers, who must work in pairs, get stranded alone; the number of rows a porter services are constantly in dispute by other carri-ers. And yet it gets done, quietly, almost smoothly, with that great French flare of not hurrying or trying too hard. There is a distinct feeling of gentleness in the way the grapes are lightly dropped into the pails, not thrown; in the way cases are carefully placed in the truck, not jammed; and in the brief handshakes and *"bonjours"* the workers have for one another as the day begins. Drop a stem with only five grapes on it, and it is sure to get picked up. All this I believe is reflected in the wine.

To carry is tough—painful actually. You spend a lot of time effortlessly emptying the small pails into the cases in answer to the cutters' calls of *"Panier!"*—the signal that their pails are full. You also spend some time talking to those around you and eating grapes. But when the case is filled and the truck is your destination, it's just you and thirty-five kilograms of grapes that seem to dig deeper into your shoulder with each step.

Normally, the man in the truck is there only to lift the case from your shoulder. With me, a new dimension was added to his job. He became, during my final fifty metres, a cheerleader—

urging me on, convincing me I could make it, and reminding me that no one had ever actually dropped a case. Each trip I completed was heralded as a victory. But as the cutters moved farther away from the trucks, the odds changed rapidly. I did a lot of juggling, and I made good use of the posts that normally hold up only the vines, but I'm proud to say I never dropped a case.

Somehow, I made it through to lunch, which began each day with the ritual of presenting every *vendangeur* with a bottle of real Burgundy. The wine I had looked forward to as a treat was now a necessity; the one-and-a-half-hour lunch that sounded extravagant was now not long enough.

The wine made for an easier afternoon. A general lifting of the spirits led to singing in various spots of the Clos des Mouche, the jokes became bawdier, and the laughter was noticeably louder. The morning was for work, the afternoon for work and fun—a pattern that held throughout the harvest.

At the end of the first day, all the *vendangeurs* were exhausted, even those who had been doing it for more than fifty years. Before leaving, I told Jackie that in lieu of money I wanted a new pair of shoulders, which he assured me would be on the next train from Paris. Since I had just hitchhiked there from Paris amid a national railway strike, his promise didn't make the outlook for tomorrow any brighter.

The *vendangeurs* assured me that the second day would be easier. It was not. I wore a leather pad on my carrying shoulder, as all porters do; however, as strong as these men are, they are not generally broad-shouldered. The pad did not cover my entire shoulder, which got badly bruised where it was exposed to the

Don't Fly Mongolia

The Uncharted-Skies Award goes to MIAT, Mongolia's one plane airline, which is building a reputation as the world's quirkiest air carrier. After one flight made three aborted attempts to land at Ulan Bator this summer, the pilot announced he was diverting to the Russian city of Irkutsk because of poor visibility. A French woman took out a simple map to look up the new destination, only to have the flight attendant ask to borrow it. After the plane had landed safely, the steward returned the map, saying, "Thank you very much. The pilot found it most useful."

case. I was sure everyone was wagering on whether I'd make it through the day.

It seemed to me more wine was consumed at lunch that day. It was, I think, the celebration of survival. Some of the students said they'd been too tired to eat last night, and one said he had gone straight to bed without getting undressed. As for me, I couldn't remember the last time I'd had thirteen hours of sleep.

The older men told stories of previous harvests, and then it was back to work. That is, for all but two of us. That day we had our first casualties of the *vendange*.

Ask Jackie how many workers he has, and he couldn't tell you. But he sure knows when someone is missing. I watched him off in the distance, scanning the vineyard and hopping from row to row. Before long a scream and a yell signalled the mystery was solved. A young French couple had strolled off at lunch, and had, from all reports, planned to spend the afternoon sipping wine and making love at the rate of 95 francs per day. Nice work if you can get it. Had it not been for Jackie, they would have wandered back to the bus at 5:30 with the others to go home. As it turned out, they went home early, on foot and with only half a day's pay. I'm sure there's a moral there about wine and love and the selection and maturity of both, but I was too tired to put it together.

At any rate, a long and beautifully warm afternoon came to a close at 5:30. I made the mistake of saying goodbye to Jackie with a firm handshake. I'd forgotten we had been up to our elbows in juice all day, and when our hands gripped, they stuck fast. For a moment I saw myself going through life with this man, sharing meals I hadn't ordered, going to movies I didn't like. Finally, we were able to push each other away with our free hands. Disengaged, we left, laughing.

On the third day, the harvest moved to the vineyards of Chorey Les Beaune, a commune of three hundred acres of Pinot grapes just northeast of Beaune. And I smiled all the way to the fields— not only had I had another thirteen hours of sleep, but I was totally prepared. I'd found a new shoulder pad that had leather reinforced by foam and had bought a thick bath sponge, which was stuffed inside my sweater under the pad. There was no way the cases were going to pain me that day. And I was right—with a quick scissors motion of his hand, Jackie made me a cutter.

Whereas carrying is periodic pain, cutting is constant ache, a continual numbness broken only when you rise with a full pail and proudly yell "*Panier!*" to the porter, who relieves you of your purple burden. Then it's back down, and you begin again, slowly snipping and picking your way to the end of the row. It is of utmost importance that a cutter have good hand co-ordination. Locating the stem of the bunch, which is always woven into other stems, or wire, or wood, is an art in itself. The white grape on a light background adds another degree of difficulty. Quickly ripping away the obstructing leaves makes it easier to see the stems.

I can remember a time during warm-up exercises at school when I had difficulty touching my toes. By 11:00 a.m., with legs perfectly straight, I was able to touch the ground with my elbows. Straightening up was the problem. Four gashes in my left hand before noon indicated that I might be adding more colour to the wine than desired. I had this horrible image of handing my pails to a porter and then asking him to throw back my finger.

In a small way, I like to think I brought the *vendangeurs* closer together. It used to be that when they finished their row they'd move on to the next section. During my tenure as a cutter, they instead gathered in one place—my row—and spent ten minutes helping me finish (or "*assistez la moustache*" as it was known).

I complicated matters by trying to talk and work at the same time, but I was anxious to find out who these *vendangeurs* really were. Most were students or unemployed youths, mainly girls. Many were housewives, who worked the harvest for extra money. Some were older men between jobs. Others turned out to be: a surfer from Miami, working to save enough money to ship himself and his board down to Biarritz; an English nanny, who worked on her days off each week just because she liked it; two globetrotting South Africans; and a young Englishman whose Dad decided his education was here that year instead of Oxford.

And then there was Maurice. Old Maurice wouldn't give his age, but it was known he'd helped plant the first vines in this area with Roman legionnaires in the third century BC. He ate non-stop, and the running joke was that Jackie needed a second storage truck just to transport Maurice's lunch out to the field each day. He was truly amazing, and the final word in any dispute in the vineyards was his.

Lunch that day, for no reason, was special. Eating with a small group of regular Maison Drouhin workers, we began with kir, a local drink of raspberry liqueur and white wine. We then proceeded with the usual bottle of *vin ordinaire* and added some food just to make the meal official. We ended with marc—a potent brandy made by distilling the skins and stems discarded during the winemaking process. Marc is drunk straight and also poured into your coffee when you're looking the other way. A fine lunch indeed. There are no details available for that afternoon.

The weather for this *vendange* had been unusually fine—hot, sunny days typical of our Indian summer, known here as the "miracle of the fall." It was so good, in fact, that Robert Drouhin decided to suspend picking for seven days to allow the grapes more time in the sun, thus increasing their sugar content, and ultimately the alcohol content of the wine. For the one hundred workers who arrived each day on two buses from the surrounding villages, it meant a holiday. For me, it meant an opportunity to work inside at the Drouhin winery in Beaune and see the vinification of the grapes we'd just collected.

Colbert is a small, very old winery, one of three operated by Maison Drouhin. I arrived at 8:00 a.m. and received a denim apron. As soon as I'd got it on, I was told to take it off—that and just about everything else I was wearing except shirt and shorts. It was time to *peger*. Until then I'd always believed that stomping grapes half nude in a barrel was something for tourists to photograph, a postcard gimmick. Not so. *Peger* is an important step in the vinification of red grapes. Once in the morning, and again at the end of the day, two of the younger workers climb into three-metre-high wooden vats, which contain the fermenting must. They vigorously plunge their lower bodies downwards, pushing a one-metre layer of skins and stems into the warm juice below—all the while clinging to the side of the vat to keep from drowning. Without this turning of the upper layer, the vat seals over, and without oxygen, the fermentation slows or even stops. Repeating this "bobbing" exercise until the whole vat is once again a homogenous liquid, is very tiring work. The temperature sensations range from very cool near the refrigeration racks that have been inserted to stabilize the speed of fermentation to very hot at the bottom, where the working of the wine bacteria causes natural heat. Two workers constantly monitor the vats of wine, one checking the colour, the other the temperature.

The girl in charge of the operation at Colbert was unable to get a good sample of the juice and informed me that I had not done the *peger* properly. I suspected her of a bit of voyeurism, but nonetheless took off my clothes and went back into the vat a second time. For me personally, the only benefit of the *peger* was that my feet and hands were now colour co-ordinated—a rich deep purple.

With the harvest postponed, the afternoon at Colbert was spent cleaning barrels, pumping the wines into holding tanks in

DO NOT PASS

The Exception to the Seatbelt Rule

While flying, you don't *always* have to buckle up, place your seatback in an upright position, etc. An American woman flying from Oslo, Norway, to New York City on Scandinavian Airlines System (SAS) skirted these regulations a couple of years ago and got away with it. It seems this woman went into the washroom of the Boeing 767 and flushed the toilet while she was still sitting on it. The evacuation system, which works on the principle of a vacuum, completely sealed the woman's buttocks to the rim of the toilet, where she remained for the duration of the flight. Unable to get up or reach the emergency button, the woman remained locked, skintight, to the bowl until "ground technicians could help her get loose." Whatever they're paying these guys, for this kind of customer service it's not enough.

Admitted an SAS spokeswoman: "She was stuck there for quite a long time." Legitimately claiming a bum wrap, the woman filed a formal complaint with SAS.

the cellar, and generally preparing for the big onslaught of grapes that would arrive when the *vendange* was resumed. A final *peger*, and I was finished for the day. Winery days begin with purple feet and end with cold showers.

The caves at Maison Drouhin are walled by two metres of concrete, and wander in all directions beneath the city of Beaune. They are part of the original fourteenth-century cellars that housed the wines of the king, the dukes, and the priests—the three rules of France at that time. These tunnels are so deep and so fortified that the temperature does not vary more than 4° C in any season, and they are always around 95% humidity—ideal conditions for aging and storage.

The next day at 11:00 a.m., the best time of the day for tasting wine, I was honoured to accompany Monsieur Robert Drouhin to his cellars to try six vintage wines, two whites and four reds. It pained me to learn that this was strictly a technical tasting, where the wine is enjoyed in every way but never swallowed. My sense of values did a somersault as I spit out a mouthful of ten-year-old Premier Cru and pretended to be pleased. My wine bias got bruised when we turned to a bottle of Beaujolais, which as a Canadian I cherished. But because Beaujolais is drunk young, and therefore has not paid its dues, it's seen in Beaune as pleasant plonk at best.

My faith in Robert Drouhin was restored when, at the end of the tasting, he collected the remainder of the wines we'd tried, and we moved on to his house for a long and non-technical lunch.

The *vendange* wrapped up with four days of cutting and carrying at the vineyards of Chorey, Savigny, Aloxe-Corton, and Chassagne—places that until then I had seen only on labels. The bus ride to Chablis was long. I bemoaned having to get up at 5:30, until our driver reminded me that he got up at 3:00 a.m., drove 175 kilometres around the countryside picking up workers before stopping for us in Beaune, and then made the two-and-a-half-hour trip to Chablis.

Unlike the Côte de Beaune and the Côte de Nuits, where some vineyards are as big as your backyard garden, Chablis is more open, a great expanse of green covering steep hills. The Chardonnay grapes that year were covered with a "rot"—one very desirable and complementary to the wine.

The most exciting day of the *vendange* was my last one in Chablis. There was great anticipation among the *vendangeurs*— the speed at which they harvested was exceeded only by the loudness of their singing. They cut short lunch, and by 3:30 we had cleaned Chablis of its grapes. The buses were quickly decorated with wild flowers and grape leaves, and we set off, like a conquering army, for Beaune. Everyone offered congratulations to one another on a *"bon vendange,"* and wine flowed in honour of the harvest. As we entered the Côte d'Or region, I realized where its name came from, for all the slopes were a bright orange-yellow gold.

Arriving at Maison Drouhin in Beaune, we were ushered in for the finale of the *vendange*, the *poulee*. Aside from the fact that buses have replaced horse carts, this very traditional festival of the grape has not changed for centuries. The first event was roll call, in which everyone was paid for their work. Once we were inside the reception hall, like the wives of landlords before her, Mrs. Drouhin was presented with a beautiful bouquet of flowers by the workers, and the festivities began. Bread and *vin ordinaire* was for the fields; now we tasted Premier Cru and Champagne. The long white tables were crammed with chocolates and pastries of every kind.

There was no sadness that the *vendange* was over, only a boisterous sense of accomplishment. For his efforts, Jackie received some very affectionate abuse from almost everyone. At some point, Robert Drouhin was able to establish silence and, knowing it could only last for a few minutes, he quickly delivered his message. The figure of 280,000 tons of grapes harvested got an immediate standing ovation and toasts all around. After two weeks of sunshine, earlier doubts concerning the 1978 Burgundy wines had been replaced with words like "*très bien*" and "*magnifique*." Monsieur Drouhin thanked everyone for a successful harvest and hoped they would return next year, as well. If he said more, no one heard him. Before thanking the *vendangeurs* personally, he led them in a hand-clapping French folk song, amid the popping of even more Champagne corks. And so on, and so on. The evening never really ended, it just faded away slowly from memory in tiny little bubbles.

Such fine people, Robert and Madam Drouhin. Michel Troubetzkoy—you were right all along—it was fun, a highlight of my life.

Pappa Germano

In 1973 I set out to conquer Europe by backpack. I was streetwise and savvy, having read every line of Arthur Frommer's *Europe on $5 a Day.*

Yes, you could see Europe on five bucks a day, but those train station benches get old after a while. So I bounded off the train into Rome's main train station with the pack on my back and the book in my hand and an arrogant attitude to boot. That's what the book said: act like you own the place, walk with purpose and confidence. Look like you know what you're doing and avoid the hawkers and shills at all cost. All I had to do was get my bearings, because I knew where I was going—Pappa Germano's Pensione. According to

Arthur, it was a wonderfully friendly B&B near the station, safe, and cheap.

Immediately I was accosted by a rotund, middle-aged Italian man with a large mustache and a small beret. "Come," he said, taking me by the arm. "I gotta the place for you."

I jerked my arm away, walked back towards the station, and pretended to be reading the local train schedule, which is in Italian. In the glass, I was watching this guy who was pointing out directions to other young backpackers who approached him. But he always turned back to stare at me. I was setting out to follow a group of three guys, believing they were heading for a similarly cheap accommodation, when the big Italian stepped in my way.

"Where? Where you wanna go?"

"I know where I'm going," I said. "Leave me alone."

As I moved to follow the others, he took two steps sideways and was in my face again. "C'mon," he said. "I gotta nice small hotel for you."

"That's it," I yelled, while waving the book at him. "You leave me alone or I'll call a cop."

With that, he grabbed the book out of my hand. I turned away to look for help, and lo and behold, there was a cop. He was about my age, and dressed in shiny black leather with a peaked cap and a machine gun hanging from his shoulder by a strap. His left hand rested on the gun, his forefinger just above the trigger. "Do you speak English?" I blurted out, stopping in front of him, interrupting his casual, languid pace.

Staring at me, he shook his head, no.

"That man," I said, pointing to the fat Italian, who was now ripping through my travel guide, as notes and business cards fall to the pavement. "He's bothering me," I said. "That man."

The cop nodded, yes, with the same indifference as before.

"I want to go to Pappa Germano's," I said loudly. Leaning to the right, I put my head in my hand, the international gesture for "bed." "Do you know? Pappa Germano?"

The cop raised his eyes slowly toward the Italian man, who was now coming quickly towards us. Then he raised his automatic weapon towards the man. I was thinking, if he shot him, that would be far too harsh a penalty for what this guy had done. The cop grunted something, pointed the rifle at the fat man again, and said, "Pappa Germano."

The Italian man collided with us, shoving the book in my face. "You see here? Paga one-forty-six. Pappa Germano's Pensione." Then he screamed, "I'm a Pappa Germano!"

"Oh," I said, looking around. I felt like an idiot. The cop nodded and smiled at me, confirming that thought. The big Italian broke into a smile and threw his hands out in front of him, looking at me like I was a stubborn idiot. It was unanimous.

"*Grazie*," I said to the cop, as Pappa Germano and I set off for his *pensione*. In less than ten minutes we were there, but it was all full up.

"How did that happen?" I asked.

"Because you no listen," he said. "All the others gotta here firsta." I recognized the three young guys from the station, the ones he'd given directions to. They were already on the way out, after stashing their packs.

I stayed across the street at Pappa Germano's sister's house. It was lovely. Lunch of pasta and red wine was included in the price.

Message to Fellow Hitchhiker: "Elliot! Phone Home!"

Two great talkers will not travel far together.
—Spanish proverb

The late 1970s, in the absence of war zones, was still a great time for backpackers to travel. I was hitchhiking out of Andorra la Vella on a fine brisk mountain morning, having spent a week walking in the Pyrenees. I was headed south out of the capital, on the highway that bicyclists took to Barcelona—a thrilling, downhill, day's coast on which they hardly had to peddle.

I spotted Elliot walking in the same southerly direction on the opposite side of the road. He was a bit of a hippie, and carrying so little gear I thought he was only out on a day hike. We nodded. Then he crossed over to my side of the road, stopped, and began hitchhiking from a spot twenty yards ahead of me. This was a clever ploy often used by hitchhikers—when the car pulled over for the first guy, it would stop at the next guy's feet.

A long time passed with very few cars, so I decided to set out walking down the mountain. As I passed Elliot—slight, early twenties in a green army jacket and ripped blue jeans—I noticed he was studying a map. As I caught a better glimpse of it, I burst out laughing. "Where'd you get the map?" I asked.

"My high school atlas," he replied. "I can't find Barcelona."

I wasn't surprised. He was holding a wad of pages he'd ripped out of the standard Oxford school atlas, and he was looking at the agriculture and forestry section on Spain.

"Here," I said, passing him a map from the inside pocket of my jacket. I had detailed Michelin maps for every country I'd be visiting, as well as North Africa. "You just out for the day?" I asked.

"No, a year," he replied. "Is Spain expensive?"

As it turns out, Elliot's backpack was standard-issue Boy Scouts of America, his boots were from his last construction job, he had a "borrowed" sleeping bag inside his pack, and he'd "acquired" the plastic groundsheet from a greenhouse in rural France. He had $100 U.S., and six months to wander his way to Kathmandu. "They got a café there on Freak Street that's totally pink, and all they play is Pink Floyd," said Elliot. I'm pretty sure it wasn't listed on my Michelin map.

My curiosity was captivated by this ill-prepared vagabond, who either didn't know or didn't care that he'd be broke in a couple of weeks at best.

We spent that day together, and a week after that. Most of that first day was spent walking down the Pyrenees, but we finally

Travel Tip

For some strange reason, all the washrooms in Europe offer the visitor a choice of two toilets. It's best to use the one with the seat. If you do use the one without the seat, I'm warning you, don't fool around with the water faucets. It's like sitting on a seltzer bottle.

Tourists Too Stupid to Travel

Asked at a Niagara Falls info booth:

Question: Can I go straight over there, to the Cave of the Winds on the American side or do I have to go all the way around and over the bridge?

Answer: Sir, water rushes over those falls at 212,000 cubic feet per second. Make sure you have a good grip on the wife.

got a ride all the way into Barcelona in the late afternoon. I spoke my best Spanish with the driver, turning to Elliot in the back seat to give him an English account of the world we were passing through.

On the outskirts of Barcelona, we circled a beautiful castle, and I explained to Elliot that it was the home of the great Dutch soccer player Johan Cruyff, now the coach of Barcelona's team.

"How come all the guards with Uzis?" asked Elliot.

"Security," I said.

"No, no," said the driver, who suddenly spoke English. "Cruyff go and no pay taxes. The *policia* wait for him to come for his clothes."

Once we arrived in Barcelona, I got a room at my favourite tiny hotel, in the Plaza Real, just off Las Ramblas. Elliot snuck in and slept on the floor, for free. I showed Elliot the best of bustling Barcelona: the student beer gardens, the tumbledown docks, and, of course, Las Ramblas, a tree-lined tribute to books, birds, and buskers.

With Elliot in tow, I upped my budget from $10 to $20 a day. By week's end, Elliot still hadn't touched his stash of cash. "Spain," he said, "wasn't nearly as expensive as I thought."

I was headed for Málaga, where I had a job waiting for me, teaching tennis at the Hotel Mijas. Elliot decided to tag along.

"Okay," I said, "but we gotta split the food."

"Fine by me," he replied, "but no hotels."

I don't know if I accepted his dare out of stupidity or because I felt myself going soft at thirty-two years of age, but I agreed. For three days we hitched and walked south along the coast of Spain towards Málaga. For three nights we slept in two farmer's fields and a barn. We spread out Elliot's groundsheet, opened his sleeping bag into a blanket, and used our packs as pillows. We ate and drank and talked by campfire. I proved to be a young thirty-two. My back, however, was sixty-seven, and fading fast.

And Elliot split the food. He was a very quick shopper. I'd give him a short list of the cheapest things we needed—bread, fruit, olives—and I'd buy the rest—smoked ham, cheese, wine. He was always out of the store with the goods packed away while I was still at the cash register. On our last day together, an elderly woman, who used her rosary to add up the bill, pointed to Elliot through the window and said, "*Ladron.*"

"No," I said, "*Americano.*"

"*Ladron!*" she repeated. Then she scooped up all my items, dropped them in her apron, and brushed her hands together twice.

"*No dinero?*" I asked.

"*Claro,*" she said, nodding. "*Ladron!*"

I paid for the stuff Elliot had taken and met him outside.

"That woman called you a thief," I said.

"That's a little harsh," he said, feigning hurt feelings. "I'm just sticking to a very tight budget."

"Europe on zero dollars a day?" I said, glaring at him.

We didn't speak for a long time, but it was hard not to like Elliot. He had this wonderful boyish curiosity and an assurance in his smile that somehow he'd always get by. He was probably letting a hot potato at home cool off while he conned his way across two continents. He probably made it all the way to Kathmandu, to the spice section of the Makhan Tole market, where they weigh and bag the marijuana and hashish. Today, he's probably selling magic convection broilers on TV infomercials, having left the PR department of Enron.

Thirty miles north of Valencia, a Spanish student in a tiny Fiat stopped to give us a lift. But he had a large guitar or bass in a cloth case in the back seat; there was only room for one. I told Elliot to go ahead, thinking I'd get a ride quicker with my short hair than he would with his shoulder-length strands.

"At the town square," I yelled, as he pulled away.

"Valencia!" he yelled back, thrusting a thumb out the passenger window.

And I never saw him again. Elliot, if you should ever read this story, call me. I still want my watch back. No hard feelings.

Mijas: Where My Money Was No Good

After the *vendange*, I went to Spain, where I taught tennis from November 1978 to August 1979 at the Hotel Mijas, in the white-washed mountain village of Mijas, in southern Spain. I had lived in Spain for six months in 1973. But since then, El Caudillo, the feared fascist dictator Francisco Franco, had died. With his passing came democracy, along with crime, drugs, and pornography. In 1973 hardly a door in town had a lock; by 1978 pickpockets plied the markets along the coast, and for a couple of dollars you could get your picture taken with a drugged lion cub on the beach.

As dictators go, Franco was a complete bastard. The mayor of Mijas, one of several mayors of anti-fascist cities during the Spanish Civil War that Franco promised to kill when he got around to it, hid in a false wall of his house for thirty years. Manuel Cortes was a thirty-four-year-old socialist mayor when he crawled through a hole in his living room covered by a framed picture. He was sixty-four years old when he crawled out. He watched the wedding of his daughter through a peep hole.

Mijas was a fairly quiet and quirky place when I lived there. At any given time, it was the ideal Spanish postcard setting. Looking up from the coast, it looked like a cluster of sugar cubes hanging on to the side of a dark green mountain. Looking out from the balcony of the villa I rented above the village, you could see clear across the Straight of Gibraltar to the snow-capped mountains of Morocco. It was beautiful, but weird.

The man who owned the villa was an American who dressed like Indiana Jones and smoked unfiltered Marlboros through a hole in his throat. He came by once while I was there. It's very unsettling to talk to a cowboy who's alternating a voice box and a lit cigarette under his chin. I remember thinking if he rigged it right, he could have been the only ventriloquist in show business to make smoke come out the dummy's nose.

There were always celebrities around. Yul Brenner owned an estate near Coín. The silver-haired British actor Stewart Granger played tennis at Lew Hoad's private club on the road down to Fuengirola. Robert Redford, wanting to buy a ranch with sudden money from something called *Barefoot in the Park*, had real estate sellers in a tizzy. Hemingway's legend loomed large in nearby Ronda. I ran into Morley Safer in a bar when both of us got up from our chairs to tell a bunch of loud Americans to shut up during a great solo by a talented local guitarist. I let Morley dress his own people down.

"Juan the Sweep," who cleaned the buses in the big square at the entrance to the town, was demanding to be called "Juan the Actor" after getting a walk-on role in a George Segal movie filmed here.

Mijas had a thriving expatriate community of Americans and Brits, failing artists and struggling South Americans, a commercially successful Dutch painter whose work belonged on the door of a fridge, a New York City pharmaceutical executive whose daughter had been murdered. And me. The Canadian who drank for free.

I taught tourists to play tennis at the elegant and overly expensive Hotel Mijas, which moulded its sumptuous two storeys along the town's mountain ridge, offering a spectacular vista of the Mediterranean Sea and the Costa del Sol below. Over a period of two days, I watched two hotel gardeners standing in the same spot, with hoses in their hands, staring slack-jawed at a topless Scandinavian woman lying on the grass. They eventually drowned two very expensive palm trees.

The tennis court was down a hundred steps or more at the bottom of the property, where a permanently locked gate faced a back street of the village. I noticed a hole had been cut in the fence surrounding the tennis court, but said not a word to the miserly German hotel owner, who tolerated me only because I was good for his business.

While I hit buckets of balls to hotel clients, a group of kids always gathered on the street, hoping to catch errant balls that sailed over the fence. These they'd promptly return to me. These kids with dirty T-shirts and holes in the knees of their pants were infatuated with the game of tennis. They couldn't afford a can of balls, much less a racquet or the price of a lesson.

I asked my buddy Javier at reception if he'd talk to the hotel owner about a free tennis program for local kids. Javier clicked his heels together and, saluting me in German military style, bellowed: "*No! Nunca! Jamas! No posible!*" Then he winked at me. Javier also knew the tennis court could not be seen from the hotel, because I'd been giving him and two other young guys from reception free lessons in the evenings.

I begged and borrowed old rackets and beat-up balls from hotel guests and friends, and got the word out to a few kids during the week: "*Gratis tennis sabado.*" The next day the key that had long locked the door of the court was taped to my lesson schedule, and on Saturday morning I held the first official but somewhat illegal Mijas Kids Tennis Clinic.

Too many kids showed up way too excited. I ceremoniously opened the door to the street, and about fifteen little kids climbed in through the hole in the fence. Then they basically went nuts. All they wanted to do was hit the ball as hard and as far as possible. They purposely hit the ball over the fence so they could chase it. It was bedlam. It was wonderful.

Eventually they wore themselves out, and we got down to some basic lessons and a few drills. And every Saturday after that became tennis camp day at the Hotel Mijas.

Gradually a strange thing happened in all the bars in town— I wasn't allowed to buy a drink. I spent every evening in bars, as did the locals. Your big meal was at lunch, and at night you bar-hopped supper: a glass of wine at the Alarcon, along with tapas —maybe a small plate of paella—another glass of wine and a tiny omelette with a small square of bread at El Gordo's. It was Hemingway's moveable feast on foot.

And every time I went to pay, the bartender would put his hands up and say: "*No, señor!*" Then he'd point to some guy, who would happen to be the father or the uncle or the cousin of one of the kids in my tennis school.

When a Spaniard offers to buy you a drink, there's only one response: *gracias*. Eventually, I had to either leave Spain or apply for a new liver. I left in September of '79 to return to Canada to strangle the editor of *Wine Press* magazine, who had been running my features on France and Spain, but only pretending to pay me.

I always believed I'd return to live in Spain one day to live and work. But things there have changed. An explosion of hotels stole the beaches from the people, the great El Horno Bar has become a souvenir shop, selling plastic donkeys filled with sangria. Tour buses get stuck in the narrow lanes of Mijas and cause traffic jams a kilometre each way. Dirt bikes scare old people in the streets.

Not long before I came to Mijas, the common mode of transportation was by donkey taxi up the steep goat path from Fuengirola. Today, a four-lane highway gets you from Mijas to Málaga in a matter of minutes.

Stop progress now, I say, otherwise there'll be no reason to travel. Everything will look like the place where you're from.

The All-New "Near Death" Vacations

As a traveller, I've done some pretty dumb things in other countries, I'll admit.

Several years ago, in Puerto Vallarta, I got quite annoyed with a bartender who continually refused to light my *perro*, or cigar, for me. (I have six cigars a year, get violently sick on two of them, and never carry matches.) Finally I asked to speak to his manager. When it was explained to me that *puro* is the Spanish word for cigar, and that repeatedly asking Guillermo to set my dog on fire was, in fact, an unreasonable request, I apologized.

Once, in Ireland, while making my way back to my room in a tall, stone hotel on the lea side of the Lee River in Cork, I caught the sight of a scantily clad woman standing provocatively on the corner. As I stepped around her, she asked, "And would you be doin' business tonight?"

"Oh, no," I replied quite innocently. "I'm over here for pleasure." It occurred to me some time later that, to an Irish hooker, my response gave out very mixed signals.

And once, while I was hitchhiking near Dundee, a mustachioed Scot with a Sherlock Holmes hat pulled over. Rolling down his window, he suggested I put my bag in the boot. Looking up from my walking boots to his deadpan face, I murmured something about "a smartass" and walked away. Scots, as I learned too late for this ride, refer to the trunk of the car as "the boot." And if you don't grasp this concept immediately, a Scot will get a real bee in his bonnet, which is in fact the hood of the car.

Anyway, I've done and said some pretty dumb things while travelling but . . . I'm proud to say that never, as a tourist or a traveller, have I walked into the middle of a shooting war.

I still can't take my eyes off the photo I clipped from page 29 of the *Toronto Star* on April 18, 2002, which shows two bewildered and disappointed Japanese tourists sitting on concrete debris in the middle of Madbasseh Square in Bethlehem, carrying only a large bottle of water, a small cloth bag with handles, and a folded map.

These two young Japanese sightseers, identified in the photo as Yuji Nakano and Mina Takashi, were turned away at the Church of the Nativity, which they had hoped to visit and actually tried to enter by knocking at the door. Unfortunately, the church was temporarily closed because it was currently at the centre of the most violent and deadly Middle East military operation since the 1967 war. The two Japanese tourists were unaware of this, even though

- the streets were almost completely deserted because there was, in effect, a shoot-to-kill military curfew imposed by the Israeli army;

- the church was completely surrounded by Israeli tanks and personnel carriers;
- sporadic shooting was coming from inside the church, where two hundred desperate Palestinian gunmen were holed up;
- the armed stand-off, now in its seventeenth straight day, had been covered by every news organization that owns a camera.

By some weird twist of fate, these two lost souls managed to get between the warring Israelis and Palestinians—which U.S. Secretary of State Colin Powell had failed to do on a five-day peace-seeking mission the previous week.

Now I've been lost between Buda and Pest. I've wandered into a black tunnel in Madeira and had to feel my way out the other side. But I have never attempted to enter the birthplace of Jesus while it was the focal point of a fire fight and missile attack.

Exactly how dozy do tourists have to be to go sightseeing in a war zone? I believe the correct medical diagnosis is "brain dead, with legs and arms fully functional." But despite their precarious position, they were not without options. They could still have:

- claimed to be the first wave of Japanese peacekeeping troops and ordered everybody to return to their pre-1967 positions;
- sought political asylum in the Felafels to Go shop across the street;
- claimed to be emissaries of Yoko Ono and begun chanting "Give Peace a Chance";
- made everyone think they were completely mad by asking for directions to Euro Disney;
- claimed Mina was about to give birth and sought refuge in the manger. (There is historical precedent for this.)

Travellers taking the road less travelled, mainly because its heavily mined, should remember the following tips: buy the really good guidebook that pinpoints foxholes and bomb shelters; when taking the Gaza city tour it's always a good idea to dress like goalie Curtis Joseph; and if you plan to work in the Middle East, always pack a copy of your dental records.

Warning to all Japanese tourists: there is a translation problem with the promotional pamphlets you're receiving from the Middle East. The sixth-century stone church in Bethlehem, widely believed to be the birthplace of Jesus, is called the Church of the Nativity. It is not, repeat, *not* the Church of the *Naivety*!

And to Yuji and Mina, I'm sending you a copy of this book in hopes it will help make your travels a little safer. I'm sending it to you at your next stop, care of the Main Mosque, Srinagar, Kashmir.

Essaouira: An Imperfect Little Paradise

While I was living in Mijas, I took a quick side trip to Essaouira, Morocco.

I went by train—the Marrakesh Express, as a matter of fact—down to Marrakesh from Tangier. At least two groups of hippies played the Crosby, Stills, and Nash song all the way down. Things disappeared faster on a Moroccan train than at a magic show convention. You had to tie everything to yourself, including your travelling partner.

"Thumbing's a bit dodgy here," said an Englishman in the souk in Marrakesh. "They caught a couple up in the mountains not long ago." He paused for a good pull on his pipe. "And they violated *both* of them." His British accent came down hard on the word "both," like it would have been okay if they had only assaulted the woman.

Abandoning my plan to hitchhike, I decided to take a bus down to to Essaouira, an enchanting Arab city built at the edge of the Atlantic. I'd forgotten that buses leaving major cities in Morocco were routinely boarded by policemen. You knew they were official policemen, because they wore British army tunics and pants from the French military. The Moroccan military kept the clothes of every country that ever dominated them. But their automatic weapons were no hand-me-downs.

So I was sitting in the aisle seat on the bus that goes to the coast, and across from me was a seventy-five-year-old man in a hooded jalaba who was smoking a joint the size of a ballpark hotdog, hand-rolled in newspaper. Which he kept offering to me. He kept shoving it in my face, even as two police officers boarded the bus and began poking at everybody's packages with the barrels of their guns.

In Morocco the contraband generally went on top of the bus, with the sheep and produce, all secured by a rope netting. The police never went up there.

"Good keef," said the old man. But there was more hashish than keef in that cigar.

I thought, that's it: he's going to foist that joint on me, the cops will cart me off the bus, and I'll be the subject of yet another documentary on a Canadian slowly going insane in a third-world jail.

But they were all smiles, those cops, as they poked our bags. When they didn't hit glass, they exited down the steps and out the back of the bus.

My whole sense of right and wrong did a somersault as I remembered they weren't looking for keef. That was legal. They were looking for bottles of Scotch, which could fetch as much as $100 on the black market in Morocco, where alcohol is illegal.

Even without alcohol, Morocco was intoxicating. Soothing and shrill at the same time, Arab music rippled through the bus with the sweet-smelling wisps of keef. A woman so swathed in robes and scarves that only her eyes and hands were naked walked down the aisle with the heads of two live chickens sticking out from under her armpits. Gazing out the window was like looking into the Bible: old, bearded men on donkeys with bulging sacks of roots hanging by their sides; women in burkas selling oranges beside the road, children choking on the dust behind the bus while

Tourists Too Stupid to Travel

The Travel Industry Association of America is currently trying to track down the people who asked the following questions of travel agents, in hopes of persuading them to turn in their passports.

Question: How long is a one-day pass good for?

Answer: What? The one you bought on that two-day special?

Question: What time does the nine o'clock ferry leave?

Answer: That depends. Do you want to sightsee in daylight or in darkness?

Cultural Misunderstanding

From a movie promo for *A Fish Called Wanda* in a newspaper in Malawi, Africa: ". . . a tale of suspense, murder, intrigue and . . . seafood!"

running to jump on its bumper. On the shoulder of the road, a shepherd stood in the shade of a scrawny tree, hissing at his goats to stay put as a brand new black Mercedes flew between him and our smoke-spewing bus. Off in the distance, I saw a shimmering image of men hunched over and moving along on stilts, which as we got closer became camels.

"Berbers," said the bus driver, pointing.

"Berbers," repeated the woman in front of me, her newborn baby staring at me with lolling eyes.

A vast sea of sand, interrupted by snow-capped mountains and dark cedar forests, brown adobe villages and mosques that tower above bustling market towns, Morocco has some of the most interesting and eclectic landscapes in all the world.

In the middle of nowhere, without so much as a shrub as a marker, someone shouted, the bus stopped, and a father and small son trotted off into the desert, hand in hand, towards an unseen home in a village beyond.

I ate orange slices and sliced hunks off a large ball of Edam cheese. After three weeks in a country with only two main dishes—couscous and tangine—anything without lamb tastes great.

Unlike the other cities in Morocco, there was no crowd of hustlers waiting to harass me at the CTM bus station in Essaouira.

DO NOT PASS

Unsavvy Traveller

Not long ago, a Polish tourist bought a donkey at a Cairo market for $500 and tried to bring it home with him as a souvenir. Egyptian airport officials refused to let him bring the animal on the plane unless he paid an additional $1,000 for cargo costs. The man changed his mind and decided to sell the donkey instead. Which is a tough sell in an airport.

I wandered down the main street, headed for the harbour. I stopped at a sidewalk table, where three American hippies drinking thick, black coffee invited me to sit. I ordered coffee while one of the hippies walked around the corner and came back with a bag of the best chocolate chip cookies I had ever tasted.

These Americans, mostly college dropouts, were part of a cave commune. They shared *everything*. The girl with the long strawberry-blonde hair flowing out from under a brown fedora giggled at the emphasis Phil put on the word "everything." As the Englishman might have said, "Everybody's violating everybody."

Phil was from Philly, Chick was from Chicago, and Flo was from Florida. I thought they were being unusually paranoid with these phony names until they explained their source of income. Each of them was ostensibly still living in the States, and each of them had a monthly benefit cheque coming in from insurance or unemployment. Once a month, the one who drew the short joint flew home (straws were hard to come by in Essaouira). The runner collected and cashed all the cheques and flew back. They were all living like kings in Morocco.

They knew of a really good cave I could rent. "Caves are where it's at, man." The hotels were too expensive, but the caves were a dollar a day. Some had electricity, all had carpeting and an ocean view: large holes eroded out of the sides of the hills along the coast, turned into a warren of apartments.

After an hour, they secured the drawstrings on their large wicker satchels and got up to leave. I felt I'd shared something special with these people, like in some way we'd known each other in previous lives. Actually, I was just really stoned.

As he was leaving, Phil said, "If you like the chocolate chips, try the macaroons. They're deadly, man."

Thank you, Phil. See you back at the cave. I believe it's my night to slay and barbecue the dinosaur.

I looked around at the place that had promised to be a quiet retreat after the madness of Marrakesh, but all I could think of was flying carpets. I stayed at a hotel that was cheap and cool, with bright Moroccan tourist posters on all the walls. I stood there staring at these spectacular scenes of Morocco, thinking I'd love to go there someday, forgetting where I was. The hotel was round, and open in the centre so that men waiting for their wives to emerge from the rooms could stand leaning on the railing looking down into the lobby.

The medina in Essaouira was all blue and white, a quiet backdrop for the souk, which was a blur of blazing colours: dyed red knotted rugs, handwoven orange kilims, jewellery made from brilliant Goulamena beads, fruit and spices that exceeded the shades of a rainbow.

In the *skala de la ville*, or woodcarver's souk, serious and mysterious men made boxes all day long, boxes of cedar and thuya the likes of which few foreigners have ever seen. Gleaming and seamless, an Essaouira box, without any help from a battery or a plug, has a built-in locking system; by touching three or four drawers, delicately and in the correct order, all the knobbed chambers, large and small, open to the owner. Forget the tactile code, and you're the proud owner of a beautiful wood-grained box with secret compartments that you'll never get into again.

In the early evening, the fishing boats docked, and one by one, the Hibachis flared up along the pier, where fresh fish were grilled between picnic tables. A short walk down the beach—and nobody I asked knew how this could happen—a Dutchman ran a ramshackle bar and served cold cans of Heineken beer. This combination was irresistible to travellers, especially the hippies, and they flocked there, often still lingering well after the sun set. Tiny orange bursts of fire flared up against the black sea, as charcoal sparked and joints were passed around.

"Hendrix lived here," said Phil, the last time I saw him. It was true. Essaouira was one of the rock star's hangouts in the sixties. Somehow, though, I couldn't see the local tourist board hanging hand-carved nameplates over the pier that said: "Jimi Hendrix did dope here."

The Decisive Difference Between a Tourist and a Traveller

Let's say you've just checked into a small hotel in North Africa and you find a dead sheep in your room. And yes, this has happened. Let's be quite clear here—imagine the sheep is dead on the hoof and in your room. The sheep is not alive and on the roof, as was the case last January with Waheeb Hamaudah in Alexandria, Egypt. Waheeb had the animal tethered on the top of a three-storey apartment building, where he was fattening him up for the festival of Erd al-Adha. It would be one of those barbaric rituals in which, with a great display of showmanship, Waheeb would slit the sheep's throat to please the crowd of religious partygoers and honour some obscure god.

Believing all sheep go quietly to the slaughter, Waheeb had no reason to be on the alert when he bent over to scoop more feed from a burlap sack and the sheep . . . what's the word in Egyptian?. . . oh yeah, Headbutt! Breaking the silence of the lambs, this woolly soldier of the animal revolution sent his would-be slayer sailing straight off the roof and onto the street below. Waheeb Hamaudah was fifty-six. Erd al-Adha is the Muslim feast of sacrifice. The meek may not inherit the earth as planned, but once in a while we win a big one.

So your average tourist on an escorted vacation finds a dead sheep under his bed and without hesitation walks onto the balcony of his hotel room and says: "Honey, call the front desk. There's a dead sheep under the bed." Quick and simple and yes, there is a good chance he'll hear a shriek from the balcony and go out to find nobody there.

The traveller, on the other hand, calls the front desk himself and says: "Yeah, I'm the guy in charge of delivering the sheep to tonight's festival. Can you give me directions on how to get there, and would there be a wine store on the way?"

Tourists miss a lot by sightseeing. Travellers experience a foreign country by taking in the local flavour . . . which, in this particular case, would be a tangy mint and garlic sauce.

To repeat, my number one rule of travel: never hitchhike on the road less travelled; it's a really baaaaaaaaaaaaad idea.

Part Two

The English: Queerer Than a Cat Fart

A tourist travels for pleasure;
a traveller takes pleasure in travel itself.

The Stupidest Hitchhiker in England, Ever

The English, the English, the English are best.
I wouldn't give tuppence for all of the rest.
—Michael Flanders and Donald Swann

I love the English. They're quirky and kind, tough but fair, wonderfully archaic in a world that dismisses history as a subject for school kids. And they're as queer as a cat fart, as John Irving might say. Eccentricity seems the norm in a country where, after hiking all day, an East Ender will ask you: "How's your plates of meat, mate?" Feet are meat, sister is blister, and your wife, of course, is strife.

Forgive me, but I find the English utterly besotted (I don't even know what that word means, but it sounds a little naughty, wot?). But you gotta love the English, and I do.

I purchased two cheap tickets to temperate and still merry ol' England for a New Year's holiday. One for me, and one for Monica Rose, who is supposed to be my photographer on many of my trips, but who ends up doing a lot of the driving—mainly from the back seat. As luck would have it, we landed in the middle of one of the worst snowstorms ever to hit the kingdom by the sea. Go ahead and ask: why would I go to England in the midst of the coldest Arctic snowstorm they've had on record? Because I was too cheap to purchase cancellation insurance. Okay?

Drifting snow and howling winds, piercing sleet and overhanging ice—even the English ale was cold. "Get the critters out," the people in the pubs kept demanding, as they watched disaster clips on the telly. "No, no," I protested. "I'm Canadian. I know about these things. Keep the critters indoors, or they'll freeze their little bums off!"

For the record, when the English are faced with hazardous icy roads, they will often call for the sanders, or, as they say in clipped British terminology, "gritters." Sometimes it's best just to sip and not be heard.

So how was my quick trip to Merry Ol'? Well, aside from the fact that I can't seem to stop saying "a bit dodgy, that," it was . . . "oh, spot on, Seth, spot on." I walked for a week from Brighton to Bournemouth along the coast of southern England with a woman who was supposed to take photos but didn't, because "she forgot her woollies, she did." We have great shots of eiderdown quilts and fireplaces in pubs.

We actually missed the worst of the storm and managed to walk, with backpacks, about sixteen miles a day along the boardwalks and cliffs of England's south shore, across deserted beaches and through gated backyards with proper little signs that said: "Mind the latch, please." From the English side of the channel, on a clear day and using binoculars, you can see clear across to France. It's amazing: even at that distance, you can usually spot the French behaving rudely.

We spent New Year's Eve on the Isle of Wight. We got the last available room on the island, at the Metropole Hotel, which was a beautiful seaside inn—back in the 1940s. I'm sure we were the last ones out before the wrecking ball came in.

You now get to meet the stupidest guy ever to hitchhike in England.

Hitchhiking Tip

Never accept a ride from the Hell's Angels biker who asks you to "hold the package gently."

We had hiked out of Ventnor, Monica and I, headed south along the coast of the Isle of Wight. After five hours on the footpaths, we decided to try to get a bus to Yarmouth, and from there a ferry back to the mainland. Of course, everything on the island shuts down on New Year's Day; there were no buses. So we began hitchhiking.

I've been to London and the British Isles a dozen times, but I keep forgetting how terribly friendly and helpful the British really are. Before long, we were picked up by a young and chatty English couple in a small, compact car.

I sat in the back seat, on the right, and the young chap—sorry, the guy—was sitting in the front left. I could not see his wife, sitting directly in front of me, because my backpack was on my lap. This guy was fascinated that we were out hiking and hitching with no real destination or booked accommodation. (In a country with a pub every mile, if not every block, I wouldn't say we were exactly "roughing it.") He asked a lot of questions, and he turned practically right around to face me when he asked them. We were having a great animated conversation, but his eyes were rarely on the road.

In England, as you may know, hedges line the rural routes, so that cars coming out of side roads have to nose out onto the thoroughfare before the driver can see both ways. Every time a car edged out in front of us, I'd gently push the guy's arm and point out the problem, because he was mostly facing me and not the motorcar speeding towards us about to end all our lives. He'd say, "No fear, mate," and turn around to talk to us again. As nicely as I could, I'd urge him to look up ahead where an oncoming lorry— sorry, truck—was headed straight for us, carrying four coffins with our respective names embossed on the sides.

This went on until I began to sweat and squirm and he began eyeing me like I had come to his country to recover from bad brain surgery.

Finally, the car pulled over at their town, and we departed with a polite "cheers" all around. That's when I said to my travelling partner, "That bleedin' rounder—sorry, that damn fool—nearly got us killed. He only looked at the road when I drew his attention to it! I was sure the crazy bastard was going to get us killed!"

And Monica said something I shall never forget. That's when she told me, and with a certain amount of merit, I must admit: "*He* wasn't driving, stupid. *She* was."

Okay, so England's first moron of the new year was an import. I had a valid passport and a right to be there. Why and bloody hell can't these people put the steering wheel on the right side of the car, that is the correct side, I mean the left side? A bit dodgy, that, wot?

Dora: One Batty Irish Landlady

God made pot. Man made beer. Who do you trust?
—From the *Irish Times*

A couple of years ago, I spent a week in north London, near Regent's Park, reading files in the library of the London Zoo. I lodged at a B&B in Chalk Farm, a fifteen-minute walk to the zoo along the Grand Canal. I had booked my room from Canada, and got an incredibly good price by agreeing to stay in an attic room and to forgo the traditional English breakfast, which contains enough cholesterol to bring down a charging rhino.

The landlady of this plain and sparse three-storey tenement opposite the Engineer's Pub turned out to be—how can I put this delicately—a freakin' lunatic. Dora was Irish, with shiny, bright, black hair. She was tall, thin, and witch-like. When I arrived, she kept me standing on the street for an hour and a half, dozing against my suitcase after an all-night overseas flight from Toronto, before she finally pulled up to the curb in a beat-up Citroën. No apology, no salutation, just rules and regulations: I wasn't allowed in the telly room, nor the sitting room, nor the back room, nor the kitchen, nor the dining area in the basement. If Dora had had a doghouse, I wouldn't have been let in at all.

My room, at the top of a narrow, winding staircase that all but forbade the hauling of luggage, had no drawers. It had a sink with pots and pans I would never use, but no place to store clothes.

If it weren't for the strange, tulip-shaped clothes tree on the landing outside my door, I'd have had no place at all to hang my things. The room also had no bed. Instead it had a pullout couch, which took up most of the room and had a metal bar that cut straight across the small of my back.

There was a perfectly good room next door, with a proper bed and even a small television set. Dora the Druid told me never to enter this room, because the woman who had booked it was due in any day now from Italy. So, essentially, I was paying $56 Canadian per night for a room at an English B&B without a bed and without a breakfast. More specifically, I paid $280 for five days at a blank-and-blank.

There were other people in the house. I heard them, but I never actually saw them. Their rules must have included coming and going by way of the basement window. I'm not sure whether Dora stayed in this house or in one nearby.

By the second day, I had loosened the light bulb in the staircase and put two empty beer cans on the step so I'd hear anybody coming up to the attic. Then I sneaked into the room next door, where I watched TV while drinking tall cans of Harp and eating chips in bed. God, it felt good. It was like camping out when I was a kid and eating strawberries after raiding Van Loon's garden.

I like to watch at least a little TV while I'm in England to make sure they're still televising dart matches in pubs and labelling it sport. I also like to confirm that the thing the English find most funny is still a man with big breasts dressed in women's clothing. And only a BBC "presenter" (anchorman) could end the big news story of the day on Hong Kong—the war that won it, the diplomacy that lost it, the history, the lives changed, and the people displaced

ONE WAY

Strangers and Other Family Members

On a return flight to Toronto, I sat next to a Canadian woman who had been visiting her mother in a London nursing home. Her family had warned her not to expect great things: her mother's mental condition had deteriorated over the past few years, necessitating the move to the nursing home.

On her second day in London, the woman summoned up enough courage to go to the small private home in East End, London. Entering the common area, she spotted her mother sitting all by herself in a comfortable chair, enjoying a sunny corner of the room. She nervously approached her mother, and got very close, so her mother could see her face. Then she asked the awful question: "Do you know who I am?" Her mother gave her a strange look, so she repeated the question. After a long silence, her mother smiled and said, "No, dear, I'm sorry I don't. But if you ask that nice lady over there in the white uniform, she might be able to help you."

And that's good travel advice—no matter how far you wander by miles, or even by mind, always introduce yourself.

by its recent takeover by mainland China—by referring to the whole episode as "the great Chinese takeout." Wot?

When I came in one night, Dora was there watching television, and I made an attempt at small talk, casually mentioning how saddened the whole world had been over the death of Lady Di. "Well," she said, "everybody in England knows Diana didn't die in the car crash, she only hurt her hip. It was at the hospital, and not the nearest hospital, mind you, that they killed her and the baby."

"Really," I said.

I was not so much surprised or even curious about the conspiracy theory that had been accepted as fact in Dora's warped little world. No, what set the blood draining from my face was that there was no lock on the door of my attic room and there were probably knives in that kitchen I wasn't allowed into. I drank more after that, mainly to produce more empties, which I stacked on the lower steps to give me an even earlier warning system against Dora—my personal foreign guest suggestion for the "Jerry Springer Show."

The only one in the house I could have a reasonable conversation with was Ester, the twenty-one-year-old blind calico cat that had been there even before the house became a B&B. Each morning, I would watch her in amazement as she'd come down into the front living room, rubbing up against the wall all the way. Then she'd take a couple of steps to her left and nick the leg of a coffee table with her left ear, take exactly six strides across the carpet and gently butt the side of the sofa with her forehead, step back, jump up, and she was home safe on the covered armoire, where she lolled all afternoon until suppertime.

After five full days, I checked out of my bedless, breakfast-free B&B. But before I did, just to spite Dora, I moved all the living room furniture around on the cat.

No, I did not do that. In fact I said goodbye to Ester and left her with my fondest wish that Dora the Demented, while flipping around the channels at night, never happens upon the rabbit scene in *Fatal Attraction*.

Even Clinton's Wax Figure Can't Keep His Zipper Up

Of all the great cities of the world, London has to be the best for walking. Massive parks, quaint canals, and long, historic rivers—I walk in London until my hands swell up and I have to hold a pint with two hands.

On Marylebone Road, on a sunny, cold Sunday morning, I passed two to three hundred people lined up to get into Madame Tussaud's waxworks. I didn't know what the attraction was until I read about it in a copy of the *Guardian* on the plane headed home. It seems the President Bill Clinton wax figure had just been unveiled, and thousands of tourists, mostly Americans, were getting their picture taken standing beside him. And just before the camera went click, they'd put one arm around his shoulder and deftly undo his zipper. Honest! I am not making this up.

This went on for days, until management caught on and a maintenance man at the museum was ordered to take a soldering iron and weld the zipper shut at the top . . . something Hillary should have thought of a long time ago.

A Madame Tussaud's travel tip: do not waste your film—wax figures are not, I repeat, *not* anatomically correct.

The Lap of Luxury Comes with a Price Tag

Shown above is the all-new British Library sitting on enlarged piles.
—A photo caption in the *London Telegraph*

With eyes strained from five days of reading in a dimly lit library and my back wrenched by the springs of the pullout couch, I fled Primrose Hill for swinging Chelsea. I went uptown and upscale, from dank to swank, in thirty minutes south on the London Tube. Beaten up and a little bowed by my B&B experience, it was with great anticipation that I checked myself into the Sloane Hotel.

This one-of-a-kind hotel sits tucked behind London's Sloane Square, well beyond the rhythm and racket of swinging, chic Chelsea. In fact, were it not for the Union Jack snapping above the entrance and the simple brass plate reading Sloane Hotel, you could walk past its facade a dozen times and not know it to be one of the most exclusive of English inns. In this neighbourhood that gave its name to the Chelsea bun—where rakish yuppies are known as Sloane Rangers—this five-storey, twelve-room hotel is a sanctum, a silent jewel set among a string of identical tall-and-narrow red brick townhouses built in the time of Queen Victoria.

It is truly one of the premier hotels of the world, and I know this because it's listed in a directory entitled *Premier Hotels of the World*. (I have a keen eye for the obvious.) From its ensuite marble bathrooms to a twenty-four-hour food-and-beverage service, the

Sloane is the epitome of elegance and comfort.

The lobby, a symmetrical scene of beige walls dramatically appointed by rich antiques and framed oil paintings, is bathed in a warm orange glow from a crackling marble fireplace. Travel-worn Louis Vuitton suitcases are stacked three high beside the uniform of a British navy admiral hanging limp on a headless mannequin. The hallway is guarded by a life-size statue of Napoleon . . . a great man perhaps, but not a very big one. All the chairs in this lobby are cushy and inviting, including the hooded white leather porter's chair that sits next to the lift. (I tell you, this place is so posh, the porter has his own porter.)

Everything in the hotel—the four-poster, queen-size Empire beds, the Japanese wardrobes, the Burmese privacy screens, the Louis XV-style canopy sofas, the pressed-glass candlestick lamps— is antique and exquisite. Every room is a decorator's tour de force, each with its own distinct personality created by a careful collaboration of colours and artifacts. It's like a museum with live bodies.

The Sloane's staff choices seem to be mandated by a United Nations resolution: one manager and a busboy from Spain, a deskman from Chicago, a guy from Australia, a woman from Poland, two porters from Vancouver, and a very elegant and cordial general manager, Rebecca Maxwell, from—wait for it—Deep River, Ontario.

After I checked in, my aching frame told me exactly what I needed: two hours of uninterrupted, unadulterated luxury. I hit the stopper and turned on the hot tap of the deep, square, red-tiled bathtub, and set a large glass of Lagavulin on the marble ledge. I placed the little television set on the foot of the bed so I could see it from the bathroom and lost myself in a long, hot soak.

For a tourist, luxury is an "upgrade." For a traveller, it's a reward.

Perusing the BBC News, I sipped the whisky slowly, breathed deeply, and toasted life's small and marvellous moments, all the while vowing never to spend another week of my life in a library basement or a loony bin B&B.

It wasn't until later that I discovered the uniqueness of the Sloane. Bundled up in my terrycloth robe and leafing through a small bedside book while propped up on my French *lit bateau* against three Lace Lady cushions, I found myself reading the price tags on the twin pressed-glass candlestick lamps with gold shades. And that's when I realized—everything in the Sloane Hotel, on every floor, in every room (except for the disembodied admiral, which has become the hotel mascot, and the front desk, which was custom-made by Viscount Linley), *everything* is available for guests to first use, then purchase.

"Selling off the silver," as the British say; everything has a price. Small souvenirs of the Sloane are neatly scattered everywhere: volumes of Thackeray's works, antique hairbrush sets, vintage timepieces by Rolex and Cartier, tiny, perfect *objets d'art*, Annick Goutal *parfums*. And the prices here are better than in the antique shops that line nearby King's Road. As I catch myself laughing in the 1.5-metre-square, carved wood over-mantel mirror in Flemish manner (circa 1899), I think: I could just reach over and pick up that phone (asking price £60) and buy the whole lot of it for £6,135 or $14,724 Canadian.

The brilliant idea, which makes the Sloane the only antique shop hotel in the world, is the brainchild of owner Sue Rogers, an interior decorator and collectible dealer by trade. One day a guest begged to buy a print hanging in her room, and a light went on. The light was a Vaughan lacquer lamp costing $2,064, and, well . . . you get the picture. *If* you have $2,080—the asking price for a framed still life called *Flowers in an Urn*. After selling seven beds in one year to American, German, and Japanese tourists, Sue Rogers went on a four-poster buying binge to antique fairs and auction houses in England and France.

I tell you, this place has so much class that if the bathtubs were only one foot deep, I'd still be in over my head.

As I walked the halls studying Edwardian prints, I sank into carpets so thick I fear short guests could go missing for days. I'm telling you, this place has so much class, the bellhop was played by Sir John Gielgud.

At the very top of the hotel is a small sitting room, where guests can have their meals or a drink. An adjoining terrace unlocks a view of roof-topped London, including nearby Royal Hospital Chelsea, which was designed by Christopher Wren. From there, with binoculars, you can see the well-coiffed staff at Harrods deftly placing the £100 price stickers on jars of marmalade.

Check in with your husband, check out with Napoleon. At the Sloane Hotel, you can shop till you drop without ever getting out of bed.

London: Where It Costs 20p to Take One

Before booking airfare to London, one thing you should seriously consider is winning the lottery. London is expensive. Really expensive.

Taking a break one night from my research at the zoo, I ambled down to the Queen's Pub at Primrose Hill and placed a £10 note on the bar. My pint of Harp—a very good English ale—was £2.65, and a bag of crisps was 80p. That's closing in on $10 Canadian, but then where else can you get "turkey stuffing" flavoured chips and a brew named after a musical instrument? I followed this up with a steak and kidney pie, and there went my budget for London on $20 a day.

Next to me at the bar of the Queen's Pub sat an old man, a little grizzled but not in the least shy. "Yank, are you?" he asked.

"No, I'm Canadian," I replied, a little too quickly.

"Canadian, you say?" he said. "Let's see—we got our Micks, we got our Spicks, we got Jocks, Frogs, Yanks, Yits, Crouts, Paddies, and Sweaty Socks . . . you know, I don't believe we have a nasty name for Canadians. Albert? Do we have a slammer for Canadians? No, I didn't think so." Turning slowly back to me, he smiled and said, "I suppose that means we quite like you people."

So I bought him a pint.

Then I told him a couple of stories about Canadians, and I heard him turn to Albert and say, "He's a real nutter, this one."

So there it is. Henceforth all Canadians travelling to England

Travel Sign

AUTOMATIC WASHING MACHINES. PLEASE REMOVE ALL YOUR CLOTHES WHEN THE LIGHT GOES OUT.
—Sign in a London laundromat

will be known as "Nutters." Sorry, I make a lousy first impression.

You want to know how expensive London is? In Victoria Station—I'm not making this up—it costs 20p to take a pee! That's 52 cents. Even if a really weird guy in a rubber jump suit stands too close to you at the trough, and consequently you can't go. No pay now, leak later policy here.

A coffee and croissant is $5, and a traditional fish and chips takeout wrapped in newspaper with a pint is $16, if you can find an English fish and chip shop these days. Then you still have to do your "please take pity on me" tourist routine to get the guy in a nearby pub to let you bring it in and eat it.

It is therefore essential that, upon your arrival in England, you acquaint yourself with the currency.

When I was there, £1 equalled $2.26. One pence was 2.26 cents. The pound notes start at 5 and go up: 10, 20, 50, 100. The pound is a small, thick coin, the size of our penny. Their penny is the size of our quarter, but thinner. There's a 5p, a 10p, a 20p coin, which is octagonal and small, and a 50p coin, which is octagonal and larger. There's also a £2 coin just like our toonie.

A wee bit confused? Okay, here's how it works.

Me: How much is this guidebook?

Shopkeeper: Wot? The guidebook? Thatta be ten quid, gov'ner.

Me (puzzled): Okay, then how about this map?

Shopkeeper: Thatta be a fiver.

Me: Okay, how about this postcard?

Shopkeeper: Wot? This here postcard? Why, that's a half a crown, mate.

Me (finally mastering the mystery of English money): Do you take Visa?

The Trafalgar Pub: A Prize Despite the Size

The pub is an English social phenomenon. The tiny Trafalgar Pub is strangely emblematic of England itself—a courageous little place set still and apart from encroaching currents, a solid rock in the middle of a muddy pond. Located on the same corner in London's Merton area for well over a hundred years, in a simple, brick house with two heavy oak doors, the Trafalgar looks every bit like an unpretentious London local. And it is. Except that it's just so damn small. There are six stools at the bar, four tables the size of large ashtrays that have small ashtrays on them, and adjacent benches for eight—maximum seating capacity, fourteen.

The "new" addition, built eighty years ago (everything in England is old), bumped total occupancy up to about twenty or so, thirty if everybody stands against the walls. "Or fifty as of New Year's Eve last," says Douglas Webb, the bubbly and balding publican, as he draws another pint of Fuller's Extra Special.

Looking around the Trafalgar, you get the feeling you're in the Museum of Modern Clutter. A large collection of knickknacks that customers have brought back from abroad is scattered around the place. Hanging from the overhead beams is a shining array of copperware—mugs, horns, buckets, and ships' lamps—all hauled down and polished once a week. Fresh, red carnations in crystal vases grace all of the tables, backdropped by deep red velvet curtains.

Over the Top Down Under

Aussies have always been very proud of their beer, but they may have gone too far with billboards for Foster's Lager that read: "So good, you won't even want to pee!" I think we're all relieved that Foster's doesn't sell fruit bars.

The genial governor of the pub for the past thirty years smiles at all the questions I ask of him and usually answers: "Wot?" Mr. Webb, in his "whistling flute," sorry, grey suit with flashy brown tie and handkerchief to boot, is a bit "Mutt and Jeff," which rhymes with deaf and rings of cockney colloquialism. As tender of the wee Trafalgar he's a man content, absolutely in his element. When he's not pulling on the long, elegant pump handles to send a frothy batch of brew into his patrons' pints, he sneaks a half of Guinness for himself and roughs up his dog, Hector, who occasionally saunters down from the living quarters up in the back. It's two-and-a-half pulls to the pint, and Mr. Webb delivers each draught slowly, carefully, with a love long lost in today's bartenders. He talks softly and modestly, and weathers easily the good-natured abuse of his regulars. You get the sense that if nobody came to this tiny tavern he'd still put a suit on every day, and he and Hector would have a jolly good time.

On the way to the loo, I am stopped by one such regular, who holds up the dice game he is playing with his three mates to ask me, "How do you find the old gentleman behind the bar?"

"Oh, wonderful," I reply. "Very helpful." I smile back at Mr.

Webb, who is artfully coaxing a pint of ale up from a keg in the basement.

"Been dead two years, he has, did you know that?" asks the ruddy-faced man, to the hysteria of the other three at the bar.

"Wot?" booms the voice of Mr. Webb.

"Telling this lad how much you mean to us all," quips the quick-tongued customer. "How we couldn't get on without you, governor. Wot!"

That kind of banter fills an English pub, and by law fulfills its purpose—a place to get away from home that soon becomes a home.

The tiny Trafalgar has been tagged with the nickname "Thrupence Penny Hop," dating back to the days when a pint of ale cost four pence everywhere else but remained three pence here. It's one of the few disappearing "free house" pubs unaffiliated with any one brewery and therefore able to serve up any ale or lager Mr. Webb so chooses. Serving a dozen different brews in a place barely bigger than a bread box is no small feat; the basement must look like a barrel factory. In addition to the name brands of draught, they blend their own special pints, and they sell a good variety of bottled brews, as well. A single glass, bar-top pantry does a bad job of warming pork pies, cheese rolls, and sausage. And, of course, packets of crisps.

Dining Out Travel Tips

• Looking around the room playing "Married/Not Married" is fine. Betting and writing down your scores is tacky.

• "Always wash your hands upon leaving the washroom" does not constitute a tip. Most people leave money.

Two regulars at the bar, Ricky Paul and Ian Rushton, are in the process of turning a game of cribbage into a marathon, progressing from pints of bitters to snifters of port in what began as one drink and a quick hand of cards. Ian Rushton introduces himself as the reigning cribbage champion of the Trafalgar. Several times.

When I ask them why they like this pub so much, unhesitating and in unison they reply, "Because the wives can't get at us here!"

They both point to the end of the bar, where nailed to the wall is "the male pleasure licence" of the traditional English pub. It lists the prices the bartender charges to answer an incoming call for you: "Just left = 30p"; "On his way = 50p"; "Haven't seen him = £1"; "Not here = £2"; and "Who??? = £5."

Of course, it's cozy and quaint, but more than that, the Trafalgar has a quiet kind of cheer about it, an enclave of ease insulated from the hectic city that surrounds it.

And did I mention it is small? The Trafalgar is so small, you can only enter sideways, and then only one at a time. This place is so small the lunch special is steak and pigmy pie. I mean this pub is so small the dart team has to stand across the street and lob the darts back in through the window.

The dull thump of a card being played on the bar, the rattle of rolling dice in the wooden gaming box, the quiet laughter from the mild ribaldry of friends—all of this is the sound of a perfect pub in old London town. The Trafalgar is the smallest and one of the best.

Part Three

Florida: That Knob at the Top of the Keys

A tourist is a gawker; a traveller, a walker.
A tourist is on vacation;
a traveller is on a personal pilgrimage.

Welcome to Florida—"Hey! I've Just Been Robbed!"

First, let me say, I hate Florida. But you have to go there to get to Key West. The Sunshine State is a 58,560-square-mile retirement home landscaped with stagnant swamps and shopping malls, and largely populated by land developers, lunatics, and people who have great difficulty voting. (As one woman from the Midwest said after the Florida debacle that eventually resulted in the disaster known as "Dubya": "Those damn people can play twenty bingo cards at once. How come they can't fill out one simple ballot?)

On one trip down to the Keys, I flew into Fort Lauderdale to pick up a car and was robbed within an hour and a half of the plane touching down. Robbed nicely, casually, and non-violently, I hasten to add. They'd have ripped me off sooner, but the shuttle bus of InterAmerican Car Rental took thirty minutes to get me from the airport to their agency lot a half a mile away. (I knew something was slightly off centre when I walked into InterAmerican's office and read this warning on the wall: "It is prohibited to drive our cars outside the state of Florida." My question: "Is there any way I might play cards for a lot of money with the guy who named this company?" By now he's probably the president and CEO of TransWorld Airlines, motto: "We fly anywhere within the continental United States.")

On my way down State Road 84, I pulled into a plaza to purchase my week's supply of sustenance—a mickey of Scotch, a

Cultural Misunderstanding

In 1987, when Pope John Paul II came to America, he was dogged by protesters speaking out against the Roman Catholic Church's stance on homosexuality. In Miami, when the old but still regal Holy See, dressed in flowing robes, took to a massive altar to give mass, he had to look across the road at a huge billboard put up by gays that read: "He's just another man in a dress."

six-pack of beer, and a bottle of Champagne—all at Walgreens. Then I went next door to Winn-Dixie to buy some groceries. I put my box of booze in a Styrofoam cooler and left it at the ten-items-or-less checkout counter, in the safekeeping of two young female clerks. I quickly grabbed some ice and an armful of food, returned to the checkout counter, and there was my Styrofoam cooler—gone!

"Ah, excuse me, miss? My cooler?"

"Oh, I thought you came and got it."

"No, if I'd come and got it, I'd still have it. Except I don't. Yes, I am from Canada, but I don't even know Doug Henning."

Now, the manager of Winn-Dixie turned out to be a very nice, sympathetic guy. He's been robbed lots of times before, but never of goods his store doesn't even stock. This heist broke new ground, even for Florida.

Meanwhile, back at Walgreens, where I had to obtain proof of purchase, the saleslady and I swapped stories. Me, ripped off in the Sunshine State before I can break a sweat, and her, dealing with a second robbery her first day on the job. The Walgreens lady was nice. The Winn-Dixie manager made good on my losses. I felt so good about it, I immediately went across the street and stuck up a gas station just so I'd blend in more with the locals.

Florida's state motto is "In God we trust." He'd be the only one, for sure. Word of advice to Florida thieves: if you use InterAmerican cars as getaway vehicles, you'd better not try to transport your stolen goods across the state line. Otherwise, you'll be in clear violation of your rental agreement.

Driving a getaway car would be the worst job you could have in Florida. Often, you can't actually see other drivers, only suntanned hands with white knuckles gripping the steering wheels. Most drivers in Florida have shrunk below the height of the dashboard.

You know that joke? The one in which the Miami nursing home residents are having a gloomy conversation about their arthritis, their cataracts, and their frequent fainting spells, until one woman cheerfully adds: "Thank God we can all still drive!" In Florida, they don't laugh at that joke. They ask the name of the nursing home, then circle it on their map as a place to avoid at all costs.

Key West: Weird Town, USA

Travel is fatal to prejudice, bigotry, and narrow-mindedness.
—Mark Twain

The journey from Fort Lauderdale to Key West is a pleasant, interesting, slightly devious drive down Interstate 95. First up is Key Largo, which is not really Key Largo, but Rock Harbor. The name was changed to cash in on the hype of the '40s flick starring Humphrey Bogart and Edward G. Robinson. And no, the movie was not shot here, as they would have you believe. At the local Holiday Inn, you can take a ride on the *African Queen*, the original steam-powered boat used in that movie starring Humphrey Bogart and Katharine Hepburn, also not shot anywhere near here.

Until you get to the Lower Keys, it's a slow and slippery drive down a strip of souvenir shops and dive shops. There's no short-age of tourist booths, and they all use the description "exotic." The most exotic thing about this drive is the International House of Pancakes at Marathon, marker mile 50. I had a huge urge to stop, get photographed in the car eating an international pancake plate, and then send the photo to the guy at the InterAmerican rental car agency: "As you can see, I'm having crepes in Paris. Just try and stop me now!"

From Key Largo to Key West, it's 106 miles of flat road and concrete causeway, all shadowed by a natural reef and heated by the Gulf Stream, which clings to the entire coast, shimmering like liquid glass from the bottom of the clear, shallow waters.

The Keys, which officially run from Biscayne Bay near Miami to the Dry Tortugas, seventy turbulent miles off Key West, were not originally linked by road; they were connected by railroad. Up and running by 1912, Henry Flagler's Florida East Coast Railway extension line was either a stroke of sheer genius or the grandest exercise in naivety in the history of American transportation. The successful completion of this amazing engineering endeavour displayed uncanny brilliance. Its utter destruction by a 1935 hurricane, a nameless 200-mph killer, made the whole concept look silly, like a model train set left out in a monsoon. Along with Flagler's folly, eight hundred people died.

Today, rusting remnants of the railroad run alongside Route 1, a sad reminder of an exhilarating era now dead and drowned in a place where wind and water have no respect for a shallow strip of topsoil tailing off into the ocean alone.

The two-lane route down to Key West is interesting, sometimes beautiful, with turquoise seas and purple jacaranda trees,

Unsavvy Travellers

A young British couple were the toast of the town after arriving from London for their dream vacation in sunny Sydney, Australia. Unfortunately, they had dealt with a travel agent over the Internet, and the town they were the toast of was Sydney, Nova Scotia. The clue that they might be on the wrong continent came after they landed in Halifax and were transferred to a small prop plane. "I'm not the best flyer in the world," said nineteen-year-old Emma Nunn, "but I couldn't see a small plane like that going all the way to Sydney, Australia." That, and the opera house in Halifax is a tad smaller than the one in Sydney, the one you can see from the moon.

After a warm Cape Breton welcome, Emma and her boyfriend, Raoul Sebastian, were having fun, but also looking forward to returning to England to strangle the travel agent.

Be very careful on the return flight, kids. There's also a London, Ontario, eh?

No Good Travel Deed Goes Unpunished

Returning home once, I cleared Canada Customs only to hit a traffic jam at the escalator in Terminal 1. All of a sudden, someone shouted: *"Uno! Dos! Tres!"* And two women leapt onto the first set of moving steps. The larger, older woman fell down first. The younger woman, perhaps her middle-aged daughter, went down trying to grab her.

Skirting the crowd, I jumped over the rail, dropped my shoulder bag on the escalator, stepped over the younger woman, and grabbed the older lady. I tried to lift her up, but her centre of gravity has sunk. In sailing terms, she was "turtled." Finally, I wrestled her to her feet, clutching her arms and wheeling her around like we were executing an allemande left in full-contact square dancing.

Then it occurred to me that if this woman had never stepped onto an escalator, she had never stepped *off* of one either. She screamed as the one safe step she had come to trust began to disappear, and with a mighty heave I lifted her up and thrust her onto the floor. We both went down in a heap. The younger woman, and those who had helped her up, plus everybody's carry-on luggage, piled into us from behind.

Meanwhile, a quick-thinking Canadian was tossing everybody's bags out of the way, so those still on the escalator wouldn't trip on arrival. With all good intentions, he kicked my shoulder bag into the wall and that's when it happened: the sudden and untimely death of Senhor Macieira from Portugal. He smashed my bottle of Five Star Macieira. You can't fault the guy, but I do think laws should be in place to have people like him flogged in public.

Surviving is a snap, I thought, as I plodded through the airport with a steady stream of brandy leaking out the bottom of my leather bag. Do-gooding, *that's* the difficult part.

and almost always tacky, with signs beckoning drivers to "Go All the Way!" to the end of the road. Going down, Route 1 is a road. Coming back, in the sights of an oncoming hurricane, it's the only exit in an overcrowded outdoor theatre after somebody has just yelled "Fire!"

The Keys, unfortunately, are following the lead of the rest of Florida, where over-development and a disrespect for nature have seen even the once great Everglades decimated, and continue to endanger its indigenous species.

The Conchs brag about their birthright —and validate it with a traditional conch shell on the family lawn—and occasionally declare independence from the rest of America. But Key West is the end of the road for the rest of the locals, displaced Americans fresh out of running room from spouses and dreams, normal life and the law. For many of its 28,000 citizens, the American Dream skids off track here and splashes into the surf in the shallow shoals of the Atlantic.

Yet there is something about the Keys, a sense of adventure, an element of risk, a feeling that something's about to happen that you've never seen before but will remember always.

Monica and I were sitting at an outdoor bar late one afternoon, drinking cold draught beer and fetching small plates of barbecue from a charity foodfest in the parking lot. As the place began to fill up, we started to clear out, until a waiter put a hand on my shoulder and said, "Stay a while. It's worth it." We did, and an hour later, without a word of warning or introduction, the great Clarence Clemens appeared and played his saxophone well into the night.

Tourists Too Stupid to Travel

Uttered by a tourist standing in front of the Victoria Park
Restaurant in Niagara Falls:

Question: Can we walk to Expo (Vancouver) from here?

Answer: You can, but you'll want to get up real early
and pack a lunch.

You see things in the Keys: a bartender wearing a necklace and
bracelets of live snakes; outrageously dressed drag queens quoting
Tennessee Williams; frantic partners dancing on a Duval Street
balcony that you swear is about to collapse under their weight; a
white witch in flowing black robes returning from shopping on a
pink flamingo bicycle with her groceries in a wicker handlebar
basket. It's a people watcher's paradise, and after a week walking
the streets, back alleys, and beaches of Key West, I can't help but
come up with a much more appropriate name for the place. When
you think about it, Key West is kind of a boring designation for
a city situated so far south. But Eccentricity City captures the
personality of the place just perfectly.

Normalcy is left behind . . . and tolerance seems to thrive.
Out-of-era hippies, would-be Jimmy Buffetts with parrots on their
shoulders, homeless beachcombers with great tans, white-bearded
Hemingway look-alikes with their captain's hats askew, gangs
of gays enjoying "San Francisco South"—all have a place in the
Keys, where a laissez-faire, live-and-let-live policy seems to rule
all encounters.

You can't help but stumble across the once close ties between the Keys and Cuba, Key West being closer to Havana than to Miami by about twenty miles. A souvenir sign from the '50s hangs on the outside wall of a bar in Mallory Square: "Fly to Havana in Thirty Minutes. $10 Plus Tax." Since 1960, the United States has forbidden its citizens to travel to Cuba, and there has been no official diplomatic communication at any level of government. A decade ago, however, this did not stop the mayor of Key West, Sonny McCoy, from water-skiing the ninety miles to Havana in six hours and ten minutes for no apparent reason whatsoever (the very same reason most things happen in the Keys).

The fire chief of Key West, Bum Farto, left office after a drug conviction and has not been heard from since. These are not the delusional ramblings of a jet-lagged mind, but actual names and events documented in the *Citizen*, the local newspaper.

Not all that long ago, Key West authorities seceded from the United States, declared the island the Conch Republic, declared war against America, and then quickly surrendered and asked for cash reparations. Wouldn't this have been an irresistible ticket for Conch Republic voters: President Sonny McCoy and his trusty V.P. sidekick, Bum Farto.

In recent years, Key West weirdness has spread to the large pet community. In the 1989 mayoral election, bar owner Captain Tony Tarracina defeated candidate Tom Sawyer by thirty-two votes, while Willoughby the Cat, a very fat and very famous local tabby, finished with thirty-seven official write-in votes. Headline in the paper: "Tony wins by a whisker!" Think about it. If Tom Sawyer had taken the cat's candidacy seriously and made a deal to win over his supporters, today Willoughby the Cat could have had Bum Farto's old job as the Key West fire chief.

In 1990 Winston the Horse was, in the words of the *Citizen*, "surprise attacked on his 'dangles' by Unknown the Pit Bull." The startled horse escaped the pit bull by taking refuge on top of a parked car. Both animal and vehicle needed extensive body repair.

In 1993 Chi Chi the pot belly pig was charged with sexually assaulting a parked Harley-Davidson motorcycle. Honest. The Harley needed a new fender, but suffered no lasting emotional damage. The pig had a pretty good defence—he thought it was just another "hog." The pig's punishment? Castration. 'Cause down here nobody messes with another man's Harley.

Also in 1993, Rocky the Chihuahua, who must be one smooth-talkin' pooch, was sued for impregnating a purebred Rottweiler. A publication ban prohibits using the embarrassed Rottweiler's name in this story, so we'll just call her Strumpet. Although the outcome of the civil suit is not known, a sentence of castration for Rocky the Chihuahua was never under consideration. In Key West, as long as it's consensual and the victim isn't 40% chrome, the damages are strictly monetary.

Benedict Thielen, one of the hundreds of writers who've made this island their home, may have said it best: "Key West is a place where the unexpected happens with monotonous regularity." Put another way by a bumper sticker I spotted: "Shit Happens. But More Shit Happens in Key West."

Key West—where America dead-ends and the bizarre begins.

That One Place, Far from the Madding Crowd

Because of its wonderful climate and intrinsic insanity, Key West has always been a haven for writers. Hemingway suffered through thirteen years of hangovers here. Tennessee Williams came for the sailors at the naval base, while Robert Frost came to be a recluse. Many Pulitzer Prize winners, such as Elizabeth Bishop, Philip Caputo, John Hersey, and Wallace Stevens, lived and wrote in these small, brightly painted gingerbread houses, heavily protected from the sun by a thick canopy of shade trees.

Key West is rife with writerly stories. Hemingway punched out Wallace Stevens here after the poet remarked that he didn't much care for the novelist's work. But then again, Hemingway was quick to duke it out with any writer, as long as they were a lot older, like Wallace Stevens, or a lot smaller, like Morley Callaghan. But the story guaranteed to raise another round of beer in any Key West pub is the one in which Truman Capote proved the power of the pen over the penis. While bar-hopping with Tennessee Williams, Capote was asked by an inebriated woman to sign his name in a circle around her navel. Which he did, to the anger of her drunken husband. Storming over to Capote's table, the man whipped out his mighty sword and bellowed, "How would you like to autograph this!" Capote replied quite calmly in that lispy, giggly voice: "I don't think I could autograph it, but I might be able to initial it."

Set back amid a jungle of palms and wild plants are houses painted in blushing pastels, tropical turquoise, and hot pink. A few are nearly as rough and ready as the boarding houses or cigar-making factories they once were. By far the most thematically unique of these houses is Authors of Key West, an elegant little writers' compound snuggled into a corner lot at the very top of Old Town. Inside the high walls and iron wrought gate is something very rare in this carnival known as the Conch Republic: quietness. Blissful, barefoot, palpable, soft, slow-motion silence that makes you want to read and write, think grand thoughts, and take long naps. In this city of salsa bands and honky-tonk bars, conch train tours and buskers, the only place more tranquil than this B&B is the City Cemetery over on Olivia Street, the permanent home of more people than presently live in Key West.

If small can be sprawling, Authors of Key West has managed to pull it off. The main building has four bedrooms upstairs and three downstairs, along with the office and breakfast nook. Just a few feet away is the pool, which is a wonderful refreshing water station but three is definitely a crowd.

There are four spoiled cats that prowl the property and five cockatiels in a screened gazebo who are very, very aware of them.

Aside from the main house, there are several small cottages scattered around the property. Each is named after a famous Key

The Little White House in Key West, a sprawling structure with a double facade and wooden louvers, is well worth a visit—but you can't sleep there. Even President Harry Truman, who called it home on ten vacations during his administration, would not be able to sleep there today. Somebody stole his bed.

West author: Lillian Hellman, Thornton Wilder, John James Audubon, Jimmy Kirkwood, and, of course, playwright Tennessee Williams, who lived just over on Duncan Street when he gave the final polish to *A Streetcar Named Desire*. I stayed for a week in the Hemingway cottage, a cozy, wooden-porched cabin complete with a stocked kitchen, an air-conditioned bedroom, a bathroom with shower, and a large living room with a TV, a small dining table, a roll-top desk, and an antique typewriter. The cottage also comes with a cat: Leo—a Hemingway six-toed cat, of course, with an attitude about what exactly belongs to him. Namely, your lap.

The rack of an elk adorns the door sill; big game antlers frame the living room wall. Framed photos of America's most revered writer, with many of his wives, hang from the walls of all rooms. An almost complete collection of early editions of his books lines the desk. The ancient Underwood is about the same age as Hemingway's famous Royal . . . "In the late evenings of that week, Leo and I sat on the porch of a cottage in a town on an island . . ." Sorry, but it's kind of contagious, if you know what I mean.

No matter what the weather, the cottages are dark; like all houses in Key West they are defended against the sun by a tangle of tropical plants, and hurricane shutters cover the windows. But each guest's quarters has a porch, or a balcony, or some kind of little outside nook.

By day, the scents of blooming bougainvillea and flowering orchid trees permeate the place. By night, lighted stained glass windows bathe everything in a soft, southern glow.

Authors is open to anybody, but there's a considerable discount offered to repeat clients and authors who leave a signed copy of a book behind. In the library of signed editions, Lisa Alther's *Kinflicks*

Travel Sign

IT'S HARD TO MAKE A COMEBACK WHEN YOU HAVEN'T GONE ANYWHERE.
—Written in the dust on the back of a bus in Wickenburg, Arizona

is popular, *The Procrastinator's Success Book* generates a lot of interest but never gets read, and local writer Stuart Woods has been known to drop by and get a reader's first-hand review of his latest Key West mystery.

A travel tip sheet, something that should be mandatory in every place offering accommodations, ensures that guests know all the best buys, favourite restaurants, local gossip, and historical information necessary for an engaging and memorable stay. Anything of importance is within a twenty-minute walk of Authors: the five public tennis courts in Bayview Park; the calamity called Duval Street with all its designer shops; Jimmy Buffett's Margaritaville; Sloppy Joe's; the Hog's Breath Saloon; the fish market, wine store, and raw bars of Schooner's Wharf; the Hemingway home; and especially Mallory Square, where in early evening the conch heads gather to bid farewell to the sun in a circus-like tradition of magic and mayhem.

Yet all is quiet on the home front. Authors always seems full, but you seldom bump into anybody except during continental breakfast hours, and even they are unrushed and uncrowded. This place has captured perfectly the pace of Key Westers: "Don't know where we're going, no hurry to get there, and still arrive too soon."

Travel Tip for Aging Boomers: Go to Florida

Feeling your age lately? Not bouncing out of bed, let alone in it, like you used to? Been getting up to answer the door, only to find that the knocking was coming from your knees? Need a temporary lift while everything with skin is falling down around you? Is that what's troubling you, Boomer? I have the answer: Florida. In Florida, where the average age is 87, every Baby Boomer, by law, is referred to as "the kid." But remember, hanging out with the snowbirds doesn't mean you're one of them. In case you're confused, here are some sure-fire signs that you're way too young to be a snowbird:

- You show up to eat at a restaurant with money instead of coupons.
- You think one Waffle Shop, Waffle Shoppe, Waffle Shack, or Waffle House is just as good as another.
- Until you actually see it happen, you wonder who the hell would play miniature golf "All Day for $5."
- You don't immediately recognize the complimentary bowl of apples at the bank as your primary weekly food source.
- When planning a day trip you don't allow for the amount of time it takes to get out of the car.
- You learn that when a woman slaps a man's face in a bar, she's just trying to keep him awake.
- And finally, you know you're too young to be a snowbird because . . . you tip.

Part Four

The Caribbean (and Mexico): Don't Trip Over the Conga Line

A tourist takes trips;

a traveller sets off on grand journeys and,

okay, trips a lot.

St. Lucia: Fame in Far-off Places

Somewhere around the fourth or fifth day on a slow and dreamy tropical island, I get the urge to start a revolution. This occurred to me last year as I walked the island of St. Lucia, the largest of the Windward Islands in the deep southeast of the Caribbean.

At first glance, St. Lucia looks like the perfect palm-treed paradise—hazy indigo images, white beaches tracing the shores of haunting volcanoes, black men with gold teeth in the market hacking coconuts in half with machetes, a kid beside a lonely road holding a live snake twice his size, women ablaze in bright cotton colours with headdresses piled high on their head, knotted according to their marital status. In a blinding blur of glaring sunlight and damp, dark shadows, St. Lucia is a feast for foreign eyes.

There is culture as well, in the Caribe style. Derek Walcott, considered to be one of the greatest English-language poets alive today, was born in the capital of Castries. Walking north along the coastal road you come across an outdoor theatre and elegant restaurant named in his honour. Look up from Marigot Bay, the naturally U-shaped lagoon James Michener called "the most beautiful bay in the Caribbean," and you'll see the mountain-top mansions of Oprah Winfrey and George Foreman. You can almost see them gossiping over the fence, she giving him best-selling books, he paying her back with burgers from his famous grill.

Like two huge black breasts bursting out of the island from a volcanic inferno, Petit Piton and Gros Piton are the landmarks of

St. Lucia, visible from miles around, the source of folklore every-where. At the nearby fishing port of Soufriere, somehow pro-nounced Soo-fret in the local French-Creole patois, people line up at several spots for island buses that may or may not show up, may or may not be going where they're supposed to go. Confusion reigns until darkness descends, a price is arranged with anybody with a van, and families headed to different destinations pile in and leave, at last, mostly laughing.

At nearby Mount Soufriere, the "drive-in" volcano hisses steam and regurgitates black volcanic muck through a rocky, pot-holed crater that looks like the surface of the moon. You used to be able to drive onto this crater and walk around the boiling holes of lava, amid the strong stink of sulphur. But one day a guide fell through a deceptively thin crust and into the active volcano. Amaz-ingly, he lived. Twelve years and many skin grafts later, he's a local celebrity. The lava pools are now fenced off to visitors, and guides are required to stay on the walkway.

St. Lucians are not the friendliest people in the Caribbean, but they are definitely the fiercest drivers. Young daredevils verily punish their minivans, driving as fast as possible over very bad roads and around hair-raising switchback curves. They pass on hills and bends, race through small villages, and slow down not a bit on mountain roads with no guard rails between them and the rocky shore below. I was certain my ride in from Hewanorra Airport was going to be my last.

And, as I said, near the end of the week, my adoration for the island waned. As the infatuation wore thin, I imagined myself as the famous and revered bearded rebel Che Guevara, collecting foot soldiers as I rode through mountain villages until we're an over-whelming army descending on the capital and sworn to do good. I'd lead everybody into the main square, and after a nine-hour Castro-like speech, I'd declare every Saturday to be Pick Up the Bloody Garbage Day.

What looked like a tropical Utopia on day one, looks like a living landfill upon closer inspection. Like most of the Caribbean islands, the shoulders of roads seem to be made of bottle caps and broken glass. The harbours look like floating dumpsters, and the beaches, except those of the hotels, look like exotic litter zones.

St. Lucia once had rolling, lush banana plantations, picture-postcard scenes in vivid greens and yellow. To protect the fruit from bugs, the banana clusters are now wrapped in bright blue bags. And when these flimsy pieces of plastic fall off, nobody picks them up. The plantations now look like they're withstanding a garbage strike. And don't get me started about the treatment of animals, or I'll start handing out live ammo to my troops back on the square.

Word of advice to Caribbean tour operators: if Canadians wanted to wallow in garbage, they'd vacation in the city of Toronto.

My Che Guevara daydream fading, I packed my bags and headed for home, mumbling to myself about the serenity to accept what I cannot change.

When I got to the airport, having survived the return roller-coaster ride through the mountains (which in St. Lucia is like win-ning the daily double), a funny thing happened. As I milled around the open-air lounge, waiting for a Royal Air flight that was the usual four hours late, an older woman broke from a group of senior Canadians and headed straight towards me.

"I'm a big fan of yours," she said, extending her suntanned hand.

"Really," I said, taken aback.

"You're that funny writer from Canada," she said, with great enthusiasm.

"Well," I said, trying to strike the right response between humility and getting her to say it again, only louder.

"I have all your books," she continued.

"Well, that's great," I said. "And thank you." Now I'm not just dealing with a fan, but with someone who puts food on my table.

"Oh, yeah," she said, "I heard you speak once at the Different Drummer author series, and you were hilarious."

Now, I have to tell you, these moments of celebrity are rare for all Canadians, save for Céline Dion, and therefore to be cherished. Frankly, unclaimed bodies back in the morgue have a better chance of recognition than Canadian writers abroad.

"And I love your radio show," she said.

My spirit went suddenly dead. I told her I didn't have a radio show.

"Well, of course you do," she said, undeterred. "You know, Sundays at noon on—"

"I am not Stuart McLean!" I said, with great irritation and edginess in my voice.

"Oh, you artists are all the same," she laughed, giving me a little never-mind wave as she returned to her group.

"I am not Stuart McLean!" I yelled after her. Why the hell don't people mind their own business, anyway?

As she faced the others with her back to me, I heard her say, "You see that guy behind me? The one with the eyebrows? Yeah,

Travel Tip

Should you be mistaken for someone famous in a foreign country, do not deny. Just say, "Ah, yeah, well, you got me. Listen, I got mugged in the market . . . could you lend me $200 and I'll have my agent contact you as soon as I get home?"

well, that's Stuart McLean." And then, lowering her voice to the depths of condescension, she added, "But he doesn't want anybody to recognize him."

I could have killed her. But, then again, I had trouble finding the market in Castries; I wouldn't have a clue where to hide a body in this country.

Jamaica: Big Mistake-a

The weather is here; I wish you were beautiful.
—Jimmy Buffett

"Crown jewel of the Caribbean," say the brochures. "Fashionable playground of the international set."

I really wanted to fall head over heels for Jamaica with its pirate past and mystic Blue Mountains, breathtaking beaches, jungle waterfalls, and colourful markets. Noel Coward's choice to build his second home, Fire Fly, here means the island could not be all bad, I thought.

Sorry, but I'm pretty much with Jimmy Buffett on this one. Jimmy wrote a song entitled "Jamaica Mistake-a" after the Jamaican military mistook his plane for a drug carrier, opened fire, and put some fair-sized holes in the fuselage.

So when the Adventure Tours brochure gushed, "Jamaica . . . a romantic choice for those special occasions . . . weddings, anniversaries and honeymoons," I say sure, but try not to get caught up in the local specialties: crime, drugs, and muggings. When the ad mentions, "everyone loves Jamaica," I have to raise my hand and say, sorry—not this visitor.

Oh, I got an unforgettable vacation alright. It brought dramatic new implications to the phrase "adventure tour."

Somebody with a sadistic sense of humour built a tourist hotel in Port Royal, near the historic ruins of what was once the headquarters of the infamous pirate Henry Morgan. Port Royal is just across the bay from the capital of Kingston. I stayed a week at the hotel. Its name is long lost from memory, and, if there's any mercy in this world, the structure was erased in 1988 by Hurricane Gilbert.

As I walked along the hallway of the tenth floor on the way to my room, and noticed all the locks had been jimmied

Tourists Too Stupid to Travel

One of the most-asked questions by people on a cruise is: "What time is the midnight buffet?"

Answer: "Sir, all ships, by law, must have a jail. Now, we're going to put you in there until you come up with the right answer."

with a crowbar, I sensed there might be a problem in the land of "No problem, mon."

The many splendours offered in the vacation package were a little overstated. The lock on the door wouldn't lock, and the washroom flooded every time I turned on a tap or flushed the toilet. The windows wouldn't open, but that was okay, because there was air conditioning . . . except for twice a day, when two-hour blackouts shut down the air conditioning, immobilized the elevators, and melted all the ice in the ice machines.

The entertainment consisted of four guys with car horns and hollow coconuts playing "Yellow Bird" at the pool bar from 10:00 a.m. to midnight every day. The music, which angered some guests and put the rest to sleep, was broken up periodically by a retired CNR conductor from St. Thomas, Ontario, who regularly stumbled into the waiters, sending overloaded trays of beer smashing on the patio beside the pool.

There was no beach, just a shoreline strewn with harbour flotsam and oil slicks. The clay tennis court had flooded and was a simmering mud puddle, a breeding ground for mosquitoes—but the net was still standing. There were small sailboats available as advertised, but a recent bylaw had made it illegal for small craft to enter this busy port off the tip of Palisadoes. Volleyball? Net in place; somebody had stolen the ball. I took an afternoon tour that included the Royal Botanical Gardens, and the van broke down on the way back to the hotel in the middle of a garbage dump.

Every meal featured suspicious little red hot dogs and goat meat. By the end of the week, most of us thought we'd been part of a tasting group for a recipe book entitled *101 Ways to Pass*

Goat Meat off as Real Food. The service was slow and sloppy and the complaints along with the "no tipping" policy created a silent war between the guests and hotel staff. I'm sure the chef's brother-in-law owned the restaurant down the road where all the hotel guests eventually went to eat.

The hotel offered "free weddings," and I'm sure some people did get married, if only because it was the only thing at the hotel to do.

The real entertainment was going down to the shore at night, sitting on the dock, and watching the reddish pink tracer bullets light up the sky over Kingston. I was told there was a small civil war going on in the capital. Or an election campaign. They are actually the same thing in Jamaica.

On the flight home, angry vacationers passed a petition around the plane detailing the highlights of this misadventure tour and demanding full refunds. I think Adventure Tours eventually issued $100 vouchers for "your next adventure tour with us." I'd be surprised if any of them ever got cashed.

The best part of this trip was the Toronto-bound flight, on which the flight attendants, sensing a mood of mutiny, opened wide the complimentary bar. It was the first cold Red Stripe beer I'd had the whole trip. The guy next to me kept pushing little liquor bottles of Scotch between the seats to the railroad retiree, who was sequestered in the window seat by a watchful wife who'd simply had enough. Each time the bar cart went by, she cut him off at the aisle.

So it was a surprise to almost everybody when the guy beside me started humming "I've Been Working on the Railroad" and the old guy jumped to his feet, drunk, and began singing at the top of his lungs. As others began to sing, he made a move to conduct the Adventure Tours Choir from the aisle and, in doing so, managed to break the only thing his wife had bought on the trip—a woven wicker purse with a hand-carved wooden handle. The first crack was the handle snapping, the second crack was the one that sent him reeling back into his seat.

It was a fitting finish to a vacation in the hot hell of Jamaica.

Instant German for Travellers

Wherever you go in the world, you come across German tourists. What they failed to accomplish in the Great Land Grab of the late 1930s, they've now achieved through tourism. They're everywhere—Morocco, Tunisia, St. Lucia, Cuba—and they're generally obnoxious. Yet when you go to Germany, the people are friendly and helpful. It's like they only issue travel visas to the very rude.

So I've created a new language—English that sounds German. It's easy, and everybody can understand it. You just make the endings rhyme a little, and throw in some official Teutonic-sounding words.

Let's say you come upon a German tourist. You ask, "Where is the parking lot for the nude beach, sir?" But he doesn't understand English. In my made-up German you would ask, slowly and with a lot of hand gestures, "Autoshtoppen . . . knockers floppen . . . knickers droppen, senhor?"

I actually used that line at the morning market in Lagos, Portugal, and later somebody delivered six kilos of dried cod to my room.

The Rain in Nassau Falls Mainly in Your Room

On a short stay, and probably only on a short stay, Nassau is a fascinating little cay unfortunately trapped between Miami hype and the genuine, slow-paced, sun-soaked Bahamas. It is a land of limping dogs and non-stop beat-up limos, unabashed opulence and families living in the backs of windowless delivery trucks. It's an island of spectacular beach coves secluded by swaying palms and moistened with the white froth of Caribbean blue waves and roadways that double as garbage dumps. You can't drink the local water, but the beer they make from it is outstanding. And at the same price as all the imports, Kalik is a colossal rip-off for the locals.

Nassau is like that—a beautiful, colourful, painful contradiction.

I was not a happy traveller when I arrived at Breezes Super Club in the Bahamas for New Year's 2002. First, I didn't want to be there. I wanted to go north instead of south, and to pay less rather than more. And I wanted to be with my dog. I wanted to stay in Muskoka at the dog-friendly Willow Beach Cottages on beautiful Lake Kashagawigamog (literally, "Great Lake of Long and Narrow Winding Waters with Way Too Many Vowels"). However, they were all booked up, so I started looking farther afield.

There are beach clubs and tennis clubs, Club Meds and Clubs Carib, and then there's Breezes on Cable Beach, south of Nassau. Breezes lets you know at every opportunity that it's not just a club; it's a Super Club.

Any Alcohol? Cigarettes? Elephants?

And you were worried about that extra bottle of tequila you were bringing back from Mexico? Several years ago, Mexican customs agents failed to notice a nearly three-ton elephant being smuggled across the border from Texas. A circus owner in Mexico City paid a smuggler $4,500 U.S. to transport the elephant in a trailer behind a pickup truck. Dozy customs officers waved it through. It happened on April Fool's Day.

The four-night stay at Breezes seems reasonable at first, until you add up all the taxes and allow for the gouging of people who travel during holiday periods. (The nerve!) By the time I begrudgingly booked the trip, I was paying much more for these four days than I'd normally pay for a week or two away.

And the day before I left, the lady from Willow Beach Cottages called to say there had been a cancellation.

Monica and I arrived at Breezes late in the evening on December 29, after a chaotic scene at the Nassau airport that involved aggressive porters hustling everyone's luggage as it came off the carousel. After a brief wait in the spacious lobby of Breezes, we were assigned a room just off the lobby, close enough to the party lounges to hear the band and smell the cigarette smoke even with the door closed and the balcony door open.

My first impression was that Breezes was not so much a Super Club as one big singles' bar with unlimited ashtrays. Yeah, that's what I go to the Bahamas for—white beaches and blue clouds brought to you by Philip Morris. I was not happy. So I marched back down to the lobby and asked for another room, one where the windows didn't rattle during drum solos.

After a long but civil battle, in which the staff at Breezes was way more polite than I was, Monica and I somehow ended up with the only available room in the hotel—the presidential suite. Suddenly, I was happy.

"The president of Jamaica stayed there last week," said the receptionist as she handed me the key.

It turned out to be only one-third of the presidential suite, the living room and second bedroom being locked and off limits to us, but I was still 33⅓% happier than I had been an hour earlier, when our room was part of the stage show.

From then on, nothing bothered us. We walked every day for four or five hours, taking buses all over the island when we got tired and ignoring the rain and the unusual cold spell that gripped the island. The wet winds that battered the island caused the post-ponement of Junkanoo, the grand all-night New Year's parade we had hoped to attend. We handled the nasty weather with the traditional forbearance of polite and plucky Canadians until New Year's Eve, when it began to rain in our room.

While sitting in the outdoor hot tub, I had noticed that the roof of the hotel was missing most of its shingles. I just thought they were replacing it. We had noticed several bulges in the ceiling's plaster, but had thought little of it. Now, suddenly, those four breast-like swellings became funnels, and rainwater streamed into the room. We scrambled quickly, catching the leaks with two garbage pails, an ice bucket, and a towel. Help came quickly, but all they could do was bring more buckets.

Hurricane Michelle had torn off half the roofs in Nassau in early November, and ours had not yet been repaired. We were on the eighth and top floor, the front line of defence against the wind and the rain. I wondered if they'd brought the prime minister of Jamaica their really nice silver-plated ice buckets and mopped up the floor with monogrammed towels. By the time we went down to dinner, the presidential suite looked more like a maple syrup sap run in Quebec than a penthouse in the tropics. Not happy once again. Call me a spoilsport, but for $2,000 for a four-night holiday, I don't think it's supposed to rain in your room.

But when we got to Pastafari, the hotel's à-la-carte restaurant, we met Tena, the best and baddest woman in all the Bahamas. She's large, she's black, she's wicked, and you can't help but love this woman. Tena with an "e" lords over the lovely and lively Pastafari pasta bar buried in the pit of cavernous Breezes.

We were first assaulted by—sorry, introduced to—Tena when we showed up for our 8:00 p.m. seating a couple of minutes late. "Downpour in 832," I said, surveying the dimly lit pasta café, where diners read from straw-bound menus by the orange glow of candle lamps. She gave me the evil eye, Tena did, the one the Italians call *la mal occhio*. "That's fine," she said, when I told her we really wanted to take our time and order each course as we went along. "I ain't goin' nowhere, hon."

Tena highly recommended I try the lobster bisque, but I declined. After I sampled a bit of Monica's I realized how very good it was. "Excuse me, miss?" I beckoned her over to our table.

"I thought you wasn't in no hurry," said Tena, and I thought I caught the reflection of fire in her eyes, maybe from our candle.

"On second thought, I would like a small bowl of the lobster bisque," I said, apologetically.

"Oh yeah?" she guffawed. Then, turning on her heels to leave, she said, loud enough for the whole restaurant to hear, "You had your chances before, honey. You ain't gettin' none a that bisque!" Throwing her head back, she turned and fled through the swinging doors into the kitchen. There was an awkward silence in the room, then everybody burst out laughing—mainly at me.

Sometime later, Tena returned to our table with a small bowl of the bisque, but I didn't get it until I promised to sit up straight and listen better.

Reluctantly Tena granted my request and brought the wine list to our table. Although she recommended the Pinot Grigio, I chose a golden bottle of Chardonnay from Chile. "You'll be sorry," said Tena. As people around us stifled their laughter, she sashayed away to wait on another table.

About five minutes later, Tena emerged from the kitchen holding a bottle of white wine in front of her. "You see this nice cold bottle of Italian wine," she said, waving it at me from half way across the restaurant, "This here's the wine that you should be having—the Pinot Grigio—but I'm giving it to this nice gentleman right here from New Jersey 'cause he listens to me." And she placed the bottle neatly into the metal chiller.

The laughter started at the table of the New Jersey couple and swept across the restaurant like a wave. "I'm glad you goin' slow, honey," she said, nodding towards me. "'Cause we gonna import that bottle you ordered." Then she stomped off into the kitchen again, severely testing the strength of the door hinges.

Tena was like a frowning Mona Lisa—every time I looked up she was glaring back at me.

By now Tena with an "e" was getting bigger laughs than the stand-up comedian from Miami who was working a small crowd in the Hurricane Disco across the hall. I might as well have had a sign on my back that read: "Official Joke of the 2002 Bahamian Comedy Olympics."

I sauntered over to the salad bar, a safe haven that Tena did not control or patrol.

Later, when our bottle of Pinot Grigio arrived at our table, Tena poured Monica a glass and then sat down in the chair beside her. "I don't know how you stand him, honey!" she said, quickly running down a list of my failings tonight. They hugged in an act of mutual remorse, before Tena finally took my order.

"I'll have the lamb chops," I ventured nervously.

"That's a good choice," said Tena, nodding.

"Well done," I said, with renewed confidence.

"No, you'll get them medium," said Tena matter-of-factly. "We won't be cookin' the life outta those poor souls." And then she went on to take Monica's order, eyeing me all the while and shaking her head.

Tena never cracked a smile throughout the evening, but her dark, flashing eyes almost laughed out loud. Tena and me—we were like a ventriloquist act. I was the wooden one, the one that only speaks when spoken to.

Not only did Tena have me laughing harder than all the others, not only did she make the evening one of the most memorable New Year's Eves I've ever had, but she proved without a doubt a theory I've been spouting for years: going out to dinner is only partly about the food. The art of catering to guests in restaurants has largely been lost. Today's waiters and waitresses deliver food. Period. What most restaurants fail to realize is that food tastes better when it's heavily seasoned with fun. In an ideal world, Tena wouldn't have to worry about tips—she'd be paid a standard salary for waitressing, which would then be doubled for her cabaret act.

When the cheesecake I did not order arrived, Tena said, "I knew you'd change your mind. You eat that now. Don't make me come back here, hon." My dinner ended on a sweet note perilously short of a spanking. I felt lucky Tena didn't send me up to my room without my brandy.

At the Pastafari, Tena *was* the sharpest knife in my back— sorry, the drawer. She knew exactly where the line not to cross was located. If I hadn't responded in kind to the first dart she lobbed my way, I know she would have moved on to a more willing victim. Tena with an "e"—the zany czar of Breeze's pasta bar. Thank you, hon. You're wonderful.

Returning to the room for a quiet New Year's celebration, Monica and I stood out on the balcony and sipped

Dining Out Travel Tips

- While cruising the salad bar, there is absolutely no need to test the effectiveness of the sneeze guard.
- If you don't like the food just say so. Telling the waitress that their doggie bags are acts of animal cruelty is the wrong approach.

Champagne as gale-force winds sent the fireworks from the nearby Sheraton Hotel sailing over our heads. The torrential rain was cold now, and came at us sideways. Inside the room, four garbage pails caught the steady streams of water coming through the ceiling. I could sense 2002 was going to be one wild and wacked-out year.

A Warning to All Travellers to Mexico

The 1,600 kilometre Mexican peninsula of prickly desert and devastating beauty that extends south from San Diego to Los Cabos is called the Baja. Looking on the map like a crooked middle finger pointed south, this cactus-covered spit of sand comes to an abrupt end at a pile of rocks that splits the Pacific Ocean and the Sea of Cortes.

Two distinctly different cities share this common point called Los Cabos. San Jose des Cabo is like a harmless town drunk, mostly napping in the shade after a few calamitous bursts from the bottle. Cabo San Lucas is like the drunk's hipper, drug-addled brother, wallowing in loud music and fast food, shooter bars, and jet skis. If you don't want to be blinded by relentless sleaze and malicious overdevelopment, don't come to Cabo. I'm sorry but any city outside of America that boasts a Jimmy Buffettville, a Hard Rock Café, and a Planet Hollywood should be nuked and rebuilt as a trailer park. Cabo San Lucas makes Atlantic City seem somehow cultured.

On the day of New Year's Eve, I checked into the Aquamarina Hotel, which is located on a strip of beach two kilometres from

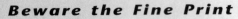

Beware the Fine Print

The What's-in-a-Name? Award goes to Michael Barson of Alexandria, Virginia, who was arrested by the FBI for selling low-cost vacations that came with so many restrictions no one could ever claim them. Barson, who kept a semi-automatic rifle in his travel office, was once jailed for two days for pulling a gun on a complaining customer. Nonetheless, consumers from twenty-one states and the District of Columbia continued to send him money. The victims, it seems, were not put off by Barson's various aliases, among them Bill Bailey, Dusty Rhodes, Skip Town, and Al Coholic.

downtown San Jose des Cabo. Like many Mexican hotels, the Aquamarina changes names every year. While I was talking to the manager that first day, I was informed it was currently in bankruptcy. I quickly learned not to be late arriving at the buffet.

The Aquamarina provided non-stop, live entertainment for its guests at no additional charge: Ernie from Barrie, Ontario. Ernie was the model who posed for the wordsmith who created the phrase: "a piece of work." Tall, lean, and not at all mean, Ernie was in his late thirties and operating with a liver that was surely in an advanced state of denial. I heard Ernie long before I ever laid eyes on him. Ernie had a low, loud voice that could be heard in nearby towns and a cackling laugh that attracted rare waterfowl from across the Sea of Cortez. My first guess was that Ernie announced goals and penalties at Maple Leaf Gardens without a public address system.

Ernie and his shorter, mostly silent sidekick Dwayne, whose name soon became "Bert" among hotel guests, began their day at the patio bar at 10 a.m., moved to the pool bar in the afternoon and spent their evenings back at the patio bar—unless, of course, they were in town for an evening of barhopping. At no time, night or day, during their week in Los Cabos could either Bert or Ernie have passed a sobriety test . . . even if they'd studied for it.

And generous? These guys were constantly buying drinks for everybody at the hotel, a fine gesture made somewhat easier by the fact that all drinks were free with their all-inclusive package.

Now normally Bert and Ernie would be dismissed as "rowdies," a couple of rubes from Barrie who if they weren't vacationing in Mexico, would be exploring the bottom of Lake Simcoe on snow-mobiles. Although they were loud, they were also lovable, a little frayed but very friendly, crass but in a classy kind of way.

Every afternoon Bert and Ernie tried and failed to get a volley-ball game going in the pool. Part of the problem was their range of movement. They just couldn't reach a lot of balls from their bar stools beside the net.

Up and down our steep-banked beach, red flags were stuck in the sand, warning swimmers not to venture into the water because of a treacherous undertow. But the fishing, apparently, was great. One day the boys announced they'd rented a fishing boat and the owner agreed to let them take it out alone. Terrific. Now there were two reasons not to go swimming—the undertow and Bert and Ernie had a boat with a motor.

The day they went fishing was known around the Aquamarina as the day the hotel went quiet. Parents let their kids out of the rooms for the first time. The hotel laid off four bartenders.

Late in the afternoon Bert and Ernie returned with an thirty-five-kilogram marlin flopping around in the backseat of their Jeep. It was quite a sight to see the vehicle slide to a stop at the entrance of the hotel carrying three excited fish out of water. Only a couple of fast-footed security guys kept them from tossing it in the hotel pool.

As Ernie explained, "We were just gonna keep it fresh till dinner." And dinner it was—carved into fillets by the chef and enjoyed by all the hotel guests . . . except Ernie who celebrated the catch a little too much and slept through the feast. For Ernie, it was the fish fry not the fish that got away.

Later in the week, I borrowed the guys' Jeep to drive up the coast to the old Mexican town of Todos Santos. Parked exactly on the Tropic of Cancer, Todos Santos is not yet spoiled, the mango groves and sugar cane fields not yet smothered in concrete. Open streetside cafés still provide a good lunch for two with Mexican beer for under ten dollars. Kiosks sell a specialty called *penocha*, a dark molasses candy from the local sugar mill.

Travelling slowly along Calle Juarex y Marquez de Leon, I had one of those drive-by déjà-vu moments. On this dark desert highway, cool wind in my hair, I stopped and stared in disbelief at one of my favourite record albums. I was thinking to myself, this could be Heaven or this could be Hell. There it was: the Hotel California, with the sound of the Eagles coming out the front door and every open window, telling me I could check in anytime I liked, but I could never leave.

The hotel plays the song nonstop, at concert volume, which echoes through the neighbourhood. And you thought your neighbour was insensitive. How would you like to have been listening to the same song coming through your privacy fence since 1976?

I spent a languid afternoon in Todos Santos and on the way back, on this roller coaster narrow highway, a police car suddenly appeared in my rearview mirror. I was speeding. They followed me for a very long time, but as they made no move to pull me over, I assumed they were running a check on the plate number. And that's when I really panicked. If Ernie's driving record showed up on their computer screen, they probably wouldn't pull me over, they'd just pull up alongside the Jeep and open up with automatic weapons.

As we neared Cabo San Lucas, they passed me, obviously in a bigger hurry than I was. No wonder, I thought, the 911 call probably came from the Aquamarina. Bert and Ernie were probably playing water polo in the pool and using real ponies.

By the end of the week, everybody had pretty much had it with the group of three bikers and their "bitches," as they fondly referred to them, who had a large suite on the ground floor and had turned that section of the hotel lawn into their outdoor party place. Aquamarina was only three floors high, so those of us above them could not escape the drifts of marijuana, the loud music, and the foul language. Even Bert and Ernie were embarrassed by these "rodders."

On the last night, they took their lewd game to another level and, with the management unable or unwilling to quiet them down, a group of us discussed a plan to go down and try to put an end to the nonsense. We agreed to give management one last try; otherwise, at two in the morning, we were going down to party headquarters.

Nobody relished the thought, but the number of disgruntled guests on the top two floors was growing.

But at 1:50 a.m. a very funny thing happened. Ernie settled things all by himself. Ernie came back to his second-floor room dead drunk. He bounced off a few pieces of furniture, removed most of his clothes, and then staggered out onto the balcony. Those of us on the second and third floor, dreading the approach of two o'clock, watched Ernie as he walked out onto his balcony, wearing only his boxer shorts. He made a kind of sweeping motion towards the sparkling ocean beyond the beach and then, in one of the most effective yet repellent show-stopping moments in the history of tourism, he puked all over the party one floor below. It was, to use a word I've come to hate, awesome.

Suddenly, people were running in panic, muttering, "Oh! God! No!"

Then Ernie went to bed, oblivious to the knocks and shouting at his door by people who were still wet from the chunk shower.

The next day the partyers paid a high price to have their clothes washed, dried and ironed by two of the maids in time for their 1:00 p.m. departure.

Yes, they were a treat, the bad boys from Barrie. And to think I wrote a book entitled *Guys—Not Real Bright and Damn Proud Of It!* before I'd ever met Bert and Ernie.

I'm a travelling psychic, I tell you, a psychic!

The Hotel Orientation Meeting: Boring but Non-Venomous

On package holidays I never attend the hotel orientation meeting. Having a beer with a talkative bartender is far more productive. So, when we were staying at the Eden Resort in Loreto, Mexico, I passed on the meeting and went golfing with Monica instead.

On the twelfth hole of the Loreto *campo de golf*, which hugs the Sea of Cortes, Monica sliced her drive into the rocky promontory of dead wood and bramble bushes along the right side of the fairway. She did this three days in a row. Every time, I climbed into this rough and retrieved her ball. Hers, and a lot of other peoples' bad shots, as well. These were brand new balls, some right out in the open, others inside crevices and under rocks.

By the third round, I had accumulated forty new golf balls and started worrying about my luggage being overweight. I assumed the other golfers were either too old or too lazy to be climbing around rock piles for their balls.

Near the end of the trip, we hooked up with a great couple from British Columbia, who were driving the length of the Baja Peninsula. Somewhere near the town of Insurgentes, I was bragging about my golf ball windfall, when Chris, who had played that course with his wife, Trish, said, "You don't go to orientation meetings, do you?"

"No," I said. "They're a waste of time."

"One word of caution about that twelfth hole," said Chris, rolling his eyes at Trish.

"What's that?"

"Rattlesnakes."

New travel motto: always go to the orientation meeting.

I'm a Great Traveller . . . but a Lousy Tourist

Everyone has a photographic memory. Some just don't have film in there.
—Anonymous

A number of embarrassing escapades in foreign lands have convinced me that I travel very well, but I tourist very poorly. One is now permanently etched in that part of my brain that flashes red like an activated jerk detector whenever the country of Cuba is mentioned in casual conversation.

In the winter of 1994, Monica and I spent a week in Santiago de Cuba at the Delta Sierra Mar Resort. I spent a lot of my time trying to hide from the pervasive and insidious Cuban curse known as "Guantanamera." In Mexico, the virus that'll keep you locked in your bathroom is known as "Montezuma's revenge." In Eastern Europe, it's "Balkan belly." In Cuba, it's music. "Guantanamera" in the elevator, at reception, all around the pool. "Guantanamera" in the aerobics class. "Guantanamera" every night by every musician who can hold an instrument. Believe me, of all the things Cuba will need when Fidel falls and freedom is restored, a new national song would be an excellent idea.

At week's and wit's end, I signed us up for the three-site Santiago City Tour to get me away from this hotel that had been trying to get its name in the *Guinness Book of World Records* for the most suicides inspired by the continuous plays of one song.

The first stop of the tour, the rum factory, was closed due to labour problems, but a representative from Bacardi was liberally pouring shots of their special Seven-Star brand as we piled off the bus. And the house band assembled in the parking lot was enthusiastically banging out "Guantanamera."

Now, I have to tell you, I hate rum. I can't stand the taste of rum. I hate rum more than Brussels sprouts, cigarette butts, and that kid in the car ad who says "Zoom, zoom." I hate rum more than that idiot Aussie who holds his mouth wide open while he torments crocodiles on camera. I'd rather drink schnapps through my nose, which I saw an old German do once in Burgundy. If he smoked, he could have been a dragon.

And my personal policy is no drinks until after dark, or after a great walk, run, or tennis match. I like to feel I've earned a drink.

But as I stood in that parking lot after twenty straight minutes of "Guantanamera," I realized this band had no intention of moving on to "Yellow Bird" or even "I Be Strokin'." And that's when, in the words of Jimmy Buffett singing about the bear on the mountain in "God's Own Drunk," "I took a slash." I couldn't carry on without something to numb my brain. It was a medicinal hit. Honest.

I have to admit, the Bacardi rep was right: this highly rated Seven-Star liquor did not taste at all like rum. It tasted like really, really high-octane gasoline going down your throat just after somebody lights it. I cried out in pain but, of course, nobody heard me over "Guantanamera."

The cigar factory was also closed due to labour problems, but that didn't stop the rum tasting at the rear of the building. And, yes, another house band was playing: "*Uno, dos, tres*, all together now . . . Guantanamera . . ."

It was becoming quite clear to me that, in Cuba, even shoeshine stands have their own house band.

This was steamy Cuba—the close heat, the hot rhythms, the spinning—sorry—the swaying palm trees. But as Monica would later remark, "It wasn't the heat, it was the stupidity!" As politely as possible, I brushed aside the offer of another glass of rum . . . and went right for the bottle. My screams of pain from the internal flames deafened me temporarily, and I drowned out two, maybe three, lines of the song.

Even with few vehicles operating on the roads of Cuba, our bus managed to get sideswiped by a Lada, and we all stood in the baking sun for an hour until another vehicle was dispatched. On a new bus and back on our way, I thought: if the famous Santiago de Cuba Cemetery is also closed due to labour problems, it's really going to ruin my day. But no, there it was—an iron-gated and whitewashed residence of aboveground tombs gleaming in a mean midday sun. Eerie? Solemn? Otherworldly? Maybe to the others on the tour, but I was elated. I felt like I'd been rescued from a fate worse than death: there was no house band in the cemetery.

Standing in the graveyard, unsteady on my feet and badly burned by the unrelenting sun, I realized I was a bit tipsy. No, worse than that, with fire burning in my belly and beading up my brow I was somewhat intoxicated. Okay, I was shit-faced in a foreign country and, frankly, it was not my fault.

And then, through blurry eyes, I suddenly came face to face with the enemy. There he was in a crooked crypt, warped by a

Tourists Too Stupid to Travel

From a turned-around day tripper.

Question: Am I on the Canadian or American side of the falls?

Answer: This can be very confusing. A good rule of thumb is: If your money is leaving your wallet at twice the normal rate, you're on the Canadian side. On the other hand, if your money is leaving your wallet at gun point, you're on the American side.

hundred years of humidity, the source of all my pain, the evil man who invented the rum that was right now making me crazy—the great Cuban rum-maker Don Facundo Bacardi. The patriarch of the Bacardi rum corporation was the *numero uno* tourist attraction on this leg of the Santiago City Tour.

Monica gave me an elbow in the ribs even before I opened my mouth. Normally, that would be the end of it. But I was, as the Brits say, tiddly. "So, Angel," I slurred to our soft-spoken cemetery tour guide, "the guy in the bent box . . . would that be a Bacardi with a twist?"

Angel just glared at me, and nobody in the group of Canadian tourists ventured so much as a chuckle. Except me. I found this so damn funny I made a kind of snorgle noise, the sound my dog makes when he tries to bark while swimming.

I probably should have stopped right there, but the seven-year-old hard stuff kicked into high gear as we passed the tomb of Bacardi's nephew, right beside the old man. Aha! The accomplice of my enemy. Angel eyed me nervously as he talked about the founding family of rum.

"So, Angel," I said, waving a hand back and forth, from uncle to nephew and back again, "a double Bacardi on ice?"

Angel shot me a dagger of a look. If looks could kill, I was at least standing in the appropriate place.

Although no one else laughed, I got quite hysterical. As Angel moved the group on towards another famous Cuban's grave, I hung back with the Bacardis, yelling after Angel, to inquire whether the rum-maker killed in that tragic shipwreck off the coast was "the Bacardi on the rocks."

That's when I got thrown out of the cemetery. Angel returned quickly and, as politely as possible, asked me to leave the tour and sit on the bus, where I'd be much more comfortable. Which I did, quietly. In the state I was in, I realized I could have a lot more fun . . . alone.

My ejection from this famous cemetery did not, however, stop me from pushing the window down on the bus and yelling at Angel one last time: "Don't forget to tell 'em the story about the Bacardi shot in the drug deal, Angel. The Bacardi with coke!"

I doubt if anyone heard me, least of all Monica who was hiding behind the tomb of the Unknown Revolutionary.

Anyway, it worked out great, because on a Cuban tour bus the air conditioner is so loud, you can't hear—wait for it— "Guantanamera."

I'd like to take this opportunity to apologize to Cuba, Angel, and especially the Bacardis. I'll never do it again . . . drink your rum that is.

Like I said, I travel alright but I'm a toad of a tourist. I have great difficulty with the "group thing." Had I stumbled upon the Santiago Cemetery while on a day hike, with nothing more than a zip-locked lunch pilfered from the breakfast buffet and a good guidebook, it would have been a great personal discovery. I'd have figured it all out, enjoyed the graveyard for its inestimable history, and congratulated myself on how my curiosity carried the day. By the time I left that cemetery, I would have convinced myself that I was one of the few people ever to have found the place, except of course for a bunch of Bacardis. I'd have believed I was a rare and special visitor, quietly in and respectfully out of this churchyard of the dead.

That's what travellers do. We don't care how knobby our knees look, trapped between khaki shorts and hiking boots. We simply seek the road less travelled—and hopefully one with a pub at the end of it. We not only make hasty detours off the beaten path, we thumb our sunburned noses at those who shuffle along behind the tour guide, beating to dust that common path. Tourists! Only on Halloween would a traveller consider wearing a Hawaiian shirt with a straw hat, knee socks, and sandals.

At the end of the day, a bit battered and bruised by shortcuts we never should have taken, still dizzied by the perilous path along the cliff's edge we could not avoid, travellers stand at the hotel bar, scanning the room full of three-meal-a-day trippers, and offer a toast to our travelling partners: "Damn tourists! Cheers."

Oh yeah, we're just stupid enough to be arrogant, as well.

I Got the Better Deal to Cuba

Sell-offs, last-minute clubs, Internet auctions—travel deals, real or imagined, are everywhere these days. In the tourist trade, cost confusion reigns.

There's nothing worse than getting to your holiday destination and discovering everybody else got a better deal than you did. So before I booked a week in sultry Cuba, I meticulously scouted out the travel market to ensure I got best value for my money. I don't normally go to this extent, but—and maybe you've heard this, as well—there's a rumour out there that a whole bunch of people were getting all-inclusive trips to Cuba for next to nothing.

Smart travellers comparison shop, and here's what my research turned up:

Cost: My trip to Cuba: $886, not including airport departure tax at Holguin International Airport of $20 U.S. Total cost to three hundred suspected al-Qaeda terrorists for their extended-stay trip to Guantanamo Bay: zero. Plus no exit tax. In fact, no exit.

Carrier: I flew economy class on Air Transat. Al-Qaeda were shackled to seats of a U.S. Air Force C-141 Starlifter. (They had more leg room.)

In-flight meal: I had lasagna, red wine, and a roll. Al-Qaeda had a rice and vegetable dish and—are these guys lazy or what?—were spoon-fed by U.S. military police. Lineups for the washroom were about the same.

In-flight movie: I saw *Kate and Leopold* and liked it. Al-Qaeda watched *The Ten Commandments* and felt Charlton Heston was all wrong in the role of Moses.

Flight experience: I had to listen to a farmer from north of Edmonton tell his life story to every person in my section not quick enough to barricade themselves in the washroom. Al-Qaeda prisoners were subjected to icy stares and verbal abuse by U.S. military guards. (Because I now know more about alfalfa than Dwayne, the idiot brother who's looking after the farm while the farmer and his wife, Emma, take a long-awaited second honeymoon in Cuba, flight experience is definitely a draw.)

Flight summary: Neither I nor al-Qaeda was allowed to carry sharp objects in our carry-on luggage. I, at least, had the option of flight cancellation insurance. Plus, my flight attendant showed me how to get out of my seatbelt.

Transfers: I spent one hour clearing immigration at the Holguin airport and forty-five minutes sitting on the hotel bus because a Canadian named Eduardo got lost in a terminal the size of your local Italian hall. Al-Qaeda prisoners, with their VIP status, were safe and secure in their compound while I was still looking for my tennis racquet at the airport's lost and found.

"Book now, fly late—we're the experts in last meal specials!"
—A small mistake in a last-minute travel ad

"For $20 more you get the continental breakfast or free parking!"
—Ad for a Toronto airport hotel

Hotel: I stayed at Club Amigo Guardalavaca. Al-Qaeda stayed at Camp X-Ray in Guantanamo Bay. No amigos here.

Reception: I was welcomed by Armando, a Cuban gentleman who made me feel I was the most honoured guest of his country since the Pope. Al-Qaeda's reception, even in a damp 30° C climate, was icy.

Accommodation: My room was small but clean, with two single beds and a shower. Al-Qaeda are staying in cages sixty-four feet square. But in fairness, I've never killed anybody. In fact, before Eduardo, I had never even been tempted. (Okay, there was also that woman in St. Lucia who mistook me for Stuart McLean.)

Upgrade: I arranged for a one-bedroom villa with balcony and a full bath. Al-Qaeda also complained about their cramped quarters, but were told to deal with their travel agent, Taliban Tours, back home.

Style: My room was furnished with modern Cuban mahogany and leather. Al-Qaeda rooms were finished in shiny Frost fence, interspersed with plywood porta-potties.

Nice touch: I got a basket of fruit in my hotel room. Al-Qaeda got free toothbrushes . . . made of rubber.

View: I could see the landscaped grounds with the mini-putt course and archery range. The typical al-Qaeda detainee is looking at the bum of the suspected terrorist in the next cell.

Atmosphere: At Club Amigo, hotel guests enjoying too much Crystal *cerveza* huddled around the bar, singing like birds. At Camp X-Ray, so far, sober prisoners were not singing like birds.

Venturing out: Around the hotel, there were lots of people selling cigars. Around Camp X-Ray, there were lots of land mines.

Meal issues: Some hotel guests were not thrilled with the breakfast buffet. Al-Qaeda guys got—I'm not making this up—Froot Loops for breakfast and, justifiably, went on a hunger strike.

Painful experiences: For me, watching our Miss Canada in the Miss Hotel Guardalavaca contest trying to sing and dance. For al-Qaeda, being shackled and handcuffed every time they leave their cells.

Drawbacks: At Hotel Amigo Guardalavaca, kids stay free. At Camp X-Ray, al-Qaeda barracks are lit by floodlight all night.

Disappointments: For me, not meeting Fidel. For al-Qaeda, no sign so far of Osama bin Laden.

Upon leaving: I'm somewhat sad, but looking forward to returning. Al-Qaeda are very sad, and looking forward to a trial.

Conclusion: Al-Qaeda guys got the best price, but I got better value for my pesos. It pays to shop around. And, as my mother used to say, always wear clean underwear and don't get involved in state-sponsored terrorism.

On Airlines, the Dead Get Better Service

I've done an awful lot of air travel these last few months, and I, like most passengers, have been subjected to annoying delays, smoky European airports, discourteous service, and the like. However, after reading a newspaper clipping from the *Vancouver Province*, I have to count my lucky frequent-flyer stars that, although a few people sitting next to me on long flights have been a little cold, none of them have actually been dead.

Donna Beaulieu, of Campbell River, British Columbia, was flying from Bali to Vancouver when, somewhere over the Pacific Ocean, the guy next to her up and died. This is true. And no, he had not just finished his in-flight meal.

The air tragedy began when the Continental flight touched down on a remote island between Guam and Honolulu, and a middle-aged man wearing only a hospital gown boarded the plane with two medical attendants who did not speak English. Normally when a man staggers into an airport wearing only a hospital gown, airline authorities have instructions to call Robert Downy, Jr.'s parole officer. Personally I hate it when I have to sit next to somebody wearing a hospital gown—when they bend over to put their bag under the seat, they always moon first class.

About three hours later, the man quietly passed away. One cause of death was immediately ruled out when flight attendants determined that neither Val Kilmer nor Adam Sandler was starring in the in-flight movie. One theory not yet disproved is that someone had just told the deceased what the same flight would have cost if he'd flown Air Canada.

It was left to Ms. Beaulieu's son-in-law to walk to the back of the plane and inform the flight attendants that the guy in 12A might need some assistance getting off the plane. Like a gurney? According to Ms. Beaulieu, the attendants then approached the dead man and put his seat into the upright position. They were about to serve the meal and, you know the rule: when the trays come down, the seats go up— no exceptions!

After the meal was served, the attendants propped the dead man up with a pillow under his head and tucked him in, according to Ms. Beaulieu, "like he was having a nap." Which was sort of true. For the sake of appearance, the flight attendants did everything short of putting headphones on the guy and bringing him a cocktail.

Here's the irony of it all: how many times have you muttered something like, "I'll be dead by the time she comes back with my drink"? And here's this deceased passenger getting first-class attention.

The man's body was removed from the plane in Honolulu. And it's a good thing his destination was Hawaii. If it had been Canada, and he failed to fill out that immigration form, he'd still be sitting in 12A.

My only question is, if you're sitting beside somebody who dies in the middle of an international flight, isn't there some way you can inherit his forty-ounce duty-free entitlement?

So, now you've got one more thing to worry about on long flights besides screaming kids and 135-kilogram pigs running amok in first class. The next time the guy beside you coughs and lapses into a deep sleep, he might just be napping. Then again, he might not be. Dead men don't push the emergency button.

The good news? They don't snore.

The Sins of a Sunday Driver

It was ten in the morning, and already sweltering in the cubbyhole rental car office tucked behind the reception desk at the Club Amigo Guardalavaca. I began signing my name all over the two-page rental agreement for the Jeep. Juan José concluded the deal

Cultural Misunderstanding

When American Airlines wanted to advertise its new leather first-class seats in the Mexican market, it translated "Fly in leather" directly into Spanish. Unfortunately, *vuela en cuero* literally means "Fly naked." This not only boosted seat sales, but did wonders for the membership drive of the Mile-High Club.

by saying, "Jess, everythin' ees injured," which I took to mean "everything is insured" (how he found out my nickname was Jess, I'll never know).

"Everythin' except la radio," he added.

I laughed, and he said: "*Si*, crazy. No?"

Complaining that running this car rental agency, which judging by my list of choices only has two vehicles on the lot, is too much work for one man, Juan José showed me how to change a flat, and told me not to speed . . . something about the police.

I pulled away from the Club Amigo Guardalavaca onto the highway that goes west to Holguin and drove slowly past a hundred or more people waiting for buses that seldom arrive. It was a colourful but sad scene: women holding babies in the shade of trees, men in army fatigues, workers with lunch boxes, old men squatting on their haunches in a semi-circle—all with eager expectant looks on their faces, though none so bold as to actually stick out a thumb.

Just past a sign with the number 40 in a circle, policemen in sunglasses and grey uniforms rushed out onto the road and jumped into the path of my Jeep. I braked and swerved, nearly hitting the slowest officer, and they were on me like the Bolivian Army taking down the Sundance Kid. Apparently I was doing fifty kilometres per hour in a forty-kilometre speed trap. The forty-kilometre zone is twenty metres long, and after that there is no speed limit. I know all this because a Cuban woman beside the road explained this to me as she casually climbed into the backseat of the Jeep.

A Cuban cop stared at me like I had been caught advocating free and fair elections. "Many people are killed on this highway," he scolded me, angrily, and then fined me $10 U.S. Yeah, but I'm sure this particular twenty-metre zone remains relatively fatality-free.

Was I mad? Hell no. He may have caught me speeding, but I got away scot-free on the uninsured radio caper.

I dropped my translator/hitchhiker off near her family's home close to the village of Rafael Freyne.

Beyond the forty-kilometre scam, there seem to be no limits and no real rules of the road in Cuba. Many drivers brandish bottles of beer, and, apparently, everybody has the right of way. "Everybody" includes parades of riders on horseback, tourists in horse-drawn carriages, motorcycles with sidecars that seat a family of five, bicycles, farm carts hauled by oxen, the occasional bus, and these huge, square Soviet-made trucks that spew black smoke exhaust so dense it temporarily blinds other drivers. And of course, the odd, mint-condition pre-1959 American cars running rust-free on $2-a-litre gasoline and homemade parts.

As I parked at the main square in Holguin, an old man, tall and wiry with tough, tanned skin, pulled an eyelid down as he faced me—giving me the international symbol that he wanted to watch my car. This struck me as not a bad idea, actually, with the liability of the radio looming large in my mind.

Fifteen minutes later, I walked by to check on things, and the old man was sitting in the driver's seat of my Jeep—no doubt passing it off as his own—and trying to pick up chicks.

For hours I walked the streets of Holguin, a tawdry but vibrant city where everybody is busy, oblivious to a modern world that left them stranded and frozen in 1959.

As tradition dictates, I climbed the 462 steps straight up the Loma de la Cruz, with its huge white cross that can be seen for miles. As you drive into the city, this mountain path looks like a steep, concrete irrigation ditch, but as you get closer the tiers of steps take shape.

On my way to the top, I inherited two young "guides," neither of whom was allowed to enter the walled *mirador* at the top, both of whom expected a dollar or two when I came out. At the very top, a couple of uniformed officials ushered in visitors. Flushed and sweating, I trudged through the gate. "*Como es tu?*"

DO NOT PASS

Savvy Travellers

A South American couple who regularly visited a church in Milan for an hour of prayer in front of a statue of the Madonna were actually charging their mobile phone from an electrical socket behind the statue, priests discovered. One of the priests said the visitors were still welcome: "Letting them charge their mobile is a bit like giving them a glass of water." Yeah, but wait'll they show up in an electric car.

asked one of the guards. "*Sediento*," I replied, hoping there was a fountain nearby. They laughed and pointed to a thatched-roof hut on the other side of the cross. "The bar is there," they said, using up the only English phrase they knew.

A bar at a national religious monument? I couldn't believe it. If this was some tacky trick by the Roman Catholic Church to lure me back to the fold, it was a good start.

An English-speaking Cuban at the bar informed me that the bar is open twenty-four hours a day, seven days a week.

"Who in their right mind would climb 462 steps at four o'clock in the morning just to have a beer?" I asked.

"Him!" he replied, pointing at the little bartender, who sat on a keg of draft, drinking Crystal lager from a can.

Of course. It was the best make-work program in the world.

The slick young Cuban on the stool next to me was too cool for his own good. Fluent in English, and an American wannabe, he wore out the f-word in our first minute of conversation. For him, everything in Cuba was stupid and backward. America was his mecca. He told me he spent three days on a raft trying to reach Miami before the Cuban coast guard hauled him home. Surprisingly, he got no jail time—instead he paid, over a long period of time, a $900 fine. "Rafting," he said, rubbing his fingers together, "is good business for the government."

He told me the most famous story in this part of Cuba: a guy went to sea with just an inner tube and a bottle of rum, and woke up hungover on the yacht of an English princess. (Fergie—you got lossa splainin' to do!) "He lives like a prince now, rich and fat," the Cuban kid said.

I felt like telling him that, according to the newspaper I'd read on the plane, the guy had recently been turned into a frog.

"The Pope was here," he said, sweeping his right hand around the bleak and dry lot with its gigantic white cross. "And Elian Gonzales, too." I'm sure those two celebrities were served their beer in real glasses, rather than recycled plastic cups.

After giving a good portion of Holguin's population a dollar each, I made a wrong turn leaving the city and followed a breathtaking but circuitous route back to Guardalavaca. Every time I stopped to ask directions, the Cuban who answered my questions would climb into the back of my Jeep. People got in, people got out. I stopped for a woman with a child in her arms, I turned down two kids who wanted to ride on the back bumper holding on to the roll bar.

From somebody's bag appeared ice cold beer. As we sailed through the mountains, I totalled up the laws I might or might not be breaking: fitting four passengers in the front seat, allowing open alcohol in the vehicle, travelling more than forty kilometres an hour, operating a limo service without a licence. The beer, I believed, was legal, but that radio should definitely not have been on the road.

When I arrived back at the hotel, Juan José checked the gas gauge and the mileage, and asked me about the radio.

"Well, it's still there," I said, adding that I never actually turned it on.

"Never mind," he said with a shrug. "No stations here."

Cuba—I love it—it's kind of a drive-thru dictatorship.

Part Five

Portugal: Home of the Cultural Misunderstanding

A tourist is happy to get home;
a traveller is happy to get home alive.

I'm Just a Flat Tire on the Holiday Highway

Quite often, I have a run of bad luck while travelling.
Not bad luck like that of the United Parcel Service worker who took a nap while loading a 747 jet at Anchorage airport and woke up in Hong Kong.

Not really bad luck like that of ninety-year-old Kitty Synocak, who flew Canada 3000 from Toronto to Stuttgart and had the time of her life chatting with the flight attendants. Only when the flight was halfway back to Toronto did somebody notice Kitty had not got off the plane in her hometown of Stuttgart.

Not horrible luck like that of Luc Blanchet, who arrived home in Baie-Comeau, Quebec, from a business meeting in Toronto four days late. Luc's not-so-great adventure began with an Air Canada flight delay that caused him to miss his connection in Montreal. He stayed overnight at an airport hotel. The next day's flight just didn't happen, and he was forced out into the cold by an airport fire alarm. After another night in the hotel, an over-booked flight forced Luc to switch from Air Canada to Air Nova. As soon as Luc got settled in his seat, all passengers were ordered off the plane because of technical problems. Luc returned to the airport lounge, collapsed from exhaustion, and spent the night in a nearby hospital ICU. The next day Luc took a train to Quebec City, and after a $780 taxi ride home, promptly sued Air Canada. Trains, planes, and auto-suggestion: "Luc, don't ever fly again."

Cultural Misunderstanding

In Portugal, Pepsi's "Come alive with the Pepsi generation" translated into "Pepsi brings your ancestors back from the grave." If that isn't an endorsement for Coke, I don't know what is!

Compared to the guy who got bitten on the ass by a scorpion that escaped from somebody's carry-on luggage on a Mesaba Airlines flight to Allentown, Pennsylvania, a few years ago, my bad travel luck is almost pleasant.

Maybe it's age. In the '70s you could give me a map and a backpack, and I could conquer whole continents in less than a dozen months with no more misfortune than occasionally sitting on the corkscrew of my Swiss Army knife. Nowadays it seems I'm the Rodney Dangerfield of travel—I tell ya, I spent my whole vacation in the airport lounge, while my luggage was sitting on a beach in Hawaii.

A recent trip to Portugal was more like a crisis management seminar than a vacation. Monica and I arrived at Pearson Airport for our flight to Lisbon the required two hours prior to takeoff. Three hours later, we were still in line with several hundred anxious passengers staring at the Air Transat counter employees, who are doing nothing except staring back at us.

Now, don't get me wrong, I love the Portuguese. Portugal is a vibrant country of postcard seascapes and breathtaking mountain vistas, a country with outstanding food and wine. However, under what they consider to be the very broad category of check-in luggage, the Portuguese will often include refrigerators, central heating systems, motorcycles, and sofas.

This flight's luggage, which ton for ton equalled all the military hardware shipped to Desert Storm, broke the conveyor belt at Pearson Airport behind Air Transat's check-in counters.

The staring contest ended when an Air Transat supervisor came up with a brilliant idea: carry the luggage twenty feet to where the belt was still working! By unanimous vote, he became our choice for Air Transat's employee of the month.

Everybody was in a bad mood as we left late, arrived late, and then spent an hour at Lisbon airport watching luggage go around a long, snaking carousel. The bad news? Our luggage was not to be seen. The good news? Hey—their conveyor belt was working.

Apparently, the luggage that refused to board in Toronto later refused to get off the plane in Lisbon. My luggage went instead to Oporto, 340 kilometres north, a lovely city I'm told and a favourite jumping-off point of my clean underwear and tennis racquet. If they based it on luggage and not passengers, we'd bankrupt the frequent flyer mileage system.

We spent another hour waiting in line, with a disgruntled group of passengers that could become a mob any moment, filling out lost luggage forms. Then we went down to the lobby of the airport to pick up our rental car. This transaction was completed so easily, I became deeply suspicious of everybody at the agency's counter.

It was dank, dreary, and pouring rain in Lisbon. After being up for thirty-four hours straight, I was slapping myself on the back of the head to stay awake as I drove up the narrow streets of Lisbon towards our hotel at the top of the highest hill in the old Graca area. The Senhora do Monte is small, clean, and quiet, with terrific views of St. George's Castle and all of downtown Lisbon. I couldn't wait to drop our passports on the front desk and pass out between the sheets.

Oddly, people on the street were waving to us from under umbrellas and inside doorways. Although I couldn't remember exactly what I had done on my last trip here, I had obviously made quite an impression on the locals. They were genuinely excited to see me.

Wow! That's why I love Portugal! The people are the friendliest in all of Europe.

The streets got narrower and steeper. The rain pounded harder, and the people kept waving. Finally, one guy jumped straight into the path of the car with his hands raised. I hit the brakes, stopping in front of him.

Travel tip: in Portugal, when people shout *"Bomberos!"*, it is not an endearing term meaning "frequent foreign visitor." It means "Firemen!" That's right, the concerned citizens of Lisbon were waving at us to stop the car because it had caught fire. Driving fast and skyward, I could not see the smoke coming out the bottom of the car. They could.

Luckily, the torrential rain put the fire out as soon as I opened the hood, and the flames were unable to burn Lisbon to the ground, which happened once before. A young girl called the rental agency for me. I can't tell you what I said to the guy who answered, but I used a word that, thanks to rock stars and rappers, has international significance.

So we were thoroughly drenched as we walked up ever more hills towards a hotel that, like a mirage on a desert horizon, seemed to be getting farther and farther away. As we trudged forward, putting one foot in front of the other mostly from instinct, the silver-lining principle of travel kicked in: things could be much worse—we could have our luggage with us.

We finally made it to the hotel, and guess what? They *had* received my reservation and they *had* held the room for me.

I'm suspicious when things go smoothly. It's a room in another city, isn't it? I asked. No. Well, it's the one you've been meaning to put a roof on, right? The one that doubles as tonight's hospitality suite for the Shriners' Spring Convention? A waterbed with a slow leak?

As usual, the room was fine. Our luggage was dropped by at midnight, and a new rental car was parked on the street in front of the hotel in the morning. And it was a gorgeous fresh and sunny morning, the kind from which new beginnings take shape.

Yes, I did have a terrific trip. Because, when it comes to travelling, although my luck quotient may not be very high, my expectation level is lower than it's ever been. And that's a good thing, as Martha Stewart might say.

Cultural Misunderstanding

An American church newsletter announced an appearance by well-known missionary and motivational speaker Bertha Belch with this ad: "Come and hear Bertha Belch all the way from Tanzania."

The Portuguese Bank: Bring Lunch if You Plan to Rob It

Everyday procedures in Portugal can sometimes be much like their castles: medieval.

On one recent trip to Portugal, I walked zombie-like down the steps of the Air Transat Toronto to Lisbon flight and onto the shuttle bus. When I walked into the customs terminal with three hundred other sleep-deprived passengers at 6:40 a.m., we very much expected to be met by customs officials. Thirty-five minutes later, a small riot erupted when three customs employees, embarrassed and flustered, quickly unlocked doors and rapidly rubber-stamped everybody through in a matter of minutes. So much for heightened security.

I eased my rented Opel out of the parking garage and began the slow, unwinding drive across the new Vasco da Gama bridge and on down to the southwest coast of Portugal. After a brief reunion with my friend Fernando, I moved my things into one of his kitchenettes overlooking the sea at Vila Nova de Milfontes (called "Milfonch" for short).

As much as I wanted to crash for a couple of hours, I remembered the banks would be closed the next day, so, functioning mostly from memory, I walked downtown and spent half an hour in line at Nova Rede, a national bank with outlets everywhere in Portugal, only to learn, when I finally got to the teller's cage, that they don't actually change money. Tough way for a bank to make

Cultural Misunderstanding

The New Guide of Conversation in Portuguese and English explains how a Portuguese tourist should articulate, in English, displeasure with being assigned a poor horse at a riding stable: "Here is a horse who have bad looks. Give me another. I will not that. He not sall know to march, he is pursy, he is foundered. Don't you are ashamed to give me a jade as like? He is undshoes. He is with nails up." Okay, but despite all his other faults, the horse is still kind of pursy.

a living—not trading in currency. Would a small *No Cambio* sign in the window be too much to ask? To judge by the way I was shooed away, it would.

So I lined up at Credito Agricola, an agricultural credit union that now sees many more tourists than farmers. At Credito Agricola they welcome new customers by trapping them in the foyer. The outside door locks behind you, and the inner door doesn't open until they approve of your appearance. "Hmm, a geek in shorts on a winter day with a ball hat and backpack? This should be fun." Bzzz—I was allowed in.

Inside the tiny office were twenty-two customers, four wickets, and two tellers, who were working so slowly they looked like Canadian postal workers on Valium. I noticed the customers were split into three lines, an odd number given the two tellers. But the lines kind of blurred and merged as everyone talked and visited with people in other lines. It was like a town hall meeting. Old men with hands behind their backs discussed, I don't know, cork trees and tent caterpillars, while women emphasized their points by slapping fingers in open palms. A baby was much adored and cooed at. It was the Buena Banco Social Club.

Heads down, the tellers were oblivious to the milling crowd. They might well have been napping. Whenever a customer completed a transaction and moved away from the counter, which didn't happen all that often, people rushed the teller from the front of all the lines. Then the losers returned to their respective lines and continued to pretend there was some sort of service system in place in this bank. A short guy with thick glasses circled the lines like a roving tailback ready to punch through any opening at the front.

Unfortunately, the woman at the head of my line was: a) non-aggressive; b) polite; and c) determined to retell the story of the Old Testament to the woman behind her. More genuflecting was going on than you normally see in a church, let alone a credit union.

Much grumbling went on in my line, as well as a few choice words in English.

"Bzzz . . ." A guy emerged from the door trap with a fistful of escudos, and went directly to an empty booth at the far end of the counter. Very subtly, he totalled his cash, wrote something on a slip of paper, and pushed it slowly behind the glass towards a female teller in an open wicket. Equally surreptitiously, a receipt was passed from the teller back to him, and he smiled and left the bank. Apparently, I was the only one who noticed this. So, now that I knew nobody spoke English, I yelled a very bad word at him.

Suddenly, there was an opening, and the rover and the woman at the front of my line hit the counter in a dead heat. It was like watching the Buffalo Bills on fourth down and goal to go, without a quarterback. Words were exchanged, hands were thrown up, and the woman backed off and returned to the head of my line because—I'm guessing here—she was only up to Daniel and the Den of Lions, and she still had the story of Jonah and the Whale to tell.

I stood in line for one more hour before I got to change my money. It could have been a lot worse. As it turned out, half the people in the bank weren't there to do business, they just came along to chat with those who had some sort of purpose in life. So they left in twos and threes, and once the baby was gone, the party seemed to peter out.

I'm telling you, the Canadian dollar dropped six cents in the time it took for me to get my money changed. The inner workings of a Portuguese bank are so disorganized, I don't think you could actually rob one without packing a lunch and checking your gun a couple of times for dust accumulation.

And yet, in the window of a shop on "the Strip" in Albufeira, I came face to face with Shop 24—where nine rows of merchandise, including vodka, Scotch, wine, underwear, toothpaste, and cooking and sanitary products are fetched for you by a robot after

Tourists Too Stupid to Travel

And the question most frequently asked by tourists in Niagara Falls: What time do you shut the falls off?

Answer: Canadians are very polite people. What time will you be leaving?

you drop your money in a slot. In the same country where it takes an hour to change money, they've got a 207-item vending machine that is operated twenty-four hours a day by R2D2.

Go figure.

Away, Home Never Looked So Good

Monsaraz is a precious Portuguese town that sits within the walls of a medieval castle. It has a restaurant and two family-run bars, a mini-market, and an art museum. It's a gorgeous ancient hilltop town with narrow, cobblestone streets and whitewashed houses.

After settling into a small pension, Monica and I picked lemons off the tree that grew up past our second-floor balcony. We marvelled at the simple rural life that exists within a European town: a backyard garden staked and flourishing, chickens pecking at grain among the pebbles, the view down the green valley and up the red path to the next town on the adjacent hill, which also lay within castle walls. It was absolutely seductive, a poor man's Tuscany.

We had dinner, the only two people sitting on the hearth of the café's fireplace. We took our brandies outside and watched daylight disappear over Alentejo in a dying fireball, then walked back to our room along the wide top of the fortified wall of the castle.

At midnight the church bells struck a dozen lazy notes, and we were asleep before the echo of the last one petered out.

At three in the morning, the horny rooster started lining up his night's work. It began with a cluck, then a few more, faster and louder, until finally the whole coop was in sexual chaos. We could hear some chickens scurrying to escape, others flopping against the walls of the roost. This racket went on until I found myself barefoot and naked on a cold balcony throwing hard, unripe lemons at them and screaming, "Shut the &#@* up!"

An hour later, when the rooster was spent, I returned to bed, promising to barbecue one of the little bastards the next day. Then some drunk on a dirt bike did circles around the castle. And the church bells kept me awake till dawn.

And I thought to myself: oh yeah, I could live here. I just could never sleep here.

Breakfast at the Hotel Vau: Adventure Tourism

Don't get me wrong—*me gusto muito Portugal*. You can make more friends in Portugal in a week than you can in France in a lifetime.

Plus it's cheap, the last great bargain for travellers in Europe. And Canadians are cheap visitors. A million snowbirds go to Florida every winter to escape the snow and subsist on "Early Bird Specials" that include two-for-one cocktails and hot hors d'oeuvre trays otherwise known as "a meal on a napkin." We're cheap. It's no coincidence that some of the stupidest kids in America come from Florida. Why? Because they're waiting tables in restaurants that Canadians frequent, and depending on tips to put them through college.

I can't believe more people don't winter in the Algarve, where

> ### *Travel Sign*
> PLEASE, NO GIVE FOOD THE GOOSE
> —Sign on a goose pen in the back streets of Lagoa, in the Algarve, on a pen in which four fat geese nervously paced back and forth, counting off the days to Christmas. And let me tell you that, in Portugal, the penalty for goosing food is having to wear non-pasteurized goat cheese in your shorts for thirty days.

there's culture, romance, and more money for your loonie. And it's peaceful.

How gentle are the Portuguese? During the great military coup of April 25, 1974, soldiers restored a semblance of democracy to the country by placing flowers in the barrels of their rifles. It was known as the Day of the Red Carnations, and nobody got shot. Oh sure, some flowers wilted badly, but that was it.

Portugal is safe and fun and exciting, but it's not exactly a model of national efficiency. In Portugal, much like their bubbly wines of the north, some services are pretty green. I mean, c'mon—unless you're part of a pride of lions about to surprise a herd of gazelles at dawn on the Serengeti plain—breakfast is not supposed to be a team sport.

Yet the Hotel Vau, just west of the Praia da Rocha on Portugal's sprawling Algarve makes a fairly keen competition out of the day's first, and some would say, most important meal. Breakfast—or, as they call it in Portuguese, *da manha*—is served in the dining room between 7:00 a.m. and 10:00 a.m. But if you get down to the dining room at 9:30 a.m., as I did my first day there, you must set out on a nutritional scavenger hunt, with just thirty minutes to collect enough items to minimally qualify as breakfast. For reasons unknown, 9:30 seems to be the time at which the Portuguese meal plan starts to look like it's been funded and organized by the Canadian Liberal government.

That morning, the automatic coffee machine, having been poked and prodded hundreds of times already, coughed, grunted, and met an untimely death. Until I get a cup of coffee in the morning, I've been told, I'm not really a pleasant person to be around. I only have one cup a day, but if I don't get that cup, I'll admit I can be a little irritable. Okay, maybe more than a little: "I swear I'll kick the crap outta that machine and eat the beans raw right out of its belly if somebody doesn't fix the freaking thing right now!"

Sorry. Where was I? Oh yeah, trying to score a little caffeine. But since the hot water for the tea was also supplied by the expired machine, my backup drug deal did not go down, either.

I found orange juice, which was actually orange drink, but there were no juice glasses. But wait—my coffee cup wasn't doing anything. And I snared a roll, a crusty but lonely roll that had been either rejected or overlooked by the seventy previous diners who got to the dining room before me.

And then the fun began. When I asked if I could get a knife, the waitress looked at me like I was nuts. Not that there was no clean cutlery in the kitchen. But why would I need a knife? There was no butter, either.

By this point, about fifty hotel guests were milling around empty food trays and unmade tables looking for food. Growling stomachs took on a rather ugly tone, like small storms threatening to unite and erupt into an in-house hurricane. Most of the guests were Canadian and were so damn polite it was pathetic, while the Europeans dealt with the problem by smoking.

The staff was in constant motion, satisfying almost nobody and accomplishing very little. They looked like the Leafs trying to clear the puck out of their own end. It was as if they had shown up for work this morning hoping to find gainful employment in the hotel and restaurant service industry after having undergone extensive training in the agricultural sector. Several, I suspected, had worked at Air Canada's courtesy desk.

A rumour began to circulate that coffee was being made in the kitchen, and the technician who had arrived to fix the automatic machine was nearly trampled in the rush to the swinging doors. Sure enough, a waiter with a tray of steaming coffee cups appeared out of the kitchen, but he barely cleared the doors before he was mugged. He disappeared back into the kitchen, empty-handed and a little afraid. I staked out a spot behind the juice bar, and when the waiter emerged with a second tray, I was on him like a junkie on a tardy dealer.

Roll and drink in hand, I returned to the table where I had placed my knapsack, only to find that two rude people had commandeered it while I was off foraging for food. They had fruit, which made them both resourceful and a potential target for a takeover.

Standing there gazing around the room and juggling a breakfast that contravened the Geneva Convention's nutritional requirements for prisoners of war, I decided that all this scene needed to descend into total chaos was a cross-eyed maitre d' and a karaoke machine. I had reached the stage where I wanted somebody to stand me up in the corner and feed me scrambled eggs with a slingshot.

I grabbed my pack and, taking a spoon and a packet of sugar with me, I found a small table and chair in the recreation room near the reception. I laid waste to my roll and coffee while watching CNN in German. And, I thought to myself, it could have been a lot worse. I could have opted for the dinner plan, which would involve steak knives and alcohol.

Breakfast at the Hotel Vau—it ain't exactly Tiffany's. It's more like an early morning scene from *Survivor*.

Portugal on the Dutchy Plan

If Dutchy Doerr didn't exist, a great cartoonist with a keen eye for quirkiness would certainly have created him. Dutchy's a character. He's fit, feisty, and fully aware of the ways of this world. He's now eighty-two, and if there's anybody his age who thinks they can beat him at tennis, I'll put up the prize money.

Plus Dutchy drinks . . . a wee bit. But not alone. That's where I come in. Set in his ways, but with a refreshing quirkiness, Dutchy can turn a run to the beer store into a harrowing adventure of epic proportions. Way back, there must be some Japanese in his ancestry, because all the while Dutchy is nodding at you in agreement, he's clearly saying no. In the end, you do it his way. Dutchy's motto is keep it simple. Then, all hell breaks loose.

After hearing my tales of Portugal, Dutchy decided to spend a month there in the fall. With his wife, Edith, and her sister, Myra, he bought a senior's long-stay package at the Hotel Auramar in busy Albufeira. I joined him there for a week of tennis, and it was, as usual, unusual.

Exhausted, and just off a book tour, I had grabbed a cheap ticket to Lisbon, rented a car, and driven to my friend Fernando's cozy two-storey inn, which sits on the high bank of the Rio Mira on the ocean side of Vila Nova de Milfontes, halfway between Lisbon and Sagres on the rocky and mostly tranquil southwest coast of Portugal. Now getting touristy, "Milfonch" is still a hard-working town as well as a vibrant vacation spot. Fernando's quaint apartments overlook the spot where the river meets the Atlantic— the very spot where Sir Francis Drake would hide his fleet, waiting to pounce on unsuspecting victims of the piracy industry.

As it was unseasonably cool, I spent three great days walking and hitching to nearby towns and reading by the fireplace. On the fourth day, I drove slowly down to the Algarve and parked at the Auramar. Dutchy had been staying in a double room at the

Dining Out Travel Tip

The Portuguese pride themselves on the abundance and freshness of their fish. Make sure you insist that your fish dish be served *muito morto*, or quite dead. And keep your knife at the ready. Despite what they may claim, a sea bass that knocks over your wine glass while trying to get at your shrimp cocktail is most definitely not *muito morto*.

Auramar for three weeks when I arrived. Accommodations would not be a problem, he had said.

At 5:30, I walked into the hotel bar, where I knew Dutchy would be conducting a post-game clinic. He was sitting off to the side at a dark table with two other Canadians. This was unusual, because we normally like to stand at the bar and pepper the bartender with questions.

"So I'm checked in?" I asked him, hoping to grab a shower before dinner.

"Everything's taken care of, Bill. No problem," he said. "Except tonight."

"Whaddaya mean?" I asked, as Dutchy got up and went around the corner to the bar.

He returned with two cold mugs of Sagres beer. "Tonight," he said, setting down the glasses, "you're not officially checked in." Then he put his right index finger to his lips.

"But, Dutchy . . ."

"Keep it simple, Bill," he said, and proceeded to describe the layout of the hotel.

Now, at least, I understood why we were sitting where the bartender couldn't see us. Dutchy was on the Unlimited Drinks Plan and as it would turn out, I was on the Dutchy Plan. From then on Dutchy was kind of my local dealer—I could have whatever I wanted, I just couldn't deal directly with the head office.

I had no idea what kind of arrangement Dutchy had made with the woman at the desk, but it was clear I wasn't going to change it and Dutchy would never let me pay.

The Dutchy Plan did not include dinner. So while Dutchy went down to the dining room with Edith and Myra, I went out to the parking lot to change into something comfortable for dinner out. While changing out of the trunk of my car, I think I may have inadvertently mooned a well-dressed Brit in a Land Rover.

Later, during the commotion of a German tour group checking in, I managed to haul my luggage up the back stairs to Dutchy's room. The key was hidden in the bowl-like lamp fixture at the door. Lying in bed, I worried that if the Hotel Auramar did a bed check, like the counsellors used to do at summer camp, Dutchy would act like he was surprised to see me and start yelling "Burglar!" at the top of his lungs. I knotted my bed sheets together in case I had to make an emergency escape without going past the front desk.

The next morning, I realized I was just as reliant on Dutchy for food as I had been for beer. He brought dried toast with a packet of marmalade from the breakfast buffet up to our room. Using some weird distillation system he had set up involving the hotplate and a soup pot of used bags, he made me a cup of hot tea. And, like most vacationing Canadians faced with a free buffet, we had enough fruit in our room to require a vendor's permit at the morning market in Lagos. I'm serious—with two blenders and some plastic cups I could have started a juice bar on the beach.

I couldn't imagine what was going to happen next. Complete with goofy smile, I was like a little kid at Dutchyland. What happened next was we played tennis and, although I can't pin this one directly on Dutchy, we got locked inside the tennis court due to a malfunctioning door mechanism. We were too far from the hotel to yell for help, and the only people strolling the grounds didn't speak our language. After a long time, and many plans, I managed to lever the latch free with a thick twig I pulled through the fence. Otherwise, we'd still be out there.

That evening, we had our beer at a table where the bartender couldn't see me but from which I could see the entertainment: Duarte, the Portuguese Roy Orbison. I'm happy to report that the Portuguese Roy Orbison is also not blind.

Although I was now a registered guest on the bare-bones bed-only plan, we still hid the key in the lamp shade. It was just more fun that way.

The next day I was dying for a coffee. Dutchy accommodated me by brewing a stronger cup of tea from his in-room still, which would make us a lot of money if we were in prison rather than Portugal.

"The coffee's bad . . . and bad for you, Bill."

We played tennis with a garbage pail keeping the door open, and then went off to lunch by the pool, where the buffet manager couldn't see me. Dutchy brought me a sandwich that consisted of a large roll, a thin slice of cheese, and a wilted lettuce leaf with a hard-boiled egg on the side. And a beer.

That was pretty much the routine: second-hand tea, high-security tennis, some walking, a bit of BBC World News, the roll-and-egg lunch, and cold but illicit beer. Oh, and almost metaphysically, Duarte, the Portuguese Roy Orbison, turned into Mandrake the Portuguese Magician every other night. My heart stopped when he picked Dutchy's pocket. If he lost Dutchy's key, I was sleeping in my car for sure.

It wasn't until my last day there that I strolled past the buffet and noticed it also included grilled fish with rice, barbecued chicken with fries, calamari, roast pork sandwiches, and a salad bar. But no, I got bread with the rumour of cheese and yellowing vegetation.

"But, Dutchy . . ."

"Keep it simple, Bill. That other stuff is full of fat."

The last evening, while Dutchy and I were shooting pool, a bossy English woman slammed the door behind us, locking us in the recreation room. Even Mandrake couldn't solve this crisis involving a missing key. It took five people, including the hotel janitor, to get us out. This incident made it very hard for me to hide from the bartender, who was part of the rescue team.

By week's end, I was not just avoiding hotel employees, but also any part of the hotel that came with a lock. I'm sure my morning horoscope, written, of course, by the Portuguese Jeane Dixon, would have advised me to avoid meat lockers and bank vaults.

Meanwhile, back at the room, or as I like to call it "Dutchy's Pick Your Own Fruit Stand," I noticed Dutchy was hiding his money in the inverted lampshade imbedded on the wall near the bathroom. Here's his logic: since the light didn't work, he figured the only possibility of being robbed was by the electrician who came to fix it. The bulb was missing, so anybody else who put a hand in there would get a pretty good jolt. And the clincher—he hadn't reported the problem. To Dutchy's way of thinking, this was more foolproof than the wall safe in the closet.

At this point, I realized I had to get out of there. I mean, I quite liked the used tea-bag brewing system, but by Friday I was insisting on a first pressing.

The best part of not being allowed near the front desk is that checking out is a snap.

It was great, and great value. Because in Portugal, a little bit of Dutchy goes a long, long way.

San Miguel: Hiking in the Land of Swollen Udders

San Miguel, of the eastern Azores group of islands in the middle of the Atlantic, is thought by some scholars to be the last remnant of the lost continent of Atlantis. This tiny bit of Portuguese paradise, 2,000 kilometres from the mainland, is a land of lush, green mountains on semi-tropic earth, crashing white and turquoise surf, and black volcanic rock formations.

Safe, serene, and simply spectacular, with the cleanest air on earth, the Azores may be the best place in the world for serious walkers and curious hikers. Where else can you climb down into the crater of a volcano and have a fresh, clear lake all to yourself? Where else can you watch a local chef cram a canvas sack full of meat, vegetables, and spices and then drop it down a hole, only to have it come back up an hour later as your lunch—a stew, cooked by volcanic heat? Where else can you strike out each day for a new town, always assured of finding a clean room with breakfast for about $40?

Fascinating in the simplicity of its lifestyle and in its natural splendour, sunny and seductive San Miguel is nothing less than glorious. But be forewarned: there are two pressing problems you'll encounter as you ramble around these islands.

First, and I'm not exaggerating, the people are so friendly and concerned, actually walking along the roads is difficult. Spotting walkers, Azorean drivers constantly stop to offer them rides. On

Tourists Too Stupid to Travel

The Travel Industry Association of America is currently trying to track down the people who asked the following questions of travel agents, by offering free in-house cat scans.

Question: Does the bus tour go to the same places that the boat tour does?
Answer: Yeah, one's just drier than the other.
Question: Is the horse manure on the square real?
Answer: No, of course not. It's like fake dog doo. Lots of tourists take some home as a souvenir. Help yourself.

the other hand, should the weather turn bad, hitchhiking is a simple matter of crossing the road and accepting a lift from the first or second passing vehicle. I've seen a lot of the Azores from the back of a pickup truck through rain-spotted sunglasses.

Second, there are way, *way*, *way*, WAY, WAY, **WAY** too many cows.

There are 900,000 cows on the island of San Miguel. That's five cows for every man, woman, and child. Believe me, when a baby is born in the Azores and has to look after five cows before he's able to walk, later in life he develops a great appreciation for toys.

Think about it—900,000 cows and one very, very busy bull. His name is Lo Velho Vaca, which in English means "The Old Cowpoke."

There are cows on the sides of mountains, cows in fields,

cows in pens, cows in barns, big cows in the backs of trucks, calves in the front of trucks, cows on trailers pulled by motorcycles, small cows in cars, big cows in downtown backyards, cows in city parks, cows on ferries, uniformed cows checking passports at the airport and looking for foreign cows trying to come into the country using phony cow ID.

When you spend a lot of time with a lot of cows, you start to go a little wacky. You start to do cow humour, or *vaca humoristico*, for the locals. Walking in the constant gaze of 1.8 million doe-like eyes changes a man. After a couple of days, just me and the girls, I began to believe there might be a whole new career for me doing stand-up bovine comedy.

First cow: Geez, Louise, have you looked at yourself lately!
              You're saggin', baby.
Second cow: Erma, go sit on a salt lick and rotate.

Don't get me wrong, they're fine specimens, bred by the very latest in agri-biological techniques. In fact, they're so sophisticated, some of these cows have done away with the traditional cow bells and can now be seen with cell phones hanging around their necks.

Cow talking on a cell phone: "Ida? There's a geek wearing a blue backpack and a Toronto Blue Jays hat headed your way. Can you get up on the overpass and drop the brown bomb on him? Ida? You're breaking up, honey."

Yes, cow humour is *meo vida*. I'm serious: when it's just you and them, you get a little psycowtic after a while. They stare at you as you walk by, from a vast sea of sad eyes. Once you've passed, they make these low mooing noises, and you know, oh yeah, you know very well they're talking about you.

It's troubling to walk by a field of two hundred cows with four hundred stomachs, and know that while they're standing silent, perfectly still and seemingly happy, they're actually roiling and regurgitating on the inside. And they all have bright orange identification plates stapled to their ears and large, almost bursting udders.

The farmers have so many cows to milk, they don't always get to some herds on time, and some udders are dragged along in such a way that they look like they should require a separate licence plate. Thank goodness they're not violent animals with dreams of a United Pure Holstein Cowland.

It makes you wonder if it was really the volcanoes, or cows with a bad case of food poisoning, that erupted to form these islands.

Azorean farmers see so many udders every day that many of them have lost interest in topless bars.

Cow: Dammit, Nordesto, would it kill you to warm up your hands?

Farmer: Ay, yi yi! Yesterday she had a headache!

Vaca humoristico: What do you call a cow that tried to jump over the moon but forgot about the barbed wire fence at the far end of the field? *Una completo castrofio*. In English, an udder catastrophe.

Two cows are sitting by the hotel pool wearing sunglasses,

smoking cigarettes, and drinking vodka tonics from glasses with tiny umbrellas. There's no joke here; I'm telling you, they're everywhere! Don't talk to me about mad cow disease—I'm still seeing cattle in my sleep.

San Miguel, a beautiful verderous sanctum in the middle of the Atlantic, where sweet and simple people are outnumbered and surrounded by far too many cows.

Has Anybody Famous Stayed Here?

That's the question all travel editors want writers to answer in their features.

I had just completed the photography and interviews for a destination piece on the snug and stately Hotel San Pedro in San Miguel's capital of Ponta Delgada. I was still a little "cow giddy," but otherwise fine. Standing in the hotel's cozy cave of a bar, with the flames from the grey basalt fireplace sparkling off the highly polished mahogany beams, I threw out the typical tourist question: "Has anybody famous stayed here?"

The eyes of the big, friendly Portuguese bellman lit up. "Jess," said Jorge Manuel de Costas, struggling, "Shawn Wing."

"John Wayne?" I asked, a little incredulous.

"John Wayne," he said confidently, and then, practising his English on me as he had said he wanted to do, he added: "But before he died, of course."

Of course, I thought, because a dead John Wayne is no fun to drink with. Plus, you can pretty much forget about a tip.

The *Levada*: Madeira's Meandering Killer Curb

Man always travels along precipices . . . his truest obligation is to keep his balance.
—Pope John Paul II

Without constant irrigation, the lush Atlantic garden known as Madeira would be nothing more than a big mossy rock in the middle of the ocean. Rainwater seeps through its volcanic crust and is all but lost in subterranean rivers, occasionally gushing forth from springs where it is least needed.

A half century ago, with calloused hands outstretched from huge wickerwork baskets suspended on the sides of mountains, Portuguese peasants created an elaborate aqueduct system, 2,150 kilometres long, of cement furrows that transport this life-giving water from mountaintop reservoirs to every growing patch on the island. These little rivulets run down the sides of the volcanic peaks, following the natural contour of cliffs and canyons in a never-ending gurgle of cold clean mountain water.

The concrete troughs themselves are about a foot deep and a foot wide, and walking curbs are attached to their outside edge, so the *levadeiros* can do repair work and remove the obstructions of rock slides and tumbling trees. The *levadas* allow the semi-tropical island of Madeira to grow every fruit imaginable and a dazzling array of flowers that would make a botanical gardener weep.

For hikers, a gentle-sloping path that encircles every mountain from peak to coast and cuts through the wilds as well as isolated villages—well, that's pure paradise.

"This one," said Lena, pointing to a thin blue line on our map. "I have friends who followed this *levada*. It's a lovely walk."

Lena is the consummate concierge of Reid's Palace Hotel in Madeira's capital of Funchal. For comfort with class, a traveller would be hard pressed to find a finer hotel in all the world than the inn that William Reid built back in 1891. There are countries that do not possess the distinguished and fascinating history of Reid's Palace Hotel.

Of the dozen different fruits in the fresh basket placed in your room each day, all, including the figs, mangoes, melons, bananas, and passion fruit, are grown in orchards bordered by a *levada*.

Monica and I couldn't wait for our driver to get to the top of Pico de Arieiro, Madeira's third highest mountain, so we could begin our *levada* hike back down to the coast. We gave short shrift to Pico dos Barcelos, where a spectacular cliffside park looks back on Funchal and serves as an outdoor craft guild for local women who knit sweaters and embroider colourful flowers onto fine white cotton. Ever rising on switchback curves, our taxi left the trees behind and entered into barren rockiness, where people fill water jugs from metal spigots that splash cold mountain streams onto the road.

At Pico do Arieiro, locals dressed in alpine peasant costumes served wine to a tour group at a walled lookout that offered a dizzying view of the valleys below. From this ancient belvedere, we started down a path that corkscrewed into the valley below. For the most part, it was a good walk along a stone-studded dirt track. We passed a few casual walkers taking photos of the surrounding towering mountains and deep ravines.

The cliffs along which you walk fall straight down to the tiny white-washed town below. The temptation is great to throw a rock far out and count off the seconds—best guess, fifteen—before it hits the rocks or a red tiled roof below. Along the more dangerous ledges, a single wire railing, hooked through the top of steel stakes, allows walkers to steady themselves.

In an hour we had descended into Curral das Freiras, literally "The Shelter of the Nuns," a village hidden in the crater of an extinct volcano, where the sisters of the Convent of Santa Clara escaped the marauding French pirates who'd come to plunder the port of Funchal in the seventeenth century. We tiptoed into the open and empty church to gaze reverently at its antique religious furnishings, which have survived for hundreds of years behind unlocked doors.

We followed a path out of town that snaked sharply down past small houses and vegetable gardens, past kids and dogs and grapevine trestles, all inaccessible by car. An old man inside the open door of a tiny wicker shop pointed us through his gated garden, and the sound of running water put us on the *levada*. Soon Curral das Freiras was high above us and then suddenly gone as we skirted a mountain and set off into a tangle of wilderness and wild flowers somewhere near Eira do Serado.

In the mountains of Madeira you're never too far from the minuscule canals. Stay on the *levada*'s curb and you can't possibly get lost, we figured. Eventually, they all wind their way to the coast. And so we hiked farther and farther into this wooded won-derland of verdant and virginal splendour, with overhanging rock cliffs above us, the valley floor thousands of metres below, the sea a bluish infinity beyond.

The ledge along which the *levada* was built got increasingly narrow. At some points it was so narrow my backpack got caught on the side of the cliff, and I had to walk sideways, facing the mountain, to get by. But the ground was dry, and occasionally we came upon a wide spot where we could step off the curb.

On one hairpin turn, the *levada* just eroded away. We got around the bend by grabbing onto the shrubs on the side of the cliff and shuffling across a porous ledge of about fifteen centimetres of loose dirt directly above what would be about a 150-metre fall into the rocky canyon below. Here, only the stakes of a railing remained, the wire or rope lost long ago.

Still game, but shaken, Monica said, as I had earlier, when we clambered over a boulder lodged on the *levada* that was the size

ONE WAY

Unsavoury Traveller

Lars Back, a drunken Swede who slurred female flight attendants and vomited on the lap of his female companion on a flight to New York, was not your average obnoxious idiot. He was the Swedish cabinet's expert on gender equality, on his way to attend a UN conference on the status of women. His travelling partner was his boss, and Sweden's female equality minister. At 38,000 feet, with unlimited alcohol, status has little to do with stupidity.

of a Volkswagen Beetle: "Well, at least we don't have to come back this way." And that became the theme of the hike—scary, yes, but it can't get any worse and, besides, we're not coming back this way.

After we overcame each hurdle, the breathtaking scenery centred us. A cascading waterfall across the valley, a treasured plot of orchard on a far-off mountaintop, our path disappearing into a dark underpass of pine trees, small white clouds floating below us—Madeira is one of the few places in the world where the descriptions in the tourist brochures cannot be exaggerated.

We stopped for lunch right on the *levada* at a particularly serene spot, passing bread, cheese, cold cuts, and the binoculars back and forth, our legs dangling over the precipice. Suddenly, two very fit American girls came around the bend, slowing down only to say hello, and stepping over us to continue along the *levada* at marching pace. We cleaned up, packed up, and set off again. It was one of the few times I'd ever be grateful for forgetting the bottle of wine for lunch.

An hour later, we stopped abruptly where the path had been washed out by a waterfall. Rocks careening down the mountain along this river had knocked out the *levada*. But we noticed a fresh path through the mud and over the stream where it narrowed a few yards down. And hell, if the Americans could do it . . . We scampered down, crossed the shallow rivulet, and climbed back onto the *levada* by pulling ourselves up onto tree limbs and through wiry brush. Our legs raked by thorns, we were mud splattered and a little bloody, but we pressed on undeterred because . . . "At least we don't have to go back this way."

And it seemed to get better for an hour or so. We learned not to look down from the sheer drops around bends. We grabbed hold of what stubble the mountain offered and clung close to the volcanic wall when we walked over the debris from rock slides. And then, at the end of a windy cliff side bend, there was no more *levada*. It just tapered off and disappeared into scrub and rock.

I was pulling out the binoculars when Monica spotted the hole, a round black entranceway to a cave. From the bubbling sound of the water, we knew the *levada* somehow went into this cave. Using the binoculars, I spotted the *levada* beginning again across the ravine at other end of this shaft.

"That's it," I said. "We gotta go back."

My biggest fear, the stuff of my worst nightmares, is being trapped in some kind of underground passageway that gets blacker and narrower until I can't move or turn around.

"We're going through," said Monica. She then detailed all the perilous obstacles we'd have to overcome by doubling back, this time going uphill for four hours, with just two hours of daylight left.

Did I mention I'm claustrophobic? At this point, a guy flying by in a sightseeing helicopter with a rope ladder could have had my life's savings in a heartbeat.

As Monica led the way into the tunnel, I grabbed hold of the top of her backpack and shuffled along behind, never letting my feet leave the floor of the cave. Seconds past the entrance, the light disappeared completely, and the echo from the splashing water forced us to shout. One step at a time, we crept through this black hole, our left hands on the wall, and our left feet dragging along the edge of the *levada*. We had no idea what was to our right, above us, or in front of us.

I practiced letting go of Monica quickly in case we were unwittingly walking into some sort of bottomless well. Okay, I didn't do that, but strange thoughts did cross my mind. I tried to remember if my will had been notarized and why I didn't travel with a Saint Christopher's medal pinned to my undershorts. I mumbled stupid little self-assurances like, "One step at a time," and, "So far, so good." And, "Jesus Christ, we're both gonna die here!"

The mind in crisis is not to be trusted. All I could think of as we felt our way through this horrid hole was the motto on Madeira's tourist brochures: "You can feel nature all around you." That and "It's a lovely walk."

It was the most frightening fifteen minutes of my life. And then we saw some light.

"There! Right there! Light! We've made it!" I gushed. We sped up now that we could see the *levada* we were walking on.

As we rounded a corner, we came upon a man in a raincoat holding a spear in the middle of the waterfall that had washed away the top of this cave. Oh great, I thought, if nature hasn't finished you off by this point, there's a man with a six-foot dagger waiting to do the job.

He grunted something, urging us to continue, and then bent over and continued to push rocks through the hole in the tunnel and off the side of the cliff with his spear. He was the *lavadeiro*, the repair man. With 2,150 kilometres of *levada* and one maintenance man in a ratty yellow slicker, I thought, no wonder we're in trouble here.

After ten more minutes of crouching and inching our way through the remaining blackness, we exited out the other side of the tunnel. We were cold and soaking wet from socks to knapsack, emotionally drained but relieved to be alive.

"At least we don't have to go back," I shouted above the roar of the waterfall, and we continued on in cherished daylight.

Not a minute out of the cave, the *levada* dipped straight down, running beside a set of narrow, moss-covered cement steps that also fell straight down. Honestly, it looked more like a corrugated water slide than a set of steps. I stopped immediately and began to turn around. Then I spotted the black hole of the cave looking back at me, and started down the slide. The tiny steps were rounded with age and slick with green strands of algae growing in the spray of the waterfall. A tangled wire lay on the ground to my right, the only thing separating us from a ninety-metre drop into the rocky canyon below.

I started down on my rear end, my hands clinging to whatever rough surface I could find on the steps and their crumbling sides. I could not turn to see Monica behind me, but I knew that if she slipped she couldn't help but take me out on her way down. Gee, I thought, so soon after the most frightening experience of my life, another one pops up to numb the mind.

From my right, I heard a woman scream, and I turned cautiously to see the two American girls, one standing safely across the ravine with a man, the other trapped on a ledge of loose rock just below us. At this point, we were halfway down the slimy stairs, with fifteen more treacherous steps to go.

"We gotta go back!" I yelled over my shoulder to Monica.

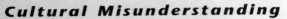

Cultural Misunderstanding

When you see a sign for *moveis* in Portugal, it means furniture. I know. I've made that mistake: the seats are really comfortable, but the storyline sucks.

A movie in Portuguese is a *filme* or *cinema*. Portugal is a good country to watch North American films, because they subtitle them instead of dubbing them, so you get the original English soundtrack. I saw *Twister* in an old dim theatre in Vila Franca do Compo, on San Miguel in the Azores. In the middle of the movie, they shut the projector down, and everybody went into the lobby for a smoke. The people, you could tell, were very nervous. "Seven tornadoes in one weekend!" they seemed to say, "I'm not going to *America do Norte* anytime soon."

"No, keep going!" she replied, shrieking above the din of the cascading water that was raining down on us.

"We gotta go back! If we go ahead, we end up there!" With great hesitation I released my grip on the right side of the steps, pointing to the scene below.

There was a long pause as we both considered our options. Going back meant scaling this slippery concrete stepladder with only the reward of the black tunnel waiting at the top. Going ahead meant ending up where one of the American girls was now stranded, the other having somehow summoned a rock climber for help.

"Just go! Just go! We can't stay here!" screamed Monica, as water poured past us. We proceeded down, bums bouncing on the flat parts, our nails scraping the sides for purchase.

Somehow we both made it to the bottom, and as we moved out of the spray from the water, I spotted the most beautiful rainbow enclosing the entire mountainside scene: a foaming river dashing over the cave and the steps, and a couple of casualties of nature immobilized below.

We were now drenched right through our packs, and our shoes squished with each step, but we moved quickly along the *levada*, which had regained its form and gentle slope. We hustled along the winding ribbon for about an hour, making great time, but with one hour of daylight left, we fully expected to wind up in that treacherous trap with the Americans.

We stopped for a water break at a beautiful tranquil opening, under a natural trestle of wild grapes, the sun beginning to set in front of us between two mountains and the sea.

"They weren't wet!" blurted Monica. "The American girls, they weren't wet."

Come to think of it, they weren't. "So?"

"So they didn't go through the tunnel. They tried to go around beneath it, that's how they got stuck down there on that cliff."

Before I could lie and say that I had also figured this out, I heard a dog bark in the distance ahead of us. Civilization. We would not, with any luck we hadn't already used up, have to spend the night in these mountains.

Gradually, the wild semi-tropical terrain became tamer, and we came upon plots of garden protected by yapping dogs, a tool shed, and finally houses, a street, and people waiting for a bus. I think the village we were in was Sao Martinho. "Funchal?" I asked a middle-aged woman who couldn't take her eyes off us. "*Autobus para Funchal?*"

"Yes," she said in perfect English, as the bus pulled up. "What happened to you?"

As we sat down, with water running onto the seats and our shoes leaking on the floor, Monica told her the story.

"My God," she said with the accent she'd picked up like thousands of other Madeiran domestics who'd gone off to South Africa for work. "They should close that one down, for sure. Five Germans died up there last month."

Dying was something we had not allowed ourselves to think of until now.

At the main entrance of Reid's Palace Hotel, we staggered past the doorman, who watched our every move with his head down, pretending not to look. Inside the lobby, which was subdued in rich red mahogany and rife with the pampered formality of British colonialism, Monica and I looked like miraculous survivors of a mine disaster. I could feel the looks and hear the whispers.

And then, suddenly, Lena was there: "So did you have a good . . . oh, my. What happened?"

Realizing I couldn't strangle her right here in front of so many witnesses, we found the wherewithal to laugh. And then everybody laughed—with us, at us, whatever.

As we entered the tiny elevator, leaving Lena standing in the lobby with a quizzical look on her face, I said, "Lena? Those friends of yours, the ones who took the *levada* down from Curral das Freiras and said it was a lovely walk? Were they, like, circus people?"

The door closed, and we limped to our room, beaten up and sufficiently scared half to death, but nonetheless alive. Showered and snug in the hotel's terrycloth robe, I stood on the balcony, the tiles still warm from the hot afternoon sun, the lights of Funchal's harbour sparkling on the water, and sipped a second cold pint of Coral. I said to myself, thank you. Out loud. Alone.

The difference between a sensational day and a horror story is all in whether or not you live to tell about it. This had been a sensational day, and one I couldn't wait to never, ever repeat.

Levada. Even now, when I say the word, a cold, damp chill goes up my back. And no matter how tightly I close my eyes, it never gets as black as it was in that godforsaken tunnel.

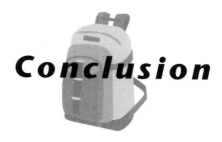

Conclusion

The Grand Adventure of Hitchhiking Is Officially Dead

I once loved the roadside art of hitchhiking and what's more, I was damn good at it. I figured out very early in my thumbing life that if your appearance put people at ease and you spelled out where you were going then you had a very good chance of getting in the car with them. Most evenings I hitchhiked home from high school, from Welland High and Vocational School to the canal-side hamlet of Dain City, having been delayed by football practice or, more often then not, detention.

When I was in Grade 12, I hitchhiked to Daytona Beach, Florida, during spring break, to discover that Canadian high schoolers were every bit as good as American college students at raising hell, projectile vomiting, and not getting the girl in the end.

I hitchhiked home from a summer job in a lumber camp in Castlegar, British Columbia, in a record three days, sharing the driving from Thunder Bay, Ontario, to Burlington, Ontario, with another guy, who was in a big hurry.

On our honeymoon, my wife and I hitchhiked from the Hook of Holland to Algeceris, Spain, and later to Vienna and Budapest. Sure there were tense moments, and it's just as well we didn't understand what the Turkish truck drivers were saying, but most of it was liberating, fascinating, and enlightening.

We spent one entire day in the middle of France standing beside a road with our thumbs out without so much as a driver slowing down. That night we returned to our tiny hotel, where the innkeeper told us the French would not pick up hitchhikers who wore jeans and sweatshirts. The next day we hauled the top-drawer duds out of the packs and once again stood in the same spot for the entire day . . . but this time looking very spiffy.

I'm sure the innkeeper had planted a sign a mile up the road that read: "Killers Ahead."

I used to hitchhike from my house in Wainfleet to the SkyDome in less than three hours and ride home after the Blue Jays game with a neighbour who worked in Toronto. I've hitched from my house in Wainfleet to Pearson airport to catch overseas flights. Thumb 'n' Fly is always more direct than Park 'n' Fly. It used to be, for me, a simple, safe, and cheap way to travel. I hitchhiked from the Peace Bridge in Fort Erie to New York City in one day to catch a Freddie Laker flight that night to London for $99.00.

My motto was: frown and they'll think you're cranky; laugh and they'll think you're a loon; but smile the smile of a man who's got a good story and a kind heart and you've got a real shot. Look good, dress clean, lose the sunglasses, and carry a neatly printed, readable sign with the city of your destination on it. This system worked for me for fifty years.

So last summer's logistical predicament—to get to Bay City, Michigan, without a car, to board the *Bluenose II* for a three-day sail down the Great Lakes and back home—seemed no problem at all to me. My plan was simple enough. I'd allow myself all of Sunday to hitchhike from Cambridge to Windsor, Ontario, and then up to Bay City, Michigan, to board the *Bluenose II*. If I was on the road by 8:30, I'd have ten hours of light to hitchhike a distance I could easily drive in six hours.

At 8:30, there I was, alone on Highway 401, with only my thumb to guide me, beside a sea of vehicles headed south to Windsor. Fresh-faced and well-groomed, I was feeling like a kid again—the freedom of the road, the anticipation of meeting new people, light on my feet and loaded with hope.

It only took me about an hour to discover that the civic motto of Cambridge, Ontario, is: Crede Nullam Personam or Trust No One. Cars and trucks were flying past me like they were volunteer firefighters on the way to a four-alarmer. In the first hour and a half, three hundred vehicles passed me by, while drivers and passengers gawked, giggled, shrugged, pointed in the opposite direction, and made stupid, apologetic gestures with their hands. I crossed myself at a car with four nuns, but that only made them laugh harder. And making faces at children who stick their tongues out at you also doesn't help.

At that point I had to ask myself, am I actually hitchhiking or just standing here looking publicly pathetic?

Somewhere around the two-hour mark, I invoked the god of hitchhiking—whose name I believe is Bert—to smite these people with a simultaneous and involuntary explosion of air bags, leaving them all oxygen deprived and lip-locked to the back windows of their own vehicles. (Each of which, by the way, had plenty of room for a medium-sized man, a small knapsack, and a neatly printed sign that read WINDSOR.)

To the skinny, freaky guy on the bicycle who rode past me three times and twice remarked "No luck yet, eh?" I will now say what I wanted to say to you then: "Oh no, I actually got a ride right to Windsor . . . but I missed my lucky spot here beside this litter-lined, weed-infested on-ramp so much, I felt compelled to return and be ignored by four hundred more heartless people who call this landfill their home!"

Cambridge. It's not even a city, you know. They killed off three perfectly good towns with character and history—Galt, Hespler, and Preston—to create one big, tawdry shopping mall with a bunch of houses and six trees. It's just an urban sprawl with a pretty, English name, and I wouldn't go back there if they gave me the key to the city, which, given what I know of them, would probably fit the front door of Guelph Correctional, anyway.

There, I said it. And I hope it didn't sound too personal or vindictive.

By the time this ugly scene ended—me not hitchhiking, but instead just standing beside a road looking stupid—approximately six hundred vehicles and three very long hours had passed me by. I don't know if you've ever seen a man reduced to hitchhiking on his knees, but it's not a noble sight. By 11:30 a.m. I realized the only way I was going to get off that ramp in a vehicle was to throw myself in front of a car and dial 911 on my cell phone.

I still don't get it. I was dressed nicely: a white polo shirt over blue shorts and white sneakers, no sunglasses, no headphones. I smiled and nodded politely at everybody as they drove by, leaving me there to rot. I mean, I wasn't exactly O.J. Simpson wearing Bruno Magli shoes and brandishing an oversized Swiss Army knife. At one point I actually checked—yes, it was definitely my thumb I had sticking out there and not my middle finger.

Buy lunch and chip in for gas, swap stories, exchange pictures of your kids and my pets, in some cases share the driving—hitchhiking used to be the most exciting way to travel, back when the world was a sociable place.

Today, fear and paranoia have created a roadside wall of mistrust between the beckoning thumb of the hitchhiker and those forbidding fingers white-knuckling the steering wheel of passing vehicles. The once great adventure of hitchhiking is now pretty much dead.

On Sunday, July 29, hitchhiking met an agonizing end in the Canadian city of Cambridge, a place where they keep their beer cold by holding the bottles close to their veins. Someday I hope to erect a small monument beside that Cambridge on-ramp: a large brass broken thumb in remembrance of the day that hitchhiking died.

Dejected, disillusioned and three other bad adjectives that start with a "d," I moved to a ramp farther down the 401. Strange Steve picked me up almost immediately, and minutes later dropped me at a truck stop at Highway 97 and the 401. Steve said he'd have taken me all the way to Windsor if his wife wasn't such a pain in the ass. (I'm guessing the woman was born and bred in Cambridge.)

Steve had thought one of his fellow truckers would gladly get me to Windsor, but when I walked around the lot I discovered they were all either sleeping in their cabs or headed for Toronto, in the opposite direction.

And to Officer Griffith of the Waterloo Regional Police, who pulled me over with his cherry lights flashing and ran my driver's licence number even though I was travelling without a car, might I just say: "Huh?" When you pull a driver over for speeding, you don't run a check on his sneakers, do you? The biggest problem I used to encounter hitchhiking on major highways was where I was allowed to stand. Now, apparently, it's outstanding warrants.

Finally, two decent young guys in a beat-up red Jeep picked me up, and since they were speeding, I was able to gloat as we overtook about a hundred of the hordes of cars that had passed me in Cambridge. (Which, by the way, is a place so devoid of kindness, donations to the local food bank actually go to a bank.)

Two trusting women picked me up in Ingersoll (now there's a town with a soul) and dropped me at London's Via station, where my dream of reliving my vagabond past fell through the cracks of Platform #1. I boarded a train to Windsor.

Once safely aboard the *Bluenose II*, I showered, watching all the grit and grime from Cambridge go straight down the drain—which is exactly where that town is headed unless they all attend next year's Friendship Festival in Fort Erie and hope some of it rubs off.

Venting, I'm told, is healthy. Hitching, today, is most definitely not.

To Dean Fosbroke

with grateful appreciation.

Bayard H. Jones

THE AMERICAN LECTIONARY

The American Lectionary

BAYARD HALE JONES
The School of Theology
The University of the South

MOREHOUSE-GORHAM CO.

NEW YORK

1944

Copyright, 1944, by
Morehouse-Gorham Co.

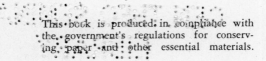

This book is produced in compliance with
the government's regulations for conserv-
ing paper and other essential materials.

Printed in the United States of America by
THE HADDON CRAFTSMEN, INC., SCRANTON, PA.

To the Memory

of

Henry Judah Mikell

Bishop of Atlanta
Chancellor of the University of the South
First Chairman of the Committee on the Lectionary

PREFACE

THIS BOOK is designed to further the understanding, and facilitate the use, of the new official Lectionary of the Protestant Episcopal Church in the United States of America, adopted by the General Convention in October, 1943, and incorporated in all new printings of the Book of Common Prayer in 1944.

Its primary motive is to furnish to the clergy of the Church a convenient guide to the choice of suitable sets of lessons, from among what some have considered to be an embarrassment of riches, in the plural alternatives of the Sundays of the Christian Year.

For this purpose, the book provides tables setting forth the sort of brief allusive indications of the subjects of Sunday psalms and lessons, which we found useful as work-tables in constructing the system. These listings do not profess to be complete summaries of contents; to make them so would impair their usefulness for ready reference. They contain just enough to identify a given passage to the memory of one already familiar with it, and to intimate the thread of the "liturgical harmony" which caused the correlation of those particular psalms and lessons into a unit of choice. In this way, they will afford to anyone with a reasonable familiarity with the Scriptures an opportunity to see virtually at a glance the nature of all the options offered on a given Sunday, to make then and there an intelligent selection of the set which he might feel most applicable to that occasion, and perhaps even to derive a hint for a desirable homiletical treatment.

In addition, it seemed worth while to embrace this opportunity to put on record the story of the framing of the new Lectionary, with credit where credit was due. Furthermore, nine years' intensive study of the subject had brought to light a clarified knowledge of the history and nature of the Christian Year, and of the problems of the use of Holy Scripture in accordance with it, such as we did not find elsewhere in any one place. We wished to make this knowledge available to all who might be interested in those subjects. It is our observation that both clergy and laity are rightly interested even in the technical phases of what is undoubtedly one of the most marvelous of all practical teaching devices in the world, the Church's comprehensive exposition of the Faith through the acted drama of the Christian Year.

In so doing, we were not unmindful of a possible value of the record of our struggles with those problems, for all those who in after years, in our own Church or elsewhere, might bring greater knowledge and ability to a task which is basic to the exercise of the Teaching Office of the Church.

BAYARD H. JONES

Sewanee, Tennessee.
Trinity Sunday, 1944.

CONTENTS

THE AMERICAN LECTIONARY

I

THE MAKING OF THE NEW LECTIONARY

THE REVISED Lectionary completed in 1943 was evolved through nine annual editions put forth for trial use by a grant of authority by the General Convention to the Liturgical Commission under the provisions of Article X of the Constitution.

The originator of this undertaking was the Rev. Charles E. Hill, a parish clergyman deeply versed in the Holy Scriptures, and gifted with admirable judgment both of literary and of pastoral values in the material to be used for public reading in the Church. Mr. Hill had been one of the foremost in the criticism of the inadequacies of the Lectionary adopted into the Prayer Book of 1928, and had been drafted to membership on the Liturgical Commission to take his part in the working out of his constructive ideas.

My own connection with this task seems to me to have been largely accidental. As a result of studies in past lectionary systems, in preparation for work subsequently incorporated in a book on *The American Prayer Book*,[1] I had subjected Mr. Hill's first suggested schedules to tabular analysis; and at the meeting of the Commission on the eve of the General Convention in 1934, it developed that I was the only member present who had done so. Consequently, when the Lectionary Committee was organized, with the Rt. Rev. Henry Judah Mikell of Atlanta as chairman, I was a little dismayed to find myself assigned to that committee to share with Mr. Hill the detailed work of perfecting the Lectionary.

For the attaining of practical results, it was perhaps fortunate rather than the contrary that neither Mr. Hill nor I were technical scholars in any department of scriptural learning. Thus we were

---

[1] Edward L. Parsons and Bayard H. Jones (Scribners, 1937).

1

untouched by academic theories or pedantic hobbies. As working parish priests, we had a single aim: to set forth as comprehensively as possible the teachings of Holy Church, in the most edifying passages of Holy Scripture.

But it was also fortunate that we had discretion enough not to linger long picking the flowers of our own choosing in the Eden of our innocent ignorance. We very early invoked the aid of the Rev. Dr. Burton Scott Easton, acknowledged to be one of the foremost New Testament scholars of the world; added him to our committee; and profited by his advice not only in his own field but also in the whole subject of the use of Scripture in Christian worship, where he has also proved himself to be a master.[2] The original Old Testament lists likewise received a minute and scholarly censorship at the able hands of the Very Rev. Dr. Hughell E. W. Fosbroke.

A little later, we secured the invaluable coöperation of the Rev. Dr. Cuthbert A. Simpson, who labored side by side with us until the task was completed. Dr. Simpson added to the qualifications of an Old Testament scholar of the first rank other endowments no less rare and valuable in their combination: a remarkable judgment of literary form, a profound sense of liturgical fitness, an unfailing discrimination of both theological and practical values, and an unlimited capacity for sheer hard work. Dr. Simpson completely redesigned the entire list of the Old Testament lessons. Moreover, unquestionably the balance and precision of our completed task is in large measure due to his indefatigable and inspired contributions.

In the use of the Psalter, Dr. Simpson associated with himself a voluntary sub-committee of his colleagues at the General Theological Seminary, the Rev. Dr. Edward Rochie Hardy, Jr., and Mr. Ray Francis Brown, instructor in Music. Dr. Hardy also rendered very valuable advice in the final allocation of the daily Lessons from the New Testament.

[2] Burton S. Easton and Howard C. Robbins, *The Eternal Word in the Modern World* (Scribners, 1937), is invaluable for an understanding of the Christian Year, and as a guide to expository preaching in accordance with its Epistles and Gospels.

After the lamented death of Bishop Mikell, the Rt. Rev. G. Ashton Oldham of Albany, accepted the chairmanship of our committee; and the work was completed under the wise and generous guidance of a man who has never permitted the affairs of a great diocese to encroach upon the daily devotional habits and the pastoral solicitude of the parish priest.

In the carrying out of the undertaking, all these various participants worked together in the utmost harmony. It developed that none of us was afflicted with any personal pride of authorship. Every one proved himself eager to abandon the work of years when a better organizing principle came to light. It happened that every major improvement of underlying plan originated within the Committee, as a result of the intensive studies which we were constantly making of various parts of the project, and our close observation of the working out of the daily schedules in two seminary chapels, as well as of our experience as preachers on Sundays.

Besides this, a very large number of comments on details were given careful consideration at every stage of our work: so that the editor of *The Living Church* was correct in stating that this "revised and thoroughly tested Lectionary . . . is uniquely the product of the whole body of the clergy; for it has been developed by actual use."[3]

The new Lectionary was enacted by the General Convention of 1943, by the passage of a resolution which specified that it "be adopted as the official Lectionary of the Protestant Episcopal Church, and the standard for Annual Calendars." We refrained from proposing that it be required that the revised Lectionary be inserted in all future printings of the Book of Common Prayer, from a desire to avoid imposing unnecessary burdens upon the publishers in war time. It might suffice for the moment if the editors of the various annual Calendars conformed to the new standard. As a practical matter, these unofficial Calendars are in virtually universal use to govern the services of the year, since few even of those who have the

[3] October 3, 1943, p. 21.

requisite knowledge to do so can take the trouble to correlate the
Christian Year with the dates of the secular calendar, making all the
adjustments for Sundays, weekdays, and occurring or concurring
festivals. What actually happens is an application of the old saying
that the best way to find Easter is to buy a penny almanac!

However, early the following year the principal publishers foresaw
the imminent necessity of issuing new printings of the Prayer Book,
and of their own motion took the very proper step of agreeing among
themselves to make this issue conform to what the Church had
declared to be its official Lectionary. The result, after due conference
with the Rev. Dr. John Wallace Suter, Custodian of the Book of
Common Prayer, and the Lectionary Committee, was to establish
what is in effect the new Standard Prayer Book of 1944. Its only
innovations, of course, comprise the incorporation into the prefatory
matter of the new Lectionary and its attendant rubrics, in lieu of
those previously in force.

While the Liturgical Commission deliberately refrained from
asking General Convention to specify that the adoption of the new
Lectionary explicitly repealed that of 1928, there is naturally no
doubt that the action taken actually had that effect. In any case, it is
to be hoped that no officiants will continue to add the old selections
as a set of further alternatives to those given in the official Lectionary. To do so would be to forfeit the principles of balance, completeness, and unity of plan, which we have been at some pains to
incorporate in our work.

To all those whom I have named, and to the great company of
clergy and laity alike who have given their time to encourage and
advise us during the progress of our labors, I wish to express my own
profound obligation. Again and again it has appeared that all who
have had any part in the work have been deeply conscious of the
greatness of the opportunity and the essential value of its objectives.

Although it is true that there is no inevitable connection of the
Lectionary with the Church's preaching, and though there is perfect

"liberty of prophesying," so that it is open to any clergyman to preach on any subject on any occasion, yet all are open to suggestions from the Scripture appointed for the day; and it is probable that the majority follow the course of the Lectionary with considerable fidelity. And herein is one of the outstanding characteristics of our Church, in that the cycle of Scriptures for the Christian Year, gently guiding the devotional thought and the public teaching of the clergy, is a marvelous preventive of fads, ruts, and misplaced emphases, and has had the effect of keeping the Church's preaching remarkably faithful to the full scope and symmetry of the riches of the Faith. As I stated on another occasion:

> The reading of prescribed Scripture, reflecting the Church Year, is the groundwork of the Church's teaching. This feature of our services has added a *lex legendi* no less important than the *lex orandi* to the attaining of a just and full *lex credendi*. Upon those mathematical-looking tables depends quite as much of the intelligent well-being of the Church as upon the text of the Prayer Book itself. The assignment of the Lessons of Scripture "appointed to be read in Churches" is in fact a supreme function of the Teaching Office, whose importance cannot be overstated.[4]

[4] Parsons and Jones, *The American Prayer Book* (Scribners, 1937), 94.

II

THE CHURCH YEAR

THE CHURCH CALENDAR is the structural basis upon which every Lectionary is built, since it is obviously impossible to have any system at all of reading the Scriptures without a fixed and recurrent time-pattern to which it conforms. The Calendar which we now have was surprisingly slow in evolving to its present state. Properly to understand our Calendar, and to evaluate the various systems of lessons devised therefor, one must have some knowledge of the way in which the Church Year has developed.

1   THE CYCLE OF SUNDAYS

The "Christian Year," as it is presented in our latest Prayer Book, is now essentially a cycle of Sundays, grouped in ecclesiastical Seasons, and carrying their weekdays with them. It is a closed system, covering every possible date of the year. Indeed, it is considerably more than complete, since it makes provision for fifty-five named Sundays, of which not more than fifty-three can occur in any one year.[1] Two, and usually three, of these Sundays go unused every year.

Such a system seems to us nowadays most natural and inevitable. Just as far as the complexities of modern living permit, Sundays are holidays from business and labor, and nearly all Christian people are then set free to observe their obligations of worship. Hence Sundays are our primary liturgical days. Ferial Holy Days of much greater intrinsic importance than most Sundays, such as Ash Wednesday, Good Friday, and Ascension Day, see their services very scantily

---

[1] As the year consists of fifty-two weeks and one day, this can happen only if January 1 (in Leap Year also January 2) falls on a Sunday.

attended, since they are seldom public holidays, and most people are engaged in earning their livings upon those occasions.

So it is a little surprising to us that this system of Sundays is a late development in the Christian Church. The early Church did indeed keep "the Lord's Day" from the beginning.[2] The experience of the Resurrection on the first day of the week, underscored by the empowering with the Spirit exactly seven weeks later on the Day of Pentecost, set in their minds the pattern of a weekly Easter. The feasts of Easter and Pentecost themselves were observed as such from the first. But apart from them, there were no Seasons, no named Sundays; consequently no special prayers or lessons proper to any Sunday.

A preparatory season of Lent before Easter, and a festal season thereafter until Whitsunday, probably became established in the course of the third century; the Council of Nicæa alludes to both as settled features. Also, tradition ascribes to the same period the Roman observance of the original three Ember Seasons, which the Western Church took over from pagan agricultural festivals.[3]

However, the Christian Year got its real start in the formative fourth century, after the Freedom of the Church. One important influence came through the growing ambition of the Bishop of Jerusalem, who fostered local pilgrimages to the Holy Places on days chosen with reference to the feast of the Resurrection, and moving in the calendar with it. Thus Ætheria, a nun of Acquitaine

---

[2] Revelation 1:10; Acts 20:7; I Corinthians 16:2.

[3] The December, June, and September seasons replaced the Roman festivals of winter sowing, summer reaping, and autumn vintage. The *Liber Pontificalis* ascribes them to Callistus (†233). Leo I (†461) added the Lenten days to conform to the Jewish pattern of four annual Fasts recorded in Zechariah 8:19. Gelasius (†496) decreed them as stated times of Ordination: possibly in the spirit of Matthew 9:37 f., more probably because they were already fasting seasons at convenient quarterly intervals; he also appointed Mid-Lent for this purpose, and the present Roman Canon 1006 §2, specifies also the Saturday before Passion Sunday, and Easter Even. None of the services in the Roman Missal have the slightest reference to the Ministry; on the other hand some of them retain distinct traces of their former agricultural setting: cf. Eisenhofer, *Handbuch der katholischen Liturgik* (Herder, Freiburg, 1932), I. 485.

who visited the Holy City about the year 385, speaks of Lent, Palm Sunday, Maundy Thursday, Good Friday, and the Ascension Day.

In this century also, certain speculations which assigned to our Lord's nativity dates chosen for mystical reasons, gave rise to Christmas and Epiphany, and festivals assigned with reference to them. In the West, beginning in Gaul in the sixth century, Christmas acquired its own preparatory season of Advent, on the analogy of Lent. East and West fixed the three Pre-Lenten Sundays also in the sixth century.

Nevertheless, at the end of the eighth century, when Pope Hadrian sent his own service book to Charlemagne, on the latter's request for a standard book to help clear up the great diversity of use in France, we find that the only Sundays which the papal court was then observing with proper prayers were Easter and Whitsunday and their Octaves, the seasons of Advent, Pre-Lent, and Lent; except for two "Ember" Sundays (our Trinity 4 and 18), none were provided for other Sundays falling after Christmas, Epiphany, Easter, or Pentecost.

Sundays not designated in the Sacramentaries and Lectionaries of this period were simply "Common Sundays." If a given Sunday were not occupied by a fixed Holy Day, the Celebrant chose such prayers as he felt appropriate, either from the rest of the Sacramentary, or possibly from manuscript collections of prayers, of which many must have been in circulation: the sole survivor of this sort of thing, the so-called "Leonine" Sacramentary, presents such an unselected accumulation, with an astonishing number of parallel services on the same subjects.

Other books of the time incorporated such material by furnishing blocks of masses and lessons, to be used wherever needed. The *Missale Gothicum* ends with six Sunday masses. The "Gelasian" Sacramentary offers eight masses after Easter, and sixteen for any Sundays. The earliest Lectionaries give Gospels for ten Sundays after Epiphany, and Epistles for ten Sundays after Easter, as well as a list of no less than forty-two selections from the Pauline Epistles, with no stipulations as to their use.

This evidence is bewildering to the modern mind. We can see how the excessive number of masses and lessons assigned to certain periods were provided with the intent that the overplus might be used wherever required—for instance, our lessons from the Catholic Epistles on Trinity 1, 2, 3, and 5 are those appointed in the old *Comes* for Easter 7 to 10 inclusive; our Epistles for Trinity 6-17 and 19-24 are derived from that Pauline list of forty-two. But how did *they* order a service whose components were at different stages of development, and definitely out of step with each other? What did they do, for example, on Epiphany 5, with a Gospel book which gave lessons for ten Sundays, an Epistle book with only four, and a Sacramentary with no prayers appointed at all? Why and how were they permitted to get out of correlation?

The fact is that these three books were separate compilations, in the hands of three different officiants, the Celebrant, Deacon, and Subdeacon. Each one made his contribution to the complete service out of the material at his hand, according to his own discretion; each developed his own book in an independent line of tradition; and no one person was responsible for ordering the service as a whole, or for planning the material. It is this independent evolution of the three constituents, in the days before all were gathered together into a single volume, the *Plenary Missal*, which establishes and accounts for the otherwise anomalous fact that the Collect, Epistle, and Gospel for most of the old "Common Sundays" now found in the Epiphany and Trinity seasons—as well as some others, notably in Lent—display no liturgical unity whatever.

Between the ninth and the eleventh centuries the Western churches progressively gathered this rather random material together, and arranged it in some sort of order to complete a system of Sundays covering the whole year. The Gallican churches numbered the Summer Sundays serially after Pentecost; and after the Octave of Pentecost was renamed Trinity Sunday in the tenth century, more usually after Trinity. Rome fought a rearguard action, and valiantly endeavored to stick to its own original method of treating the secular year as primary, and intercalating movables into it. Accordingly Rome did not treat the Summer Sundays as a single series after Pentecost—much less as "that great season of the Holy Ghost" which some visionaries, ignorant of the history of the subject, have been fain to find—but as a number of groups of Sundays, tied to outstanding Roman festivals. There might be five Sundays after the Octave of Pentecost, or none—the variability of the Church Year was taken up at this point, avoiding displacing the Sundays of half the year with the same wide swings as Easter. This was the next best arrangement to a fixed Easter, and it is a pity that it did not endure. They appointed one Sunday before and six after "The Apostles" on June 29, five after St. Lawrence on August 10, and six after St. Cyprian on September 14.

Ultimately, however, the specious clarity of the Gallican series commended itself to the Franciscan order, and a Franciscan pope secured the adoption of the Franciscan Missal and Breviary as the basis of the standard Roman use after the Council of Trent. Meanwhile, Rome had been very reluctant to accept the festival of Trinity Sunday, and finally did so in 1334 at the expense of the First Sunday after Pentecost, which it displaced, and which remains to this day in the Roman books as a Sunday service which is always celebrated on a weekday!

Even at the Reformation the story was not quite finished. The English Prayer Book of 1662 made provision for a Sixth Sunday after Epiphany,[4] and four Office Lessons on the Second Sunday after Christmas; although the latter did not attain the dignity of a Liturgical Day, with a proper Epistle and Gospel of its own, until the American, English, and Scottish books of 1928.[5]

[4] Previously, the service for Epiphany 5 had been repeated on the rare occasions (only with Easter at its last four possible dates) when there *is* an Epiphany 6. The Roman service for this day is also very late.

[5] The service for the feast of the Circumcision was previously repeated until the Epiphany. The Roman Missal still does something very similar, any Sunday between Circumcision and Epiphany being designated as of "The Holy Name of Jesus," with a service virtually a doublet of that of the Circumcision.

2   THE FIXED FESTIVALS

While we have treated first the evolution of the Sunday cycle, since for us it remains of primary interest and importance, it must be pointed out that the first pattern of the Liturgical Year to appear was not a system of Seasons, but a gradual accumulation of Anniversaries. The earliest of these to leave a record is found in the document known as *The Martyrdom of Polycarp*, a circular letter of the Church of Smyrna recounting the execution of their venerable and venerated bishop in the year 158. This letter speaks of his burial with the first recorded Requiem Eucharist, and the appointing of an annual day of commemoration thereafter. Such anniversaries were known to the early Church as the "Birthdays" of the martyrs into the life eternal. As time went on, they became numerous, and were regarded as the turning-points of the year; we have seen how the Roman Church regulated the Summer Sundays with reference to them.

These were joined by another sort of anniversary, that of the "Translations" or days of the removal of the bones of Saints whose dates of martyrdom had been forgotten to their permanent resting-place in shrines erected to their memory. The earliest of these is June 29, the day of the Translation of SS. Peter and Paul in the year 258. Finally, anniversaries of the dedication of important churches were added to the list: for instance, the Transfiguration of our Lord on August 6 goes back to the dedication of the fourth-century basilica on Mount Tabor, the traditional Mount of the Transfiguration.

As a kind of postscript to this natural development, in the early Middle Ages the makers of calendars, who regarded a blank date as a sort of professional insult, found or made some pretext for completing the lists of certain classes of Saints, and for inserting commemorations of notable worthies which had not been included in the local Roman categories. To this period belongs the final rounding out of the roll of the Apostles, several of whom receive no more than a mere mention in the Gospels and Acts, and the story of whose lives and deaths survives only in the most tenuous and legendary tradition from the troublous early days in which they lived.

One of the most frequent complaints at the Reformation was the excessive number of Holy Days observed as holidays from labor. In reducing these commemorations to a reasonable number, the framers of our Prayer Book had no information as to the actual relative antiquity of their observance. They probably considered that they were achieving the end of preserving the most primitive festivals when they confined them to persons mentioned in Scripture. This in fact they did not do, since most of the feasts of the minor Apostles were of distinctly late appearance.

The fixed festivals which we now observe with a proper service comprise six festivals of our Lord, his Nativity, Circumcision, Epiphany, Presentation in the Temple, Annunciation,[6] and Transfiguration;[7] twelve festivals of fourteen Apostles,[8] SS. Paul, Matthias, Philip and James, Barnabas, Peter, James, Bartholomew, Matthew the Evangelist, Simon and Jude, Andrew, Thomas, and John the Evangelist; two of Evangelists not Apostles, SS. Mark and Luke; and five others, the Precursor St. John Baptist, the Protomartyr St. Stephen, the Holy Innocents,[9] St. Michael and All Angels, and All Saints.[10]

[6] That the two festivals naming the Blessed Virgin are primarily to be classified as Festivals of our Lord appears from the fact that they are provided with a Proper Preface of the Incarnation.

[7] The Transfiguration appeared very late in the West, having been adopted at Rome in 1457 by Pope Calixtus II in commemoration of the victory over the Turks by armies commanded by John Hunyadi and St. John Capistrano, and made the "title" feast of the patriarchal Basilica of St. John Lateran. Its association with a papal victory and a papal Church may have influenced Cranmer to eliminate it. It was restored in the American Prayer Book of 1892, the Canadian of 1922, and the Scottish and English of 1928.

[8] Note that St. Barnabas is specifically named as an Apostle both in the title and the Collect of his Feast; St. Paul in the Collect only.

[9] St. Stephen and the Holy Innocents, together with St. John the Evangelist, had long had a close association with the Christmas season, as the traditional "Companions of Christ."

[10] The somewhat formal nature of this list is rather underscored by the way in which the Feast of Christmas, together with the Annunciation nine months, and St. John Baptist six months before, set a convention for placing other Holy Days on the twenty-

These festivals represent, and presumably are modeled upon, the classifications of the Saints in the diptychs and litanies of the early Church.

3 THE CONFLICT OF THE TWO SYSTEMS

The Church Calendar therefore is made up of two different systems, which are combined in each successive year to a different result: the old Roman Civil Year, dependent only upon the revolution of the earth about the sun,[11] composed of the dated days of the twelve months, and containing the Fixed Festivals; and the distinctive Christian Year, made up of weeks determined by the Sundays, and grouped in variable ecclesiastical Seasons—all ultimately dependent upon the date of Easter: and as this in turn was fixed by the Passover, the ultimate base of the Christian Year is the Jewish Calendar, as ordered by the cycles of the moon.

The original Roman books treated the Civil Year with its sequence of fixed Holy Days as primary, and Sundays and other movables as incidental, fitting the latter in as best they could under the months in which they were most likely to fall. Indeed, the Roman Church has never entirely accepted the Gallican scheme of a complete pattern of Sundays covering the year: the Missal provides several special festivals attached to certain numbered Sundays in various months, which supersede the services of the Christian Year;[12] and the Breviary carries the numbered weeks after Pentecost only through the Eleventh: from August through November the primary computation is according to the weeks within the months, with the Christian Year

fourth and twenty-fifth of their months: which appears in the case of SS. Paul, Matthias, Mark, James, and Bartholomew.

[11] Or more strictly, upon the relation of the axis of the earth to the sun. Our computations of time follow the tropical, not the sidereal year; being adjusted to retain the Seasons at the same dates, instead of letting them move backward twenty minutes a year by the Precession of the Equinoxes, as would be the case if we counted a complete revolution of the earth in its orbit, as measured by the position of the stars.

[12] This method is still on the increase; witness the recent assignment of the papal festival of "Christ the King" to the last Sunday in October.

element reduced to the Antiphons and Collect, with further lessons for the Third Nocturn of Matins on the Sundays.

As we shall see later, there are many complications in reconciling the fixed dates of the Civil Year with the shifting pattern of Movables. Cranmer in the Preface to the First Book of Common Prayer said:

> Moreover, the number and hardness of the rules called the Pie, and the manifold changing of the service, was the cause, that to turn the book only was so hard and intricate a matter, that many times there was more business to find out what should be read, than to read it when it was found out.

Accordingly, it is not surprising that Cranmer, whose chief announced objective was to secure the systematic reading of the whole Bible throughout the year, arranged his lectionary for daily Morning and Evening Prayer almost wholly on the basis of the dates of the Civil Year. The cycle of Sundays had no Proper Lessons, but took those assigned to their calendar dates. Only twenty-two festivals had any Proper Lessons whatever; only five were supplied with a complete set of four.

This system was very simple and orderly, as there were only ten movable festivals which broke the regular reading of the Scriptures in course by supplanting one or more of the lessons assigned to their dates with selections especially chosen for the occasion. The twelve Fixed Feasts with Proper Lessons were simply interpolated into the sequences; interrupting without superseding them.

Gradually, however, the succeeding Anglican books increased the assignment of Proper Lessons. In 1559, for instance, proper First Lessons were designated for all Sundays and Holy Days.[13] The first American Prayer Book of 1789 filled up the Sundays with Second Lessons also. And our book of 1892 brought the number of

[13] The Church of England had no system of proper Second Lessons for Sundays until 1922; reading the New Testament lesson for the day of the month on which a Sunday happened to fall.

Proper Lessons for the movable days to a very considerable figure: they were required on all Sundays, Ash Wednesday, all of Holy Week, the Monday and Tuesday after Easter and Whitsunday, and the Ascension Day; and they were provided for optional use on the thirty-three other days of Lent, and the Ember and Rogation Days. This made a minimum of sixty-four days a year on which the lessons in the calendar must be superseded by Proper Lessons, and a maximum of 109 days on which they might be so cancelled.

Now a plan under which the substitution of special "topical" lessons is permitted to obliterate nearly thirty percent of the comprehensive general course, was in fact a complete breakdown of the basic undertaking to read the whole Bible in the course of the whole year. The only practicable method of restoring it was to return to the older plan of the Christian Year in use before the Reformation. This pattern in itself is no more complicated than the secular calendar; and Cranmer himself had removed the chief obstacles to using it by reducing the number of Fixed Holy Days.

This solution was adopted by America, Scotland, England, and Canada in their latest revisions of the Prayer Book. It largely cleared up the intolerable situation of the conflict between the movable days and the fixed assignments, as it existed before 1928. The one problem which it raised was exactly the reverse of that which faced Cranmer. Under his plan, the incidence of the Fixed Holy Days was the one thing which did not clash with the courses of reading, which were simply suspended for the particular days, and flowed around them without intermission. Under the new system, these fixed days are the one thing which does inevitably conflict. But such collisions are enormously less numerous than those which had grown up by the time of our Prayer Book of 1892. They occur on only from fifteen to eighteen weekdays in any year.[14] When they occur, they cause a

---

[14] Of our twenty-five fixed Festivals, the six from Christmas to Epiphany fall on a dated tract interpolated into the Christian Year pattern, and therefore do not conflict with the latter. SS. Andrew, Thomas, and Matthias, and the Annunciation are always transferred from a Sunday, and hence always conflict. Of the others, from one to four

hiatus of one set of lessons at Morning Prayer, and two at Evening Prayer, in the weekday courses. There is no help for this situation, short of the adoption of a Perpetual Calendar. There is, however, the palliation that the next year the superseded lessons will be restored to their places in the courses; at which time entirely different ones will prove casualties.

4 VARIATION OF THE SEASONS

Though the use of the "Christian Year" reckoning is perfectly simple in practice, it entails some grave mechanical problems in ordering the courses of a Lectionary. Some Seasons vary slightly in length; others really drastically. Provision must be made for their maximum extension, but in such a manner that a radical curtailment to their minimum dimensions will not irremediably mutilate a given course.

a) *Seasons Dependent upon Easter*: the more considerable of these variations is due to the fact that Easter swings up and down the calendar with a sweep of thirty-five days, carrying with it all the weeks from Septuagesima through the last-numbered Sunday after Trinity—a total of thirty-nine to forty-four weeks of the year.

This Trinity series (not including the Sunday Next Before Advent) may have as few as twenty-one Sundays, or as many as twenty-six. Proper Collects, Epistles, and Gospels are provided for twenty-four. If there are fewer than this number, the overplus is omitted; if more, the one or two missing Sundays are supplied by appending the so-called *Dominicae vagantes* or "Wandering Sundays," listed as the Fifth and Sixth after Epiphany.

---

in any year must fall on a Sunday; where they merely displace one set of Proper Lessons with another. To these conflicts may be added those of the autumnal Ember Days, which, unlike those of the other three Ember Seasons, cannot be fitted into the Christian Year courses, since they vary from the week of Trinity 12 to that of Trinity 17. As they cancel one-half the lessons of the week in which they fall, in 1943 we left their use optional, as they had been in 1928.

Thus we are absolutely sure of only twenty-one weeks in the Trinity Season proper. We are reasonably assured of twenty-two, which occur with all but the last two possible dates of Easter. We have twenty-three with twenty-six dates out of the thirty-five and twenty-four with nineteen possible dates. These all occur more than half the time: hence normal courses may reasonably run to the end of the twenty-fourth week; bearing in mind, however, that they may be subject to varying degrees of curtailment.

b) *Seasons Dependent upon Christmas*: The balance of the year, outside the three-fourths or more regulated directly by Easter, moves in a much smaller orbit, determined by the revolution of the days of the week around the fixed date of Christmas.[15]

1) The Advent Sequence: Christmas is always preceded by five Sundays: four counted "in Advent," and one entitled that "Next Before Advent." These Sundays are a liturgical unit, being in fact the five Sundays "Before the Nativity" of the Gelasian Sacramentary and the liturgical Lectionaries until the eleventh century.

Local Roman use never observed more than four Sundays. The Gallican held out for its own "St. Martin's Lent" of the six or seven Sundays which intervene between St. Martin's Day on November 11 and Christmas. Finally Gregory VII accepted the disputed Gelasian Fifth Sunday Before the Nativity and adopted it as a fixed feature of the year, but rechristened it the Last Sunday after Pentecost. It unmistakably belongs, however, to the Advent sequence and teaching.

The dates of occurrence of these five Sundays are actually determined by the relation of the last of them to Christmas Day, since obviously Advent 4 cannot fall later than December 24, nor earlier than December 18. The rule that designated Advent 1 as that nearest the feast of St. Andrew on November 30 is only a convenient coinci-

[15] As the "Sunday Letter" is itself determined by Easter, even this group is not exempt from the influence of that primary festival of the year. As soon as the date of Easter is known, every date in the Christian Year is determined.

dence; but so convenient that it may have something to do with the reluctance of Rome to concern itself with the full five Sundays as in and of the Season.

The "Wandering Sundays" also, when used in this place, are properly pre-Advent rather than post-Trinity. Their teaching is eschatological; in which fact indeed lies the reason for their double use in either of two widely separated connections. They may bring the Epiphany theme to its ultimate climax in the final and supreme Manifestation of the Last Judgment; or they may apply this same thought to usher in the Advent Season.

Just as the three Pre-Lenten Sundays reflect a temporary use of a Lent three weeks longer than that ultimately determined upon, so these three pre-Advent Sundays on occasion echo the Gallican use of a "St. Martin's Lent." They should be accounted not as Sundays added to the Trinity Season, but interposed between that Season and Advent proper. The cumbrous rubric on page 224 of the Prayer Book confuses many as to their real use by indicating that Trinity 25 shall use the service for Epiphany 6 when there are twenty-six Sundays "after Trinity," but shall take that of Epiphany 5 when there are twenty-seven. This could be made simpler and more accurate by saying:

> If in any year there be more than twenty-five Sundays between Trinity Sunday and Advent Sunday, the service for the Sixth Sunday after the Epiphany shall be used on the Second Sunday before Advent. If there be twenty-seven, the service for the Fifth Sunday after the Epiphany shall be used on the Third Sunday before Advent.

At all events, in order to indicate clearly the true sequence of the courses of lessons at the end of the Christian Year, we found it necessary to adopt these terms of a Second and Third Sunday before Advent in the tables of the new Lectionary.[16]

---

[16] If we had numbered these weeks forward from Trinity, instead of backward from Advent, there would be no way of indicating that it was the week of Trinity 25,

2) The Days Surrounding Christmas: Between Advent 4 and Epiphany 1, the Church Calendar is compelled to desert its principle of dependence on the cycle of Sundays, and to revert to the old Roman system of the dated days of the Civil Year; inserting intervening Sundays as best it may. The reason is that Christmas, the second ranking festival of the year, and its related days—St. Stephen, St. John Evangelist, the Holy Innocents, the Circumcision, and the Epiphany—are all calendar days, outranking and displacing any Sundays on which any of them fall. Two Sundays "after Christmas" may occur within this period, and are duly included in the tables; but the calendar takes no account of weekdays to be regulated by them. All days between Christmas and Epiphany, not occupied by any of the foregoing festivals, are listed by the calendar dates December 29 to 31, and January 2 to 5.

The necessary change of method at this point is like an interpolated change of key in a musical composition: one must get into it, and then out of it again. Advent 4 may fall exactly a week before Christmas, permitting a leisurely modulation to the new key with a whole week of preparatory lessons provided from Monday through Saturday. On the other hand this Sunday may be the day before Christmas; in which case the transition is very abrupt, the lessons for Christmas Eve supplanting those for the evening of Advent 4.

Likewise, the First Sunday after Epiphany may be the day after the festival, or a whole week later. To modulate out again from the short tract of dated days between Christmas and Epiphany, back to the "Christian Year" system of weekdays dependent upon Sundays, it is necessary to extend the dated days through January 12.[17]

---

not that of Trinity 26, which ought to be omitted when there were twenty-six Sundays "after Trinity."

[17] To avoid encroaching on the courses which begin at Epiphany 1, we followed the practice of the Breviary by inserting a note in the Lectionary indicating that the topical, and discontinuous, Proper Lessons for these dated days in the Epiphany Octave should come to an end at the following Sunday.

3) The Epiphany Sequence: The interval between Epiphany and Septuagesima Sunday is filled by the Sundays after Epiphany. Septuagesima may fall as early as January 18. Therefore there is always one Sunday after Epiphany; two, with all but the three earliest dates of Easter; three, with twenty-five dates; four, with eighteen; five, with eleven; and six, with the last four dates only.

Thus the Epiphany Season shares with the end of Trinity-tide the adjustment for the variability of Easter. Just as the Trinity season has a normal length of twenty-four Sundays, which occur more than half the time, the same is true of four Sundays after Epiphany. And again as in the case of Trinity-tide, this normal duration is filled out, when Easter is at one extreme of its range, by adding the two "Wandering Sundays."

It may be added that these Sundays wander out of the calendar of the year entirely more than half the time. Epiphany 5, used in the series from which it takes its name with the last eleven dates of Easter, is pre-Advent with the first five. Epiphany 6 on the other hand is post-Epiphany with only the last four dates, and pre-Advent with the first twelve. Both go entirely unused in either place with the nineteen central and most frequently occurring dates.

5　THE RECONCILIATION OF THE CALENDAR

The annual problem of fitting together the ever-shifting pattern of movable and immovable elements into the calendar dates of a particular year raises problems of a complicated nature. The first American attempt to provide answers to them is found in the Tables of Precedence on page LI of the Prayer Book. This Table, however, is not altogether complete and precise. In actual practice it has been found necessary to fall back in some particulars upon the rather more comprehensive treatment of the English book of 1928; though even that is not exhaustive, as will appear. Since, therefore, no Anglican Prayer Book has yet entirely solved all the contingencies which are capable of occurring; since it is desirable that our next Prayer Book should contain definitive solutions of them; and since in the meantime there is need for the guidance of the editors of annual Calendars: it may be of use to present the analysis which we have developed from our own experience in applying the Trial Lectionaries during the last nine years.

   a) *Occurrence*: The first problem, and the only one treated in the American Prayer Book, is the occurrence of a fixed and a movable commemoration upon the same date. Two solutions, according to circumstances, are applied to this. Certain Sundays, Holy Days, and Seasons are absolutely privileged, and compel the transfer of any other observance to the first "open day," that is, the first weekday thereafter which is not itself already occupied by a Holy Day. These privileged days are: all the Sundays in Advent, Pre-Lent, and Lent, together with Easter 5 and Ascension 1;[18] Ash Wednesday, and the Ascension Day; and all the time between Palm Sunday and Low Sunday, and from Whitsunday to Trinity Sunday, inclusive.
   Accordingly, four Holy Days are never solemnized on a Sunday: St. Andrew and St. Thomas are always transferred to a weekday by the Sundays in Advent; the Annunciation is always displaced by the Sundays in Lent, as well as by the whole period of Holy Week and Easter Week; and St. Matthias by the Pre-Lenten and Lenten Sundays, as well as by Ash Wednesday. St. Paul and the Purification are displaced when they fall on the Pre-Lenten Sundays; St. Mark and SS. Philip and James by Easter Week, and the latter also by Easter 5 and Ascension Day; St. Barnabas by Whit-Week.
   In all other cases, the second solution applies: a Holy Day falling upon any other Sunday than the above takes precedence of it; all

[18] The mention of Ascension 1 is otiose, since it never conflicts with any other Day in our Calendar. The special rank of Rogation Sunday hardly seems desirable— it is not so given in the British books—and there appears little reason for displacing SS. Philip and James for it merely in its aspect as an agricultural festival; which emphasis in turn neutralizes any importance this Sunday might otherwise be conceived to have as the Last in the Easter Season.

services are of the Holy Day, and the Sunday is reduced to a "Commemoration," its Collect being read after the Collect of the Holy Day.[19]

Similarly, the fixed Holy Days take precedence of movable feriæ other than those listed above. St. Thomas prevails over an Advent Ember Day, and reduces it to a Commemoration; and so with St. Matthias occurring on a Lenten, and St. Matthew on an autumnal Ember Day, SS. Philip and James on a Rogation Day, and St. Andrew on Thanksgiving Day.

b) *Concurrence*: The other problem is that raised by what is know as the "concurrence" of two Holy Days falling upon successive dates, so that the service provided for the evening of the first day is brought into conflict with that assigned to the Eve of the second day. The American Prayer Book supplies such services, but makes no provision whatever for resolving the conflicts. In this matter the English and Scottish books furnish some detailed directions, but no comprehensive rules, nor do they solve every possible case. In some instances it is necessary to appeal beyond them to Roman practice. Their underlying principles, however, appear to be as follows.

The general fact which we have noted, that the fixed commemorations on the calendar dates anteceded the growth of the Christian Year, and remained the primary reckoning in the West, appears in the fact that where at all possible the Fixed Festivals retain their observance complete, with both First and Second Evensong, when brought into juxtaposition with a Movable Feast before or after.

Thus when a fixed Holy Day falls on a Saturday, the English book specifies that "then Evensong on Saturday is the Second Evensong of the Feast, the Collect of the Sunday being added after that of the Feast." The exceptions to this are Advent Sunday, whose Eve sup-

[19] Independence Day is a fixed date, but not properly an ecclesiastical Festival. A special Rule of the Liturgical Commission in 1943 left it to the discretion of the officiant whether to let it take precedence of a Sunday on which it fell, or to transfer its observance to the following day.

plants the evening service of St. Andrew, and Passion and Palm Sundays prevailing over the Annunciation. To these most certainly should be added Whitsunday (which we have provided with special psalms and lessons for its Eve, which is something neither we nor the English have done for the three Sundays of lesser importance named by them) when St. Barnabas falls on the Saturday before.

Likewise all Sundays whatever, regardless of their rank, or of the manner in which they may compel the transfer of any festivals occurring on their days, yield to the service of the Eve of a Holy Day which falls on the Monday following;[20] the Collect of the Sunday being read after that of the Feast.

A like prepotence of fixed over movable days appears in the case of St. Thomas in concurrence with Advent Ember Days before or after, St. Matthew with the Autumnal, and St. Matthias with the Lenten Ember Days, as well as SS. Philip and James with the Rogation Days; and of course should be applied to Thanksgiving Day in our book, since it has no Eve, and is in effect only a solemn votive commemoration assigned to a date by the Civil Authority.

[20] However, Palm Sunday, Easter, and Whitsunday are automatically protected from this sort of incursion by the "closed weeks" which follow them. Trinity Sunday, now stripped of the like protecting Octave which it once had in the Sarum Rite, but still a Cardinal Feast, after which half the Sundays of the year are named, certainly ought to be provided with the same protection.

The British books experiment with a requirement to transfer certain feasts to the Tuesday rather than the Monday after Advent, Low, and Trinity Sundays. The idea seems to be to protect the evening service on these days in the same manner as Easter and Whitsunday. If so, this device is illogical, since it does not take in Lent 1 and 5, which have the same rank as the three mentioned; and incomplete, in that it does nothing for the cases where festivals fall naturally on the Mondays involved. And is it desirable? The argument is that the Roman Calendar is so crowded that a certain telescoping of observances is necessary there, which is not required with our sparse commemorations. But this is fallacious: we are not dealing with a blank Calendar, but with one filled with continuous readings of Scripture in course. It is a gain to eliminate one day's supersession of this course by placing the service of an Eve on a Sunday evening, where, as mentioned above, it merely exchanges one Proper Lesson for another. Besides, the Sunday cycle is actually enriched and varied by the occasional substitution of the provisions for a Holy Day. Indeed, the rules which protect fourteen Sundays of the year from ever being supplanted by a Festival, and exclude four Holy Days from ever being observed on a Sunday, would be too one-sided if it were not for the provisions which open all Sunday evenings but three to the solemnization of an Eve.

But the Cardinal Feast of the Ascension retains all its services intact, when SS. Philip and James comes the day before or after, with commemoration of the Saints' Day. Likewise Ash Wednesday (which has no Eve) preserves its evening service, with commemoration of St. Matthias, when that festival follows the next day.

No Anglican book gives any rule for the unique contingency of the concurrence of St. Mark with SS. Philip and James, on the rare occasions when they are brought into juxtaposition when, with the last four dates of Easter, one or both are transferred after Low Sunday. This is really the problem of two days of equal rank, for which the Roman rite has two solutions. One, that of dividing the service between them, is not available with the different structure of our service. The other is the precedent of the three festivals following Christmas, and the two days following Easter and Whitsunday. In these cases there are simply no Eves at all; but the Collect of the following day is commemorated on the evening of the first day. This solution should certainly be adopted here.

III

THE USE OF SCRIPTURE IN WORSHIP

THE DIRECT use of the Bible in the Anglican services of worship is demonstrably greater than that of any other Christian body, ancient or modern, Catholic or Protestant. The neglect which the use of a dead language had caused to befall the systematic reading of Scripture at the daily services before the Reformation, we far more than made up, achieving a standard which no other Protestant Church, rejecting any system, has shown itself able or willing to maintain.

The history of the use of Holy Scripture in Christian worship is deeply interesting; and we found a consideration of it indispensable to intelligent and constructive work in the revision of the lectionary.

1 HOLY WRITINGS

All the great religions of the world have recorded their essential teachings in sacred books, which each religion reverences as a divine revelation. No ancient faith is, however, properly a "book religion," in the sense that it started with a book, as certain modern sects have done, or as a narrow Protestantism without historical perspective sometimes assumes that Christianity did. In each there was the same course of development: first a living movement, taught and propagated "mouth to ear," and preserved, sometimes for considerable periods, in oral tradition; then, as the movement gathered strength, a fertile production of written records of its origins, fervent presentations of its principles, outpourings of devotion; and at length the formative period of that religion closed with an authoritative collec-

25

tion of its classical writings as its "Canon of Sacred Scripture," by a process of selection from among its early books.

The content and extent of such Scriptures are very various. They may comprise some or all of these chief classifications: Historical, with the narratives of the heroic ages of the faith; Theological, containing their doctrinal revelation of God; Ethical, with precepts of right conduct; and Devotional, with collections of hymns, prayers, and even complete liturgies of worship.

Judaism and Christianity are alike in being historic religions; they are entirely unique in the sense *in which* they are historic religions. They are not merely religions *in* history, or *with* a history, as are all others: they are religions founded upon history, based upon facts, grounded in things which really happened—while all other religious systems are only developments of philosophical or devotional speculations. Brahminism, Buddhism, Zoroastrianism, Mohammedanism, all present ideologies in the dress of mythologies. Only the Jewish-Christian line is firmly factual. The very content of its beliefs and the pattern of its worship are definitely linked to events which actually occurred. In this very fact lies the cosmic validity of the Christian faith, as the revelation of God through history.[1]

We therefore find that these two religions stand together again in a special emphasis upon one particular group of their historical books—what may be called their "charter narratives" of the life and teaching of their founders. By the time of Christ, the Jews had classified their Scriptures into the Law, the Prophets, and the Writings.[2] Both the great religious teachers, and most of the basic historical narratives, were grouped together into the second of these divisions, and all later history, as well as all ethical and devotional matter, was relegated to the third; but the first, comprising the five books

---

[1] *Cf.* a most brilliant setting forth of this principle from a somewhat unexpected quarter, in Charles Clayton Morrison, *What is Christianity?* (Willett, Clark & Co., Chicago, 1940).

[2] Luke 24:44.

of the Pentateuch, was exalted as the Jewish Charter Narrative, embodying the life, work, and teaching of their great leader, Moses. In liturgical use, the "Law" was the ritual climax of the synagogue service, accompanied by significant ceremonies of respect and attention. This precedent was exactly followed by the Christian Church with regard to the ritual use of the four Biographies of its Founder, which bear the significant title of "Gospels"—the "Good Tidings" of God's condescension and man's exaltation.

2   LITURGICAL USE OF SCRIPTURE

While all religions make their Scriptures the basis of their teaching, they vary considerably in the part that the reading of those Scriptures may take in their services of worship. There is, in fact, no necessary connection: many even of our own offices are performed without the reading of lessons. The Brahmin Vedas and the Zoroastrian Avestas stand at one extreme, consisting of little but liturgical matter. On the other hand the collections of the teachings of Buddha are not much used in worship, as this cult is more a way of personal salvation than either an authoritative doctrine or a corporate devotion.

Although one early document known as the *Didaché*, which contains definite liturgical forms, was included in the list of Sacred Books in Egypt in the fourth century, it happens that Christian forms of worship never became embodied in the accepted Canon of Scripture. This was fortunate, since it left Christian worship free to develop on an autonomous basis. It is true that this development was frozen in sacrosanct unalterable forms in some regions, and that such forms assumed great authority in practice, even to the supplanting of the use of the Scripture itself.

On the other hand, none of the many particular prayers quoted in the Bible were adopted into Christian rituals, with the sole exception of the brief and comprehensive form imparted by our Lord himself. The Lord's Prayer, at first used only in private devotion,[3] eventually came to be a part of all Christian services of whatever sort.

But the Psalter, the collected Hymn Book of the Hebrews, was adopted outright by the Christian Church, and has been used from that day to this. It is directly or indirectly the parent of all our other songs of praise. The "Evangelical Canticles" are simply New Testament psalms—the earliest outpourings of Christian devotion taking the accustomed forms of Hebrew poetry. These also have been adopted into our services. Subsequently, ecclesiastical canticles in the same general mode of poetic prose were composed upon the model of the Psalms. And finally, paraphrases of the Psalms into modern verse were the precursors of our metrical hymns.

Besides these contributions of scriptural elements to the structure and adornment of Christian services, the Church continued the custom of the Synagogue of reading passages from the Scriptures for edification, and also as the basis of a discourse grounded upon them, applying them by way of exposition, instruction, or exhortation—in other words, a Sermon. An instance of a synagogue service, containing a Lesson and a Sermon, is recorded in Luke 4:16-22. And the first description of the Christian Liturgy, written by St. Justin Martyr in the year 148, mentions both: "The memoirs of the Apostles or the writings of the Prophets are read as long as time allows. Then when the Reader has ceased, the President gives by word of mouth his admonition and exhortation to follow these excellent things."[4]

3　Liturgical Publication of Christian Scriptures

It was definitely the use of certain books at the Eucharist by the Church which established them as Christian Scriptures. From first to

[3] *Didaché* c. 8.
[4] I *Apology* c. 67.

last, liturgical use was intimately involved with the publication and the acceptance of the elements of the biblical Canon.

Each of the first three quarter-centuries of the Church's life contributed a characteristic Lesson to the Liturgy. During the first of these, the only Scripture which existed was the Old Testament, which the Church from the beginning adopted from the use of the Synagogue, and acclaimed as a Prophecy fulfilled in Christ.

About twenty-five years after the Resurrection, a new element began to appear, in the form of important Letters from the great missionary Apostle, St. Paul. These were definitely "published" by reading them serially at the Christian services.[5] When each church had finished the Letter addressed to itself, it exchanged Epistles with a neighboring church.[6] A very little of this sort of thing sufficed to cause the Letters of the founding Apostle to be recognized as Christian Scriptures, and to establish "The Epistle" as a fixed feature of the Christian service.

Another quarter-century brought forth the first of the Gospels; to which each of the next three decades added another version of the Biography of our Lord. As these circulated throughout the Church, they were read at the Liturgy in the same manner as the Prophecy and the Epistle. Containing as they did the definitive form of what had always been the heart and center of Christian preaching, they were incorporated into the service with the same ceremonial solemnity which had been accorded to the reading of the Law in the use of the Synagogue.

This method of procedure did not quite stop at this point. The remainder of the first century of the Church's history was rounded out by the appearance of the subapostolic writings, such as the General Epistles and the Apocalypse of the New Testament, as well as the Letters of Clement, Ignatius, and Barnabas, and the little treatise of the *Didaché*; all of them published in the same manner

[5] I Thessalonians 5:27.
[6] Colossians 4:16.

by being read at the Liturgy. Some of them found a permanent place in the Church's Liturgical Lectionary, and therefore ultimately in the official Canon of Scripture, and some did not, according to the Church's judgment in the course of the next two centuries as to their content of apostolic authority.

Though the early Syrian Liturgy bears traces of once having had as many as five liturgical lessons, and though some surviving Vigil services in the Roman missal exhibit plural lessons to the present day,[7] nevertheless the three Lessons established in the first three generations, the Prophecy, the Epistle, and the Gospel, remained the basic norm, and the earliest stages of all national rites possessed them. Ultimately, even three were felt to overload the normal service; and every surviving rite[8] has reduced them to the two New Testament lessons for ordinary occasions. The Ambrosian, and to a lesser degree the Roman, retain the Prophecy on certain days as a third lesson, and rather more often substitute it for the Epistle.[9]

4 THE LITURGICAL LECTIONARY

During the first two centuries of Christian history, and probably through most of the third, the Eucharistic Liturgy was the only corporate service for the whole congregation. This was the period within which we have seen that first the publication, and then the acceptation, of the Christian Scriptures, were linked organically to their liturgical use. The Liturgical Lectionary was therefore the original one; and it always remained primary. The reading of Scripture at the daily Hours of Prayer, as they afterwards arose, was copied from the usage of the Liturgy, and the selection of the Scriptures to be read

[7] Especially Ember Saturdays, and the Eves of Easter and Whitsunday. Easter Even has no less than fourteen lessons.

[8] Except the Armenian, and that last vestige of the ancient Gallican known as the Mozarabic.

[9] The Book of Common Prayer affords six examples of the Prophetic Lesson retained, and the Epistle omitted: Purification, Annunciation, Ash Wednesday, St. John Baptist, Advent -1, and Christmas 2.

there followed the lead of the methods which had been evolved for the Eucharist.

The original method of the Liturgical Lectionary, that whereby the Epistles and Gospels were first "published," was the reading of a book in consecutive serial sections until it was finished. This is known as the *lectio continua*. It possessed no selection for subject or occasion, no fixed divisions even into definite portions. The Celebrant determined the length of the lessons, making a sign to the Reader when he thought that a sufficient portion had been read, and a suitable stopping place reached. Such a method is obviously that of Justin Martyr's "as long as time allows."

The Eastern Churches have gone on to develop this primitive procedure in a straightforward line. The sermons of St. Chrysostom in the fourth century show that there was a system of continuous readings at various seasons, each selection linked to those preceding and following, and each to be expected at the same date every year. And the Orthodox Church to the present day has a regular pattern for reading the Epistles and Acts, and the Gospels, in order throughout the ecclesiastical year, on Sundays and weekdays alike, in such a way that the climaxes fall on the great days, and afford them Scriptures proper to their occasions.

The Western Church started upon this road. Augustine, Leo the Great, and Gregory the Great align themselves with Chrysostom in the method of the lectionaries which underlie their collected sermons. The fact that the Western lectionaries took another turn and acquired a distinctively different character from the Eastern is due to some diversities in the development of the Christian Year in the two regions.

Apparently the East, from quite an early date, had a clear concept of a cycle of Sundays covering the entire Church Year; but a whole millennium elapsed before the West finally adopted such a system. During all that time, the Latin Church clung to the old Roman civil calendar of months and days as its basic reckoning. Anniversaries at fixed dates formed its first outstanding features, and remained as its pivotal points of reference. Sundays as such were of no particular importance in the scheme, and were quite as capable of being treated as "common days" liturgically as so many weekdays.

Consequently, during the time when the East was perfecting its method of reading the New Testament in regular courses at the Liturgy, the West was far more concerned with choosing lessons by topic to fit the particular occasions. In the whole Festal Cycle between Advent and Trinity, the West has only one short course, the reading of Romans 12-13 on the first four Sundays after Epiphany. Otherwise, there is no principle of arrangement in this period other than selection for appropriateness of subject. The result is that the great days have Scriptures quite as apposite as the East, while the lessons of the associated Seasons are rather more so, not being complicated by a simultaneous attempt to carry out a continuous cycle of course-readings.

In the rest of the year, between Trinity and Advent, the reasons for the Western assignments are extremely obscure. From Trinity 6 to 17, and 19 to 24, there is a series of selections from the Pauline Epistles, arranged in scriptural order, of relatively late appearance, and excerpted from a much longer list of forty-two, drawn up apparently for use at discretion, and appearing in the earliest Epistle-Lectionary. But the principles which governed the designation of the Gospels remain unknown. No explanation, or combination of explanations, covers more than a fraction of the cases. The following summary represents about all that is now known or surmised, and probably nearly all that will ever be recovered about a development which left little or no contemporary record.

The Eastern Churches read the Synoptic Gospels on what we call the Sundays after Trinity, and St. John, accompanied by the Acts, on the Sundays after Easter. We do the same with the Gospel at the

Liturgy;[10] and the Roman Breviary so uses the Acts at Matins. This probably goes back to the time when both East and West were following similar systems of reading in course. But while the East developed this matter into closely knit continuities, the West shows no order whatsoever in the selection of either the books or the chapters of the Gospels. Evidently unknown disruptive forces have been at work: all that remains of whatever original pattern there may have been is only a sort of general seasonal appropriateness, much like the Western specialty of the use of the Catholic Epistles between Easter 1 and Trinity 5.

Throughout Trinity-tide, no general principle of allocation of the Western Gospel lessons is discoverable. Certainly they are neither sequentially nor chronologically arranged. There are some correspondences—which even their discoverers admit may be merely coincidences—between the Gospel for the Sunday and the Old Testament lesson read serially at Matins; both were read at the Third Nocturn of that service: a possible though hardly a probable return-influence of the Offices upon the Liturgy.[11] Again, some Gospels were certainly selected with reference to the local Church at Rome where the papal Station[12] was held: e.g., Sexagesima at St. Paul's, Lent 4 at Holy-Cross-in-Jerusalem, Trinity 5 at St. Peter's; and in at least one case it is possible that the choice was influenced by an adjacent festival —Advent -1 by St. Andrew's Day. But the list as a whole is completely at random. It is just as likely as not that it represents an inclusion into a permanent scheme of passages chosen arbitrarily at some time or other for no other reason than that the officiant happened to feel like preaching about them—i.e., they may be survivals of a purely ad libitum stage.

Since there is a serial arrangement of the Epistles during Trinity-

[10] Except that a single Gospel lection from St. John appears on Trinity 21. (The Sunday before Advent does not belong to the Trinity sequence.)

[11] Adrian Fortescue, The Mass (Longmans, London, 1914), 260.

[12] Originally perhaps simply the Bishop's annual Visitation to a parish church; later magnified with the attendance of the entire Papal Court.

tide, and no arrangement whatever of the Gospels, it is obvious that it is usually a waste of ingenuity to try to find some kind of "liturgical unity" of theme between them here. The modern Roman series, which dislocates first by one, then by two Sundays, the somewhat older matching of Epistle with Gospel which we have inherited, is no better and no worse than our own. It is simply the fact that the two liturgical lessons in this part of the year have no more in common than might any other two passages of Holy Scripture. Any "liturgical unity" which may be detected is a coincidence or an eisegesis.

The Gospels for the Sundays of the year were never intended to be a complete and self-contained system. They are in fact a partial survival of a much more comprehensive collection in medieval use, which made full provision in addition not only for the fixed Saints' Days, but also for all the Ember and Rogation days, every day in Lent, and the entire weeks after Easter and Whitsunday, as well as for Wednesdays and Fridays throughout the year. This ampler collection was reasonably comprehensive, though even this was completely unsystematic:[13] it was an accumulation from many sources rather than the working out of any consistent method or plan.

Therefore it is no great wonder that our Sunday Gospels show some considerable defects as a whole. They include some very inferior passages; they omit some very valuable passages; and they display a number of needless duplications. The "Miraculous Feedings" preöccupy three Sundays of the year, Lent 4, Trinity 7, and Advent -1, in absolutely equivalent forms. The Gospels on Epiphany 6 and Advent 2 are a "concord" of two Evangelists covering the same essential matter. Another concord exists in St. Luke's "Great Supper" on Trinity 2, which is a doublet of St. Matthew's "Marriage Feast" on Trinity 20. On the other hand, some thirty magnificent passages from the Gospels go unused in the liturgical Lectionary for the Sundays.

[13] W. H. Frere, *Studies in Early Roman Liturgy* (Alcuin Club Coll. XXX, Oxford, 1934), II. 88.

Two of the most unsatisfactory assignments were altered in the American Prayer Book of 1928: on Trinity 9 the "Unjust Steward" of Luke 16:1-9 was dismissed in favor of the adjacent, and unused, "Prodigal Son" in Luke 15:11; and on Epiphany 4 the "Gadarene Swine" of Matthew 8:23 was supplanted by the "Centurion's Servant" from Matthew 8:1-13. It is perhaps a little unfortunate that this last is itself a doublet, though not a very close verbal parallel, of St. John's incident of the "Nobleman's Son" on Trinity 21.

These and other defects of the Liturgical Lectionary will doubtless receive judicious and conservative consideration in future revisions of the Book of Common Prayer. It is not possible to perfect a permanently satisfactory lectionary for Morning and Evening Prayer, until some of the defects of the underlying Liturgical Lectionary have been remedied.

Nevertheless, in spite of its apparent faults; in spite of omissions, repetitions, and inadequate selections; in spite of the fact that it is a somewhat fortuitous collection, and neither a scientific, a systematic, nor a comprehensive plan: the Liturgical Lectionary as it has come down to us is absolutely basic to the character of the Church Year, and the primary guide to the Church's teaching. It is an indispensable guide to the construction of any other lectionary for other services, which is to be kept in any sort of correspondence with the Christian Year. And though not all-inclusive in itself, it is quite sufficiently representative of the riches of Holy Scripture. Its deficiencies are very readily supplemented by an Office Lectionary which is based upon it, and which in use shares with it the principal Sunday services; and the resulting total plan for the reading of Scripture can be made entirely systematic, and completely comprehensive.

5   THE BREVIARY SYSTEM

When the observance of the daily Hours of Prayer came into being, they followed the pattern of the early Liturgy in reading the Scriptures in course, associating certain books with particular seasons of the year.

Though the Rule of St. Benedict required lessons at Matins on Sundays and festivals, the weekday services had no continuous system of lessons until the seventh century, when Gregory the Great added them to ferial Matins. This service has always remained as the only one which carries a regular series of readings, the so-called "Chapters" at other Hours consisting of little more than a selected text.

By the ninth century there was a fully developed course of reading the whole Bible at Matins. Isaiah was begun at Advent Sunday, Genesis (followed by the rest of the Heptateuch) at Septuagesima, Jeremiah in Lent, Lamentations in Holy Week, the Acts in the Easter season, Samuel and the Kings after Trinity, Ezekiel at the end of October, and the Wisdom Literature filled out the conclusion of the Church Year. Obviously this was an elaboration of the Liturgical Lectionary of the fourth century, which commenced Genesis at the vernal beginning of the year, and read the book of Acts at Eastertide. Moreover, it seems very probable that it was the existence of this comprehensive course at Matins which tended to release the Liturgical Lessons from any responsibility to cover the field in order, and allowed them to be selected for such topical and local reasons as we have seen to be identifiable in a few cases, and presumable throughout the apparent lack of any system in the liturgical Gospels for Trinity-tide. At least, the development of this plan of the Breviary lessons, and the filling out of the Sunday cycle of masses, took place concurrently during the same period.

Originally the books assigned to these Seasons at Matins were read through continuously and completely on Sundays and weekdays. But long before the time of Cranmer, the system had decayed, so that he rightly complained that "they were only begun, and never read through." To this day the Roman Breviary preserves only a simulacrum of the Lectionary of the ninth century, and affords only a kind of "token" review of the contents of the Scriptures.

6 THE OLDER ANGLICAN LECTIONARIES

At only one point did Cranmer make any use of the ancient traditions of a seasonal use of special books. The system of the First Prayer Book assigned the whole Old Testament (including the Apocrypha) straight through the dates of the Civil Year in alternate chapters at Morning and Evening Prayer—the single exception being that Isaiah was put out of course in late November to coincide with Advent. The New Testament (omitting the Revelation) [14] was read through three times, the Gospels and Acts at Mattins, the Epistles at Evensong. Some twelve fixed Holy Days supplied with one or more Proper Lessons were inserted into this pattern. Although provision was made for ten movable Festivals, including Easter, Whitsunday, and Trinity, there were no Proper Lessons for any other Sundays.

This general method of the use of the Civil Calendar remained basic in all Anglican Lectionaries through our Prayer Book of 1892. The only significant change in 1892 was that the New Testament was now read through only twice, once each at Morning and Evening Prayer, with the Gospels always at one service, the Acts and Epistles at the other; except that the Revelation was assigned to both services in alternate chapters in the latter half of December.

The Elizabethan Prayer Book of 1559 provided the rest of the Fixed Feasts with First Lessons taken from the Wisdom Literature, and assigned *seriatim*, just as the days occurred in the Calendar, with no attempt whatever at appropriateness. The American 1892 for the first time filled up all Lessons for these days, selected for suitability to their occasions.

Proper First Lessons for Sundays also date from 1559. No doubt the interlude of the revived use of the Sarum Breviary under Queen Mary had recalled to mind the value of the old use of particular

---

[14] In this Cranmer followed Quiñones. Perhaps the use of the Revelation by such visionaries as the Anabaptists did not commend it to people of that period.

books to mark the Seasons. And as the Sunday cycle was the only part of the "Christian Year" pattern found in any Anglican Lectionary before 1892, the Elizabethan revisers did well to adapt the Sarum plan to the Sundays. Isaiah, begun in Advent, was continued through the Sundays after Epiphany; Genesis at Septuagesima was followed by selections from the rest of the Heptateuch through Trinity 2; the four books of Kings covered Trinity 3 to 13; then followed excerpts from the Prophets (including Ezekiel on Trinity 16); and the year was concluded with chapters from Proverbs after Trinity 21.

This Sunday schedule from the Old Testament has been preserved in principle in all the English books until now; even the Revision of 1922 affords only minor modifications and alternatives to it.

The American books also kept this outline, except that our First Prayer Book in 1789 began Genesis at Trinity Sunday; substituting Jeremiah and other Prophets between Septuagesima and Ascension.

This book also for the first time filled up Second Lessons for all Sundays. Selections from the Epistles in order occupied the evenings, as had hitherto been the custom of the English Lectionaries for week-days. The Sunday mornings from Advent to Easter offered a sort of synopsis of salient events of our Lord's life chosen from the Gospels. The book of Acts was read from Easter 1 to Trinity 10; and the balance of the year was eked out with excerpts from the Four Gospels in order.

This plan remained in 1892, with only such changes as extending the reading of Luke 1 and 3 to cover the mornings of all four Sundays in Advent, with chapters from the Revelation on their evenings; and concentrating the entire Sermon on the Mount on the three Sunday mornings of Pre-Lent.

We have already considered the factors which caused England, Scotland, and America to abandon this older Anglican plan as obsolete. Our Lectionary of 1928 belongs to the new order, and indeed is a preliminary stage of the Revision of 1943. As such, it will be discussed in the following chapter.

IV

THE REVISION OF THE LECTIONARY

THE PRINCIPLES which guided the formulation of the new American Lectionary of 1943 did not consist of any abstract philosophy of the Church's teaching, nor any doctrinaire theories of the use of Scripture, but emerged as the outgrowth of the Committee's personal experience under three previous lectionary systems: the inherited plan of the American Prayer Books since their beginning, as revised in 1877 and included in the Book of 1892; the interim of the use of Experimental Lectionaries during the last Revision; and the system adopted in our Prayer Book of 1928. We shall proceed to consider the lessons of that experience, and the principles which a criticism of these three systems brought to light for our guidance in the making of our revision.

1 THE LECTIONARY OF 1892

Although the plan of the Lectionary of 1877-1892 had, as we have said, been rendered definitely obsolete, and though many details of it now seem so conservative, it was nevertheless much in advance of any other Anglican lectionary in existence at the time, and possessed some valuable features, neglected in 1928, which we have thought worthy of restoration in the Lectionary of 1943. Such are the sequence of lessons from the Gospels in Advent and from Epiphany to Easter, and the timing of certain historical courses.

The treatment of the Sundays in Advent as a forward-looking expectation of the Nativity, by the reading of the early chapters of St. Luke, was really a revival of the oldest concept of that Season. The apocalyptic expectation of the Second Advent was, and should remain, a secondary theme. For this same reason, however, we transferred the reading of the Revelation, which 1892 had on Sunday evenings in Advent, to the weekdays; finding that for Sunday use this book had more significant force on such occasions as Easter and Ascension.

So also, although the Sundays from Epiphany to Easter might for the most part be treated topically, it appeared desirable to keep in mind the value of the plan of 1892 in retaining an outline thread of the narrative of our Lord's life and teaching.

Now of course the change of method in 1928 which brought all weekdays into the pattern of the Christian Year relieved the Sunday cycle of its sole responsibility of setting forth the books of the Bible according to the Christian Seasons with which the old traditions of the Church had associated them. This could now be done, as advisable, in the separate courses on weekdays, instead of trying to cram them into the Sundays in a series of excerpts which, in the nature of the case, had to be reduced to almost as much of a skimming synopsis as the present method of the Latin Breviary. All Sunday lessons could, if desired, be devoted to a topical treatment of the distinctive teaching of the day, based upon the Epistle and Gospel.

Yet it remained desirable that the Sunday series should continue to present as a whole and in reasonable continuity two great narratives, the History of the Chosen People, and the Acts of the Apostles. In the weekday series, the History might well revert to the old system since the fourth century, of beginning Genesis at Septuagesima; for there alone, as will appear, would it find sufficient space to be given intact, without inconvenient omission from the variability of the Christian Year. But on Sundays, the American plan is obviously superior to the English. There is an evident appropriateness in reading the majestic account of the Creation on Trinity Sunday,[1] whereas no one remembers the original rationale of Septuagesima as identified

---

[1] In 1928, these historical selections ran from Trinity to Trinity 15, and Trinity 19 and 20. The weekday series began with Advent 1.

with the beginning of the year. Moreover, begun at Trinity, the long narrative is free of interference with any other sequence; while it is quite alien to the dominant themes of Lent and Easter-tide, with which it is involved if begun at Septuagesima.

Again, the 1892 Lectionary was sound in beginning the book of Acts on the Sundays following Easter, since its earlier chapters contain apostolic preaching on the Resurrection which is indispensable to fill out the teaching of this season; after which, there is all of the Trinity season available for the full development of its long narration of the establishment and extension of the early Church. On weekdays, however, it seems a mistake to try to crowd it all into Easter-tide, as the British books do: it may most suitably be begun at Ascension, which has its exordium as the liturgical Epistle of the feast; after which it may continue at leisure, without excessively long portions, until it is concluded at Trinity 9.[2]

2   THE TRIAL LECTIONARIES OF THE LAST REVISION

In the earlier stages of the last Revision of the Prayer Book, experimental Lectionaries, annually revised, were issued by a special Committee headed by the Rev. C. B. Wilmer, D.D., and authorized for trial use, exactly as has been done during the last eight years. These Trial Lectionaries paralleled the revision of the lectionary in the Church of England, which was in process at the same time, in adopting the "Christian Year" pattern; and likewise in abandoning the principle of single lessons absolutely required at each Sunday service, in favor of a system of choices between alternatives. Thereby they opened up a great variety of material not formerly used on Sundays; and many of us found them most educative in affording new vistas of the scriptural ground of the Faith.

Unfortunately, however, they were rather too much engrossed with

[2] In 1928, Acts occupied weekdays from Whit-Monday to Trinity 5. On six Sundays, it was used topically only.

an emphasis on ancient Hebrew history, symbolically interpreted as prefiguring the drama of the Redemption of mankind in Christ. Now it is true that there are some analogies between the career of the Chosen People and the earthly life of the Son of God. The climaxes of the great deliverances of the nation from captivity in Egypt and in Babylon furnish parallels to the liberation of man from sin and death at Easter. Every lectionary realizes this, and employs passages embodying the high points of this Sacred History at Holy Week and Easter. But it is quite impracticable to cramp the whole of the historical narratives into the narrow—and variable—space of the Sundays between Advent and Easter. An attempt to do so results in a skeleton outline of events of minor interest in themselves, embodied in passages of indifferent value for edification. In the close series of great Christian commemorations in this "Festal Cycle," it is impossible to maintain any interest in the political vicissitudes of the Jews; this sort of thing seems simply an intrusion and an irrelevancy. In fact, this method provoked a decided reaction, and precipitated a debate, which has never since been altogether stilled, as to whether it was worth while to read the Old Testament *at all* in a Christian Church!

Moreover, the choices of the Trial Lectionaries were on too elaborate a plan, so that they broke down under their own weight. The matter was arranged in two- and even four-year courses. Most clergy, encountering what they considered unreadable passages in the assigned courses, abandoned them altogether in favor of an *ad libitum* use of the alternatives. And then it was found to be too much of a nuisance to look up eight lessons, in order to sift out two which one could use. Besides all this, there was a great deal of duplication of lessons even in a single course; and lumping them all together, as most of us did, simply made a confusion worse confounded. A check of one stage of this scheme revealed one favorite passage proffered for use on no less than sixteen different occasions of the year!

As a result of this experience, we concluded that there are great advantages in a plural choice of lessons for a given Sunday, to suit different kinds of congregations and different preferences of the clergy, and to enable preachers to apply a variety of homiletical treatment in following the systematic teaching of the Church Year.

But if there is to be a lectionary embracing optional alternatives, the choice of them must be absolutely free, not in the form of such fixed annual courses as the English Lectionary suggests and the Scottish requires. No General Rubric will make an American clergyman read a passage which does not commend itself to him, so long as other matter is available; hence any system of compulsory courses is predestined to break down in practice.

Moreover, the principles of selection must not be left to the memory or the discretion of the officiant; they must be "built in" to the tables of alternative lessons. This can be done by assigning to every Sunday such Scriptures as have a real appropriateness to the occasion; and then checking these assignments in such a manner as to assure that, no matter what passage might be chosen for any occasion, it would not be read out to the long-suffering congregation within a reasonable period, and, where possible, not again in the course of the year.

3   THE LECTIONARY OF 1928

So much dissatisfaction had developed with the overweighted schemes of the Trial Lectionaries, that, when in 1925 Bishop Slattery sponsored a much simpler and more lucid plan, it was incontinently adopted, virtually by acclamation, for the Prayer Book of 1928.

This Lectionary reverted to the old plan of no alternatives, with only a single First and Second Lesson assigned to each Sunday. If that were to be the program, it devolved upon its makers to choose out the very best passages in all Scripture for the Sunday lessons, and furthermore to see to it that these passages were fully representative of the entire cycle of biblical teaching. This Lectionary does not meet this test. It is composed primarily of "favorite passages." This one fact accounts both for the enthusiasm which greeted it at the first, and also for the outcome, that the welcome accorded to it was so short-lived.

So far from trying to use the not unlimited occasions of the Sundays of the year for as wide and comprehensive a choice as possible, these favorite passages were repeated over again in other connections, often in the thinly disguised form of a parallel from another Gospel, and frequently at disconcertingly close intervals. Thus the narrative of the Baptism of our Lord, which occurs in St. Mark's version as the Liturgical Gospel on Epiphany 2, was appointed in St. Luke's account on Advent 3 Morning Prayer, and in St. Matthew's on Advent 4 Evening Prayer. The Centurion's Servant, Gospel for Epiphany 4 (Matthew), occurred on Septuagesima Morning Prayer (Luke), and Trinity 19 Morning Prayer (Matthew). The Triumphal Entry, Gospel for Advent 1 (Matthew), was also Lent 6 Morning Prayer (Mark) and Lent 6 Evening Prayer (Luke). The Visit of Nicodemus, the Gospel for Trinity Sunday, was also the morning lesson on Whitsunday; and the Good Samaritan, Gospel for Trinity 13, the morning lesson for Trinity 12. Altogether, there were twenty-five such passages from the Gospels assigned to fifty-two places in the Liturgical Gospels and the tables of Sunday Lessons.

The defects of *scope* of this lectionary, which were an inevitable result of this excessive preöccupation with favorite and familiar selections from the Gospels, appear in the extraordinarily small room given to the rest of the New Testament, of which it has the least number of lessons of any known lectionary—twenty-six out of 110 Second Lessons for Sundays. Of these, eleven are from the Acts, three from Revelation, six from the Catholic Epistles, six from the Epistles of St. Paul; but three of the Catholic Epistles and five of the Pauline were duplicates of Liturgical Epistles. The remarkable result is that from the entire Pauline corpus, only *one* lesson was offered which did not already occur in the liturgical list!

A similar preference for narrative to exposition affected the selections from the Old Testament. The Sunday schedule had seventy-one lessons from the Heptateuch and the historical books, where 1892 had forty-nine, and only thirty-three from the Prophets and Wisdom Literature, where 1892 had sixty-five. Here again the intellectual element in edification was subordinated to the story-telling recounting of events.

These outstanding inadequacies of the Lectionary of 1928 created such dissatisfaction that within ten years after its first appearance General Convention sanctioned the further series of experiments which have just been concluded by the adoption of a new revision.

It remains, however, to speak of some of its virtues, which were considerable. The majority of the passages selected were attractive; their chief defect was that they did not cover the ground. Furthermore, for the most part they were chosen on a new principle of great value and vitality. Instead of filling up a series of blank spaces with selected chapters chosen in mechanical rotation—something a child could do—its makers had asked themselves the elementary question, What gives its teaching quality to the Christian Year? and found the answer in the basic Liturgical Lectionary, the ancient assignment of Epistles and Gospels to the cycle of Sundays. Topical lessons, closely attuned to the keynotes of the liturgical Scriptures of the day, had always been used on the outstanding festivals. Why not extend this process to all Sundays? And in fact this lectionary carried out this idea of integrating all the services of the day around the central Eucharist, and reënforcing its lessons with further illustrations, sidelights, and applications at the other services, with a very considerable finesse, much of which indeed was too subtle to be properly appreciated by the most clamorous objectors to the system.

Accepting, then, the major contribution of the Lectionary of 1928, the principle of coördinating the lessons of Morning and Evening Prayer with those of the basic Liturgy, as the Church's outline of its teaching for the year, it devolved upon us to deal with this lectionary's major defect, insufficient coverage of the riches of Holy Scripture in the Sunday series.

Much of the answer to this was already predetermined by our experience with the Trial Lectionaries. We had resolved, positively, to provide plural choices of lessons on Sundays; negatively, to proceed by a simple tabular analysis, the use of check-tables of books and chapters of the Bible, so as to be cognizant at all times of just what portions of Scripture we were including and omitting. In this way we need not wait for painful experience to show up duplications of passages already used in the scheme; the method of making it would eliminate them before it was ever offered to the Church.

We realized of course that a complete elimination of repetitions is neither completely possible, nor even altogether desirable. A passage like I Corinthians 13 is of too supreme a value to be confined to the Epistle on Quinquagesima, where in the whole course of the year it might be heard only by a handful of people at an early service. Even the great Christmas Gospel, the beginning of St. John, receives a fuller glory, and serves a wider use, when repeated as the morning Lesson on Trinity Sunday.[3] Nevertheless, controlled by the method mentioned, out of 540 Sunday Lessons in the 1943 Lectionary, only eleven passages are repeated on a second occasion in the pattern of the year, and only twelve more duplicate liturgical Epistles or Gospels; all at such intervals, and in such connections, as to cause no distress in practice.

In detail, we considered that matter from the Gospels must be assigned *from a Harmony*, to avoid the reiteration of the same thing in only slightly different words.[4] And as a general rule we desired to avoid repeating in the Lessons matter already preëmpted by the Epistles and Gospels, since in most parishes the Eucharist replaces Morning Prayer at least once a month as the principal service, and therefore its lections are brought into the same sequence.

---

[3] Both examples are taken from the Lectionary of 1928, and are items deliberately retained in 1943.

[4] There were twenty instances of this fault in 1928.

4 REMAINING PROBLEMS

Proceeding on the basis of the foregoing inferences derived from experience with these three lectionary systems, there were still some matters which required further consideration.

a) Use of Gospels and Epistles: First, the proper proportioning of matter from the Gospels and the Epistles involved questions raised but not solved in both the 1892 and 1928 Lectionaries.

The American plan of filling up the Sunday evenings with lessons from the Epistles had never proved very happy in practice. It may be observed that originally the Gospels were spoken, while the Epistles were written. Hence the condensed literary style of the Epistles, and their elaboration of theological thought, often make them difficult to follow when read aloud, and no less difficult to preach about. The General Rubric of 1877 which allowed the substitution of the passage from the Gospels assigned to the corresponding day of the month[5] was a provision which had much appeal for tired clergy on Sunday evenings, since almost any passage at random from the Gospels furnishes a good background for an extempore sermon.

Of course, with the new system of the "Christian Year" pattern, there is no longer any lesson for the day of the month to fall back upon; but we could permit the substitution of the Gospel for the Day. And also, we decided to carry out systematically and completely a plan which the British lectionaries approach without quite attaining, and to provide an appropriate Lesson from the Gospels as an alternative to whatever passage from the rest of the New Testament might be assigned, at *every* Sunday service.

But we did not propose to slight the matter from the Epistles, as the Lectionary of 1928 had done, in a natural but excessive reaction

[5] In form, this was a reversion to the English method, which had few Proper Second Lessons for Sundays, and regularly took those assigned in the monthly Calendar. In fact, it was a confession of the insufficiency of the American provisions.

against the heavy schedule of whole chapters assigned to the Sunday evenings of the year. The apostolic Epistles present some luminous interpretations of the intellectual meanings of the Christian faith, all the more penetrating because it was then so new, and Christian thought still in its vital *status nascendi.* They also extend and apply those ethical implications of religion which were such a profound and central feature of our Lord's own teaching.

We therefore resolved to pay no attention to the old complaint of "too many Epistles" which had arisen under the former American system. On the contrary, we proposed to increase the coverage of the matter available, and used selections from the Epistles very freely everywhere on Sundays where their subjects were applicable; but of course topically, and in much shorter sections, confined for the most part to a single theme. While we hoped in this manner to encourage the use of this most valuable matter, in no case would we compel it, since there was always a Gospel alternative at hand. Lectionaries are used in other places besides colleges and cathedrals; and we determined that no Lay Reader in a little Indian mission should be deprived upon any Sunday of a suitable selection from the simple Gospel story.

b) Topical vs. Course Methods: We also gave some further consideration to the respective merits of the topical method of utilizing the Scriptures, and the method of reading them in course. We have seen that the 1928 Lectionary was governed by the topical plan throughout the year, instead of confining it to the Festal Cycle from Advent to Trinity, as former lectionaries had done; but it also contained a certain amount of course-reading of Hebrew history in Trinity-tide.

The reading of a series of passages from the Bible in coherent order has a definite cumulative value. In the daily lessons, it comes into its own. But in any Sunday sequence, there must be much omission, since absolute continuity and absolute comprehensiveness within the limited number of Sundays available are incompatible and unattainable objectives. But usually, when a given book is reduced to a course of excerpts, the chain is broken: it loses its continuity as a true series, and becomes merely a list. Some great narratives are capable of surviving this process, and may even be improved by the resulting condensation. But in general there is no merit in filling in successive dates in the calendar with excerpts merely arranged in the order in which they occur in the Bible. This may be a convenience to the makers of a lectionary; it has little or no value to the users. It is our opinion that our lectionary, with its topical basis of unity of thought, has a superior rationality to the listing of chapters in a mechanical order. To the eye, our lists have no order; and one brash individual once enquired of me if we had made the assignments by shaking them out of a pepper pot! To the mind, there is a very real order: they have been carefully arranged by the logical congruity of their subjects, rather than by the accidental contiguity of their occurrence in the sacred text.

We had already determined to follow the thoroughly tested precedents of the American tradition, in excluding course-reading from the Festal Cycle from Advent to Trinity, and including it between Trinity and Advent. Trinity-tide is not properly a Season, in the sense that Advent, Epiphany, or Lent are Seasons. It does not present any particular part of the life of Christ; it does not declare any special doctrine. It is devoted to the practical phase of Christian living, as the Festal Cycle unfolds the theological implications of the Christian faith. It is therefore open to any sort of course-reading, without disturbing any other continuity in possession of the field. Indeed, it shows the way, by including the Pauline list of liturgical Epistles between Trinity 6 and 24.

As there is too much History to be concentrated in a single course on these Sundays, we divided it. The "traditional" period, from the Creation to the entrance to the Promised Land, was assigned to Sunday mornings, accompanied by Second Lessons chosen topically to reënforce the Christian meaning of those primal events in the foundation-period of the Chosen Nation, which are so often given a spiritual interpretation in the New Testament. On Sunday evenings we took the history of the Hebrew Kingdoms. As this latter and often more political narrative had few natural New Testament corrolaries, we made no artificial attempt to supply them, but allowed the narrative of the Book of Acts simply to run concurrently with the History. It is interesting however to observe how the underlying unity of Holy Scripture as a whole often supplies some real common element to the chance collocations of these two series at the same service, just as it does sometimes with the Epistles and Gospels occurring during the same period.

Now in the earlier years of our Trial Lectionaries, we provided only two sets of alternative lessons on all the Sundays of the year. This meant that in Trinity-tide one of these choices was filled by the historical courses; and if any one did not elect to follow one of those, the remaining lessons became obligatory without recourse. The manifold implications of the Trinity Epistles and Gospels could be supplied with only a single set of topical illustrations; and as they usually follow quite independent themes, they demand treatment along more than one line. This was a serious infringement of the liberty and variety which characterized the Sunday lessons for the rest of the year, and which was a part of our objective for the whole of it: the more serious, because Trinity-tide is extremely rich in vital applications of the Christian faith to the task of Christian living. This part of the year, even more than the Festal Cycle, called for the most generous treatment, and the most comprehensive reënforcement of its manifold meanings, if full justice were to be done to its opportunities. Therefore we determined to add yet a third set of choices for these Sundays, restoring the system of topical assignments to two sets, like the rest of the year.

At this point our check-tables of used and omitted matter revealed that we had ample material at hand for one complete set. This we placed on Sunday mornings. In addition, there was enough from the Old Testament for another list of First Lessons; but there was not enough more usable material in the New Testament for an entire set of twenty-four Second Lessons.

Now we thought of the permission of our new General Rubric, permitting the use of the Gospel of the Day as the Second Lesson at any service. This was an inherently valuable permission, especially since we had refrained from reduplicating the liturgical Gospels as lessons at Morning and Evening Prayer on other occasions. The only drawback to a wide use of it might be the difficulty of finding just the assigned First Lesson which would go equally well with the Gospel. Our lists at that time showed at least two cases where paucity of matter had compelled us to put the liturgical Gospel, with some added context, upon the Sunday evening of its day. Why not carry out this idea throughout the Trinity Season; accompanying the Gospels with First Lessons chosen very specifically to give them background? This solution was adopted; and the resulting assignments may be found as the second choice at Evening Prayer from the First to the Twenty-Fourth Sundays after Trinity.

c) *Number of Choices*: Some persons have suggested that we have now offered too many alternatives; particularly in view of the fact that few churches now have regular Sunday evening services, and still fewer have them on the summer Sundays, which happen to be precisely those for which we have given the most numerous options.

While the conditions as to the disuse of Evensong in America may, however regrettably, be as represented, they did not cause us to weaken in our resolution to supply, as far as humanly possible, *enough* choices to fit every sort of congregation, and every reasonable variation of taste and judgment on the part of the officiant, on every occasion of the Sundays of the Christian Year.

We wished our provisions to discourage something which perhaps no system and no authority can ever entirely prevent, namely the custom of some individualists of arbitrarily supplanting the official lectionary of the Church with selections of their own, designed to support a particular course of sermons. At least a wide latitude of choices of Scripture, all chosen for appropriateness to their occasions, should furnish an invitation and a challenge to explore these new riches, and a suggestion of the advisability of conforming one's personal homiletical plan to the Church's comprehensive outline of its teaching in the Christian Year.

Likewise we have paid little heed to the resentment with which some conservative souls greet unfamiliar tracts of Scripture, with the same stick-in-the-mud attitude which always raises automatic complaints about anything new in a new Hymnal. We have always provided other and easier lessons which they can use instead. Most men will welcome the new matter because it is new, and come to love it as it becomes familiar. In any case the ampler menu will be a boon to conscientious expository preachers in the course of long rectorships, offering a new approach to old truths after more obvious ones have been exhausted.

Therefore, instead of narrowing choices, we have deliberately enlarged them, by permitting the Epistle as well as the Gospel of the Day to be used as a Second Lesson, and by allowing any assignment of psalms and lessons on a given day to be used at either service, morning or evening.

The only drawback to all this is the difficulty of making a ready and intelligent choice from all the material provided. The brief subject-summaries of the Sunday lessons in this book are an attempt to facilitate such a choice.

But a great deal can be done for the practical utilization of the material, by a right arrangement. In the first place, First and Second Lessons are coördinated in pairs, which a General Rubric indicates are intended to be used together. This obvious device was the fruit of experience; we are almost ashamed to admit that we did not think of it until 1939. Originally, we had simply filled in the whole schedules of Old and New Testament lessons independently, from salient suggestions of the Epistles and Gospels. The natural result was that the two lessons at a service might, and frequently did, have nothing to do with each other, since one might illustrate an idea from the Epistle and the other from the Gospel, or they might follow two separate leads from the one or the other. It is a great wonder that the Church tolerated such work at our hands! To be sure, the experience with the 1928 Lectionary shows that there are few clergy alert enough to detect a "liturgical harmony" between lessons at the separate services of the Communion and the Offices; but anyone at all can see whether two lessons at the same service do or do not harmonize with and reënforce each other.

While no criticism whatever reached us from the Church in this matter, fortunately we observed this glaring defect of plan ourselves in time to remedy it, and to perfect the resulting coördinations in subsequent editions to a considerable degree of refinement. The effect of this change is that the alternative now lies not between eight several lessons on a Sunday, but between four pairs. Even in Trinity-tide the third choice at each service is obvious to anyone as part of a historical series; and while a single occurrence of it can of course be elected at any point, it will normally be used or left as a whole.

Then again we were careful to assign as the first choice at Morning Prayer the set of lessons which we consider to be on the whole the most generally profitable and usable selection. This was a concession to the average mind, which is apt to take the first thing at hand. Then we arranged the other options at the two services to secure balance and variety: avoiding placing two virtually equivalent treatments of the same theme under the same service, when more than one subject was to be presented; and avoiding also a disproportion of material from either the Epistles or the Gospels at the same recurrent place in the Tables (i.e., first or second choice at either service throughout the scheme).

In this way we effected what amounts to four complete and fairly balanced annual courses of sets of lessons. Any clergyman in the habit of choosing regularly a given set, morning or evening, is reasonably assured of a comprehensive course for the year. It would be quite possible for a man with a single service a Sunday to continue for four years without retracing the same ground.

We also arranged that one of the First Lessons on each Sunday morning should have a particular congruence with the Epistle and Gospel for the Day; and provided by General Rubric that this Lesson, distinguished by a star in the Tables, is available for use when shortened Morning Prayer with one lesson immediately precedes the Holy Communion. This is to implement the rubric on page 10 of the Prayer Book. While this permission for a combined service severely curtails Morning Prayer to a point where it has a mere proclitic function, so that the user can hardly flatter himself that he has said the Office as such, yet it has some value as an enrichment of the Communion, whose Pro-Anaphora is thereby expanded to include the ancient Prophetic Lesson, and further psalmody.

d) *Length of Lessons*: From the first, we gave careful attention to the question of a proper liturgical length of the lessons assigned. Archbishop Cranmer adopted a whole chapter of the Bible as his unit. A few curtailments of obvious irrelevancies were made in subsequent books; but the system remained virtually intact in our book of 1892, which still averaged twenty-five verses a lesson. The Lectionary of 1928 shortened this to eighteen verses, without quieting a widespread demand in the Church for still shorter lessons.

No doubt the increasing use of the Holy Communion at principal services had a good deal to do with this demand. The Gospels average less than eleven verses; the Epistles less than eight. And it had come to be recognized that any service is overloaded which is provided with three sermons—two of them in the words of Holy Scripture. There is a general impression abroad that the Episcopal

Sunday morning service is longer than the average Free Church service. It is not: by actual test, it is shorter; but with the old length of lessons, it was certainly. heavier! It is a somewhat important though little realized liturgical principle that tedium in any service does not arise from its total length, but primarily from concentrating too much of the same thing at a time.

Cardinal Hugo's division of the Bible into chapters in the thirteenth century was constructed on rhetorical rather than logical principles. The chapters commonly have a satisfying beginning and ending; but they often divide a subject midway, and still more often they include several entirely different subjects. The paragraphing of the Revised Version attempts to follow logical divisions, and is a much better guide; though sometimes a slightly different partition will do quite as well, and sometimes the necessity for apportioning an exceptionally long passage into approximately equal sections in the daily lessons will result in some compromises; and sometimes, especially on Sundays, it is of advantage to take a leaf from Cardinal Hugo's book, and seek an effective beginning and ending.

In a Lectionary whose basis is primarily topical, the unit of a lesson is obviously a passage covering a single theme. This principle was followed, at least in part, in 1928. That Lectionary, together with the British tables of 1922, made considerable use of a new and important means of attaining unity of theme. This was the device of eliminating irrelevant matter not only from the beginning or end of a proposed passage, but from its middle. It proved particularly applicable to the Old Testament writers, who often offend modern ideas of unity and continuity of treatment. They frequently rejoice in an antiphonal kind of contrast, praising God and execrating their opponents in alternate breaths. In application, the resulting omission of verses looks peculiar in a Table, and has aroused the ire of some clergy whose conservative inertia apparently rebels at even the very simple task of marking the lectern Bible lightly with pencil to indicate the deleted verses. But it is remarkable how often this apparent hop-skip-and-jump progress through a chapter makes an integrated, straightforward, and effective lesson out of what would otherwise be a mass of hard names, digressions, and unpleasant matters, which would have to be omitted outright.

The result of our work is that the Lectionary of 1943 has an average of thirteen and one-half verses for the Sunday lessons. This is probably sufficient for the time being; especially as some old-fashioned clergy have audibly wondered if it is worth while to ask the congregation to sit down for some ultra-short lesson of perhaps only six verses. There are a few of these, especially on Sundays and Holy Days, where some quite particular point in the Second Lesson is so fortunate as to find some real background, but of unhappily limited dimensions, in the much less developed thought of the Old Testament. We would gladly have made such First Lessons somewhat longer, if the context or even the book from which we drew them had contained anything more which was even remotely appropriate to the subject. But we did draw the line at confusing the picture and lessening the effect of what we did give, by including a passage on some totally different matter, merely for the sake of satisfying some arbitrary measuring-rod of "liturgical length." A jewel is enhanced neither in beauty nor value by mounting it with a larger weight of the matrix in which it was found.

As for one suggestion that the lessons must be longer, because people do not settle down to listening until a few verses have been read, it must be replied that such a habit, where it exists, is certainly the result of too long and turgid lessons in time past. Experience with shorter lessons has shown already that congregations are quite willing to give them their attention from the beginning, when they find that such attention is going to be demanded, and will not be abused by interminable monotonies.

In any case there are not many very short lessons—none whatever as short as some Epistles—and as far as possible they have been excluded from the first choices at Sunday Morning Prayer. There may be some cause to regret the old lessons, with their long, leisurely, varied progress to what was sometimes a very fine rhetorical effect. It may, however, be pointed out that such opportunities are not lost to those who desire them. The General Rubric which permits the officiant either to lengthen or shorten any lesson at discretion, will enable him to read the whole chapter in which it occurs. To be sure, if he does so, it must be on his own responsibility; we cannot guarantee to him the protection from the repetition of the matter thus employed which we have been at pains to work out for the Tables as given.[6]

But such considerations or regrets do not alter the fact that the majority of people in the Church did desire shorter lessons, and many were chafing at the tediousness and irrelevancy of some parts of the Old Testament. Hence as a general rule, we aimed to give the lessons in their minimal form, for the reason that it is much more difficult to shorten a passage intelligently than to lengthen it. It is quite open to anyone to "omit the omissions," or to extend a passage to any desired length.

[6] The man who finds Matthew 5:1-16 assigned as a Lesson for Septuagesima, and who from old affection for the Lectionary of 1892 reads the whole chapter on that occasion, must not complain when he encounters Matthew 5:27-35 appointed on Lent 2.

V

THE LECTIONARY FOR SUNDAYS

A$_{LL}$ $_{THE}$ current Anglican lectionaries are in agreement in providing separate courses for the Sundays and the weekdays of the
year. The great majority of the laity regularly hear the Scriptures
publicly read only on the Sundays; it is, therefore, necessary that
the Sunday series should be complete in itself, and should cover comprehensively as wide a field as possible of the best passages of
Scripture.

The minuter details of the manner in which we applied the lessons
of those experiences and experiments, which we have recounted
above, will appear in a study of the individual assignments. It must
suffice here to give some account of the ways in which we endeavored
to give an adequate presentation of each ecclesiastical Season as a
whole.

1   ADVENT

The name of this Season, the *Adventum Domini* (the "Coming of
the Lord"), was originally intended as a synonym of the Nativity—
Christmas Day is the day of Christ's "Advent" into human life at
the Incarnation. Sundays in Advent are primarily Sundays Before
the Nativity—which we have seen to be exactly what they were named
at the first.

But the Church also saw the Incarnation in the fulness of time as
a cosmic event, pivotal for all human history, and occurring against
the far majestic background of his dread future Coming at the con-
summation of all things. This secondary theme is not absent from the
liturgical lessons of any of the Advent Sundays; and it flowed backward, coloring the Sundays of the variable pre-Advent Season.

A certain measure of arbitrary judgment was necessary in arranging the Lessons in accord with these dual themes of this Season. It appeared to us that "Apocalyptic" teaching, beyond a certain point, is not very profitable. It was obviously an outright misconception on the part of the Apostolic Church that there was to be a *speedy* Coming of the Lord at the end of the world. Later apostolic reflection realized that the Lord *had* come with power at Pentecost; as for the end of the world, no man knows the times or the seasons. The illimitable majesty of the divine sovereignty; the grandeur of the divine plan; the inevitable certainty of death and judgment for each individual: such lessons are undoubtedly of practical value. But if the selections from apocalyptic material are continued over too great a tract of time, a preacher following them may readily come to the end of applicable themes. Then the danger, as is well-illustrated in the preaching of the premillenarian sects, is that all the grand imagery of the ultimate Eschatology may become little more than an escape from present reality.

An early Easter may bring into the Christian Year three pre-Advent Sundays, all distinctly colored by eschatological themes. Certainly seven weeks of this kind of matter would be quite disproportionate to its intrinsic importance in the scheme of the year. We decided to give full reign to Eschatology and Apocalyptic in that variable pre-Advent period—it would be of advantage to make all the relevant passages available in exceptional years—but to stop the systematic setting forth of such material with Advent Sunday. It is inherently more suitable in any case to the end rather than the beginning of the ecclesiastical year.

Besides, the Reformation saw a small but important shifting of the center of gravity of the Advent Season. Though the Epistle and Gospel for Advent 2 are emphatically apocalyptic, the First Prayer Book seized upon a significant text in the Epistle referring to the Holy Scriptures as the theme for a new Collect, which has stamped the Sunday for the entire Protestant world as "Bible Sunday." The effect of this Collect, with its note of the fulfilment of all Christian hopes in the Saviour, has been to extinguish any stress on the Second Advent on this Sunday, and to join it to Advent 3 and 4, which are dominated by the figure of St. John Baptist the Precursor, in an increasingly emphatic Expectation of the Nativity.

It was for these reasons that we gave primary emphasis to the original meaning of the Advent Season by assigning as first choice at Morning Prayer that feature of the Lectionary of 1892 which we have already mentioned, the first and third chapters of St. Luke, which recount the Annunciation and the preparation for the Lord's birth and mission. The secondary themes of the Season have not been entirely suppressed, however, and may be found in due measure in the other alternative lessons, although not in as outright a form as in the pre-Advent Sundays.

2   CHRISTMAS

The First Sunday after Christmas is observed only three years out of every seven, being supplanted at other times by the four festivals following Christmas. A Second Sunday occurs four years out of seven, when the previous Christmas falls between Wednesday and Saturday inclusive. When these Sundays are celebrated, they give an opportunity for continuing the Lucan narrative begun on the Sundays in Advent, with the Nativity itself,[1] the Presentation in the Temple,[2] and the meeting with Simeon and Anna.

3   EPIPHANY

The Sundays following Epiphany were originally treated as "Common Sundays." The earliest list furnished Gospels for ten Sundays,

[1] This passage of course occurs as the Gospel for the early celebration, and the Lesson at Morning Prayer, on Christmas Day itself; yet there is no real substitute for it on the Sunday after.

[2] N. B.: When Christmas 2 occurs on January 5, the first morning lesson will be duplicated by the Gospel of the Purification falling on a Sunday four weeks later.

for use as required between the Epiphany Octave and what is now Mid-Lent—i.e., not only before the Pre-Lenten Season was established, but before Lent itself had been extended to its present dimensions. To some extent the Sundays After Epiphany are still Common Sundays, as their green color intimates.

Nevertheless, there is more real consistency in Epiphany-tide as a true Season than appears at first sight. The Epistles look irrelevant, with their short course from Romans 12-13 on the first four Sundays. The application of this seemingly diverse material in these chapters is not at once apparent. The unity of their diversity, and the clue to their consistent teaching, is found in the fact that the original Epistle for the Day of the Epiphany contained this keynote in Titus 2:11: "The grace of God that bringeth salvation hath appeared to all men, teaching us that, denying ungodliness and worldly lusts, we should live soberly, righteously, and godly in this present world."[3] It was in accordance with this that the series from Romans was selected, as applying in various ways the basic precept of Romans 12:2: "And be not conformed to this world: but be ye transformed by the renewing of your minds." Thus the Epistles for Epiphany 1-4 present a moral application of the Manifestation of our Lord in human life, in the same way as the moral meaning of the Resurrection is conveyed in the stirring text, "If ye then be risen with Christ, seek those things which are above."

The Gospels also, as reassigned in 1928 to remove the effects of certain confusions of 1549, are an intelligible series, carrying on the outline of our Lord's life begun in the Christmas Season, and expressing outstanding phases of the Epiphany idea in the form of Manifestations of the power of Christ's divinely enabled humanity.

The lessons chosen for these Sundays therefore variously reflect the moral teachings of the Epistles, and the Manifestations of the

[3] The Eastern Churches still use this Epistle on the Epiphany. The Western first adopted it for that purpose, but transferred it to an early celebration on Christmas, where we now find it, when the doublet festivals of the Nativity and the Epiphany were discriminated.

Incarnation. But it has also been increasingly in the mind of the Church that Epiphany-tide has a special message in the important matter of Christian Missions. In the Eastern Church, the Epiphany was originally the celebration of the Nativity; and it still remains there as a generalized Manifestation in human life. The West differentiated it to the commemoration of the Visit of the Magi; whence our subtitle to the Feast presents it very specifically as a Manifestation *to the Gentiles*. This is not an accidental catch-word. The religion of the Incarnation in the nature of the case must be *missionary*, and continually and increasingly *manifested* to all men. Therefore, throughout this tract we have consistently "seeded," in such places as they were appropriate, lessons on the great theme of Missions.

4 Pre-Lent

We have seen that when, in the sixth century, both East and West adopted the three Sundays before Lent as an introduction to the Great Fast, it was by way of reminiscence of former extreme extensions of the Lenten Season.[4] There is an obvious practical value in this "penumbra of Lent," which is not itself a season of fasting or penitence, but which, possessing traditionally the reduced solemnities of omitted *Gloria in Excelsis, Te Deum,* and *Alleluia,* acts as an interlude modulating from a major to a minor key. The First Sunday in Lent may fall as early as the fifth Sunday after the Epiphany: if there were no modulation, the transition from a joyful to a penitential Season would be altogether too harsh.

In the West, however, two other influences color these Sundays. One is that there are traces of a still earlier usage having nothing to do with Lent. Septuagesima was originally determined by the Vernal

---

[4] Thus Ætheria speaks of a Lent of eight weeks at Jerusalem, which is confirmed by Durandus when he says the Greeks began it at Sexagesima. The latter also asserts that monks commenced the fast at Septuagesima.

Equinox, and counted as the first Sunday in the year.[5] We therefore find the Gospels for Septuagesima and Sexagesima reflecting respectively the spring preparation of the vineyards and the sowing of seed in the fields.

The other factor arose out of the invasion of Italy by the Lombards in 568. This incursion caused the gravest fears at Rome; and Pope John III appointed the four Sundays from Septuagesima to Lent 1 as a cycle of special intercession, with solemn Stations at the churches of the four traditional Patron Saints of the City in inverse order of the rank of the Churches, visiting successively the two extramural churches of St. Lawrence and St. Paul, St. Peter's, and finally St. John Lateran, the then papal Cathedral.

The Collects for the first two Sundays reflect the impending peril, which indeed endured so many years that these services became fixed as permanent features of the Roman Year. The Epistles for the three Pre-Lenten Sundays form a unit. They are all taken from the Letters of St. Paul; and they present in turn the figure of the Christian Soldier, the Christian's undefeated conflict with overwhelming adversities, and the final triumph of Christian charity.

The liturgical Scriptures of this Season therefore comprise intimations of a two-fold spiritual call: to arms and to labor. The topical method carries these interpretations into the lessons. In this way, Pre-Lent affords a further integration of the moral applications of the Incarnation which have been found in Epiphany-tide, throws an increased emphasis on religion as being dynamic, not escapist, and presents salvation as wrought in us, rather than for us. As an introduction to the great Penitential Season, it strikes the key of a Lent which shall not be merely a spiritual "Retreat" (too often conceived as literally a *retreat from reality*), but a positive self-discipline in active and effectual conflict with the soul's inveterate enemies, the World, the Flesh, and the Devil.

[5] The extension of the Lenten Season has now pushed Septuagesima back to late winter, falling between January 18 and February 21.

5 Lent

The Season of Lent did not originate as a Fast, but as a final period of intensive preparations for the solemn Baptisms on Easter Eve. Its duration of six weeks seems to be a natural figure, grounded in the peculiarities of the human disposition. It is still a favorite, and judicious, term for final instructions for Confirmation, since experience shows that less time will hardly cover the necessary ground, yet it is difficult to hold a heterogeneous group of people unanimously together over a longer period.

The Fast was a later and gradual development, extending progressively backward from Easter. In the time of Irenæus it occupied forty hours, on Good Friday and Easter Even. Then the commemoration of the Passion was spread over all of Holy Week; then expanded to a fortnight (a fact of which the name of Passion Sunday is a reminiscence); then to three weeks, back to what is now Mid-Lent.[6] Then it was protracted to the whole period, and even, as we have seen, beyond it: only to have the Church find again that six weeks' duration was enough for a time of concentrated attention. The actual number of fasting-days, in East and West, was thirty-six: interpreted as man's offering a tithe of the days of the year to God. The identification of this period with our Lord's Fast of Forty Days in the Wilderness was an afterthought; and the adjustment of the four extra days beginning with Ash Wednesday to give that precise figure dates from the time of Gregory the Great.

The effect of this rather spasmodic extension upon the character of the Season has been rather unfortunate. No Season of the year carries a greater devotional and practical importance, yet no Season is more lacking in a unified plan. Passion Sunday alone is both truly unified and suited to its place in the series. The Epistle and Gospel for Palm Sunday have a perfect liturgical harmony—but they repre-

[6] The relaxation of the strict Fast on the Eve of Lent 4, which the French celebrate as *Mi-Carême*, is a reminiscence of the time when this occasion was *Carnival*.

sent only the latter part of the original provision for this Sunday, which formerly ushered in Holy Week with the historical narrative of the Triumphal Entry at the preliminary Blessing of the Palms, which the Reformation removed from our service; and the lections which remain belong to the plan of the following week, which recites the Passion according to the Four Gospels successively: so that our service would be more appropriate to Good Friday than to this Sunday which saw our Lord's Last Entry into Jerusalem. Lent 4, which once began the Season, gives for its Gospel the Feeding of the Five Thousand: originally intended to serve as an allegory of the Eucharist, and as such, quite suited to open a season of spiritual refreshment, though the pertinence is completely obscure to the modern mind; but it got its Epistle from the circumstance that the papal service was held, again not inappropriately, at the Church of Holy-Cross-at-Jerusalem: and the beautiful local allusion to "Jerusalem which is above" is hardly compensation for the arid Rabbinical argument of its context. Lent 3 is derived from the preparations for the Baptism of the Neophytes: its Epistle refers to their instruction, and its Gospel to their exorcism from the Powers of Evil. Even in Lent 1 and 2, where there was a real attempt to secure Scriptures proper to their occasions, Epistle and Gospel follow entirely diverging lines.

The salient themes of the liturgical Scriptures are all important and applicable to the Season; but they are uncommonly difficult to correlate either into a single message on a given Sunday or a consistent course for the whole period. Certainly no Season has a greater requirement for a system of alternative lessons to cover its manifold implications. After a number of tentatives, we concluded that the best we could do with the pattern now before us was to exploit the two separate lines of the Epistles and Gospels for the first four Sundays: Fasting, and Temptation; the forsaking of Carnal Sins, and the Prayer of Faith; Christian Nurture, and the Renunciation of Evil; the Liberation of the Spirit, and the Food of the Soul. Then Passion Sunday is integrated with the mutually inclusive themes of the Priesthood and Sacrifice of Christ; and Palm Sunday may be treated either for the Triumphal Entry, or the Passion itself.

For the first three Sundays in Lent, these lessons have been so allocated that anyone following the same first or second choice both morning and evening will cover both themes completely; though on Mid-Lent, the Eucharistic discourse of St. John is divided into mutually supplementary portions at the first choice both morning and evening—the other suggestions of the day being distinctly subordinate are relegated to the second position. Likewise, anyone following down the same choice for the first five Sundays will find a consistent course for the season, which a little ingenuity can correlate into a certain sort of unity.

At all events, we did the best we could with the material available; and do not see how we could improve the plan without altering the Liturgical Lections, which, of course, we had no authority to touch.

6   EASTER TO TRINITY

The time from Easter to Whitsunday was called "The Pentecost" in the early Church. It was an unbroken season of rejoicing, celebrating alike the Risen Life, and the expectation of the Coming of the Spirit. This is the reason why the Gospels from Easter 3 through Ascension 1 are such strong anticipations of Whitsunday that an expository preacher taking them in turn must exercise some care not to arrive at that Festival with nothing further to say on that subject. This also may account for the most ancient custom of reading the Book of Acts at Easter-tide; its narrative is almost wholly of events which happened after Pentecost.

Later, the Forty Days of the Risen Life were explicitly set off by the Ascension Day; and a somewhat unintelligent Gallican influence brought in the Rogation Days as a sort of three-day Lent before the Ascension, and likewise even effected the practice of fasting on the

Ember Days within the Whitsunday Octave itself. It is well that the American Church has reclassified the Rogation Days as merely "Days of Solemn Supplication"—not necessarily fasting; and the requirement ought to be removed likewise from the Whitsuntide Ember Days.

In the treatment of the Sundays after Easter, we confined the events of the Day of the Resurrection to Easter and to Low Sunday, following the lead of the Gospels for those days. The original system of liturgical lessons covered the Resurrection Appearances completely during the Octave; our dropping of proper Eucharists for the weekdays after Easter Tuesday has left the liturgical provisions incomplete, and it is fortunate that we are able to supplement them by the lessons.

We thought best not to follow the Gospels for the remaining Sundays by assigning lessons containing further anticipations of Whitsunday, but instead to carry out consistently throughout the Season the Easter theme of Resurrection to Eternal Life. Too often Easter is dropped from consideration as soon as its Octave is over. It seemed well to underscore the fact that the Sundays After Easter are not like those after Epiphany or Trinity, essentially Common Sundays, but like those in Advent and Lent, intrinsically *of* the Season.

Thus while Easter 2 and 5 have subordinate themes, of the "Good Shepherd" and of the Rogations for the future harvests of the year, respectively, and while appropriate lessons have been provided for these themes, nevertheless the primary Easter message has not been pretermitted on those days, but finds expression in other lessons at each service.

It may be noted that Easter-tide offered great difficulties in the matter of First Lessons, and still more in the Psalms, since belief in immortality was not universal among the Jews, and at best was vestigial and undeveloped before the time of our Lord. The Apocrypha is invaluable here. Our choice of First Lessons and Psalms seems to be

the best available: though much of it is more acceptable for its rejoicing note than for any contribution of thought; and many of the
lessons would be as appropriate on Christmas or any other great day.

The Sunday after Ascension we did not wish to treat as a mere
"Expectation Sunday," proclitic to Pentecost. Unhappily under modern conditions only a small fraction of any congregation can attend
service on the festival, which of course far outranks the following
Sunday in ecclesiastical dignity. If they do, they are not likely to hear
a sermon. The exaltation of Christ the King; the entering of our
great High Priest within the veil; the return of our Lord in our flesh
to the Heavenly Fatherland: these meanings of the Ascension are so
important that we found the normal provision of two sets of lessons
at each service inadequate to express all the meanings of this somewhat neglected festival; and we anticipated our treatment of Trinity-
tide by providing this Sunday with three.

Our treatment of Whitsunday will be obvious: except perhaps for
the Second Lesson at the second choice at Evening Prayer. There the
expression, "The words that I speak unto you" (a Hebraism for "the
things whereof I speak") "they are spirit and they are life," is offered
as a text for the consideration of the work of the Holy Spirit *in the
Sacraments.*

Trinity Sunday arose as a reinterpretation of a "liturgical harmony" discovered between an Epistle intended for an "All Saints'
Sunday,"[7] and a Gospel appointed for the Octave of Pentecost and
reflecting the year's second great occasion of solemn Baptisms. As
these passages were not deliberately selected to set forth the Church's
faith in the Triune God, they are not perfectly adapted to that purpose. Here again the Lectionary can supplement the liturgical selections, and this has been done with Lessons explicitly mentioning
Father, Son, and Holy Ghost, or, in the case of the exordium of St.
John's Gospel, giving the cosmic background of God's Eternal

---

[7] The Eastern Churches still commemorate All Saints' on the Octave of Pentecost; a
use which prevailed for a time in the West.

Being, as correlative to the narrative of Creation on this Sunday, which begins the grand course of Hebrew History.

7 TRINITY-TIDE

The Sundays after Trinity are devoted to the practical applications of religion to life. They are governed by no predetermined plan to develop the doctrine of the Church or the narrative of the Life of our Lord in logical order. They are essentially "Common Sundays," which could quite as well have been arranged in any other order. They are simply what Bishop Frere called them, the "Summer Sundays."[8]

Nevertheless, we should cleave to the Anglican tradition of naming them the Sundays "After Trinity." This designation has always distinguished Northern Europe, the region which gave birth to the Festival of the Holy Trinity, and which has always preserved the oldest pattern for the Sundays, as against the Italian-dominated South, which was very late in adopting the Festival, and has maladroitly and only very incompletely accepted the framework of the Sundays. Not only the Lutherans, but also the Dominican and Carmelite orders, adhere to the North-European reckoning "After Trinity." There is no historical ground, there is certainly no theological ground, for preferring the nomenclature "After Pentecost." It seems rather a pity that the Federal Council of Churches, in its first moves toward recognizing the Christian Year, should have elected to desert the lead of the two great Protestant communions which have always retained the Christian Year, in favor of the appellation employed by Rome.

The allocations of the liturgical Scriptures in this tract are only on the most general principles. The Gospels for all Sundays except Trinity 21 are from the Synoptics. That is nearly all that can be said about them. We know the reasons for the assignment of only four

[8] *Studies in Early Roman Liturgy* (Alcuin Club Coll. XXX, Oxford 1934), 235.

of them. That for Trinity 5 was appointed at Rome for the Sunday before St. Peter's Day; and Advent -1 may have been influenced by the following St. Andrew's. Trinity 4 and 18 are former assignments for the Ember Sundays in June and September. Any clues which ever existed for any other Sundays have now been utterly lost.

The Epistles fall into three groups. Trinity 4 and 18 again are Ember Sundays, now no longer in connection with their weeks, and in any case with a somewhat remote application of their subjects to the times of ordination.

Trinity 1-3 and 5 are those appointed in the earliest extant Epistle Lectionary for Easter 7-10. Like the rest of this list in Easter-tide, they are from the Catholic Epistles. This continuation of the Easter series into Trinity-tide helps to bind the Seasons together. These Epistles have a certain warmth and urgency which serves to initiate this "practical" portion of the year with something of the power of the moral applications of the Risen Life which glorifies the Easter Season.

The rest of the Epistles form a series of excerpts from the Epistles of St. Paul in exactly the order in which the passages occur in the Bible. Yet we have seen that they are simply a list of selections, so spaced as to have little continuity of teaching. Perhaps, as Dr. Easton suggests, they may not even be the best possible selections;[9] yet we find them very fairly comprehensive and representative, a strong setting forth of the salient teachings of the great Apostle.

The problems of apportioning lessons to this part of the year have been sufficiently discussed in the preceding chapter. Here it may suffice, for convenience, to summarize our method.

The first two sets under each Sunday service treat outstanding suggestions of the Epistle and Gospel in a topical manner. The second option under Evening Prayer in all cases repeats or includes the Gospel of the Day.

The third choice at Morning Prayer offers a course of Hebrew History from the Creation to the Conquest of Canaan, accompanied

[9] *The Eternal Word* (Scribners 1937), 166.

by Second Lessons of New Testament correlatives. At Evening Prayer, this third alternative carries on the historical narrative from the time of Samuel to the Captivity; with a concurrent course summarizing the Book of the Acts of the Apostles.

8 FIVE EUCHARISTIC SUNDAYS

Interspersed among the foregoing Seasons, we found we had a separate problem with one group of Sundays, where the Liturgical Lectionary itself most conspicuously fails to meet the requirement which we found essential for our work in the Office Lectionary, namely that of avoiding the repetition of the same matter on different occasions. These comprise the "Miraculous Feedings" which so unhappily preöccupy no less than three Sundays of the year, Advent -1, Lent 4, and Trinity 7; together with the doublet of St. Luke's "Great Supper" on Trinity 2 and St. Matthew's "Marriage Feast" on Trinity 20. Dr. Easton made us the fertile suggestion that these five all actually belonged together in the mind of the early Church: moreover, that they supplied an answer to a puzzle of long standing.

It has always been a source of much surprise to newcomers to our fellowship to find that a Church which regards the Holy Communion as central to its worship apparently makes no allusion to that Sacrament in the Scriptures for the Christian Year. Neither the great discourse on the Eucharist in the Gospel according to St. John, nor St. Paul's account of the Institution and the meaning of the Sacrament, is read at the Liturgy on any Sunday. Moreover, neither passage appeared even in the Sunday Lessons in the Lectionaries of 1892 and 1928.

According to Dr. Easton, the reason for this apparent neglect in the Liturgical Lectionary is that the Church recognized (quite correctly) that the Miraculous Feedings were cultus-meals, and prototypes of the Agape-Eucharist; and likewise interpreted the Great Supper and the Marriage Feast as allegories of the Lord's Supper.

The primitive devotional and homiletical habit of mind preferred the concrete pictures presented by these mystical types to the far more direct expositions of St. John and St. Paul. Thus so far from the Holy Eucharist's not being represented in the liturgical Scriptures for the Sundays, the original intent of the Church was that it should occupy a tithe of the year!

With this understanding, the way was open for us to illustrate and supplement the intimations of the Liturgical Lectionary most effectively for the somewhat different modern mind. The Institution of the Eucharist appears on Advent -1; on Mid-Lent, the gift of Manna, and Isaiah's mention of food and drink "without money and without price," accompany St. John's Eucharistic Discourse in two supplemental sections; and on Trinity 7 we give a Lesson from the intimate utterances of our Lord to his Disciples at the last *Agape* according to St. John. This secured the use of the most salient passages, and seemed to us to be enough. Trinity 2 and 20 received different treatment: the former by emphasizing the theme of Hospitality; the latter by a very strong pair of lessons underscoring the prophetic and Christian ideal of Marriage as such—another Sacrament which most certainly should have its place in the Sunday Lessons, and receive definite homiletical application at least once in every year.

9   RESULTS

In all these ways we endeavored to use the Liturgical Lectionary as a basis for the Sunday lessons, in order to draw out its own implications and applications as fully as possible, and also to supplement it where it needs it, so as to afford a completely rounded presentation of the Church's teaching on faith and conduct from the wellsprings of Holy Scripture.

In spite of a considerable shortening of lessons, the plan of multiple choices has enabled us to take in much more territory for the Sunday cycle, so as actually to surpass the scope of any previous method. Nearly every passage in the Bible suitable to edification is now to be found on some Sunday. Between the Liturgy and the Offices taken together, almost the whole corpus of the harmonized Gospels is thus included. Thus the treasures of Holy Scripture are really more thoroughly opened and comprehensively covered than in any former lectionary. And therewith there is less duplication of matter in the Sunday tables than in any plan since the making of lectionaries began in the seventh century.

The new General Rubrics have been enlisted to enhance these objectives, with their explicit provisions for free choice among plural alternatives, for exchanging morning and evening assignments at discretion, for substituting the Epistle or the Gospel of the Day for the Second Lesson at either service, and the like. These permissions will facilitate the freest possible utilization of what the cumulative work of the last nine years has endeavored to make the richest possible provision for the use of Holy Scripture as appointed for all the occasions of the Christian Year.

VI

THE LECTIONARY FOR WEEKDAYS

THE PURPOSE of the system of the courses of lessons for weekdays is still that which Cranmer attributed to the originators of the method of the Breviary: "For they so ordered the matter, that all the whole Bible (or the greatest part thereof) should be read over once in the year."

Cranmer's qualification is a necessary one. Every lectionary must have a certain amount of omissions. Even Cranmer found certain tracts an impossibility for public reading. He omitted a genealogical chapter from Genesis; nine chapters on the ordering of the Tabernacle from Exodus; twenty-four on the ceremonial law out of the twenty-seven chapters of Leviticus; nine on the levitical regulations from Numbers. He found Ezekiel so obscure that he prescribed only nine out of its forty-eight chapters; except for a few passages on Holy Days, he omitted the book of Revelation; and he completely passed over the books of Chronicles, Maccabees, and the Song of Solomon.

The bulk of the Old Testament is so great that if the daily lessons are to be shortened from Cranmer's whole chapters to such dimensions as we have found most desirable for Sunday use, still more must be omitted. But this can be done selectively, passing over obscurities, digressions, and nonessentials as they occur, so that the result is actually to improve the coherence and interest of an extended narrative, and to present the outstanding highlights of such books as Proverbs and Job without the tedium of interminable commonplaces. This method also rescues tracts which Cranmer found unusable by entire chapters; thus we have derived twenty-seven readable lessons out of eighteen chapters of Ezekiel.

With the structure of the Christian Year as a basic pattern, it is no longer necessary or desirable to take the books of the Bible mechanically in their scriptural order. At Dr. Easton's suggestion, we also rejected the plan of the English Lectionary of 1922, of arranging the books of the New Testament in the order in which critics of the present day believe that they were written. Such a plan has no particular value to anyone except a professed scholar; and it is probable that the lectionary would have to be revised every few years, as the critics proceed to a different conclusion. Instead of either of these, trial and error convinced us that the most practicable and valuable plan was to assign the various books to those Seasons whose length they fit, and to whose tone their general character is most appropriate. Sometimes one of these factors is dominant, sometimes the other.

The longest continuity for which we had to provide is the grand review of Hebrew History. As in the case of the Sundays, it is too long to go in a single series, and must be divided. Just where, depends on when it begins.

We have seen that in the fourth century Genesis was begun in the spring, then counted the beginning of the year. The Breviary fixed this at Septuagesima, and the Church of England still retains this, at both Sundays and weekdays. Cranmer selected January 2; the American 1928, the first week in Advent. This however is not desirable; the weeks after Advent 4 and before Epiphany 1, and from Epiphany 2 to 6, are of uncertain occurrence, and the resulting erratic omissions from the course are not tolerable. We found we were on sure ground if we reverted, with England and Scotland, to Septuagesima for the daily series. At Morning Prayer, this course runs without omission caused by the variability of the Christian Year,[1]

---

[1] From Palm Sunday to Low Sunday, and Rogation Sunday to Trinity, this and most other courses are suspended in favor of a short tract of topical lessons appropriate to the obvious requirements of Ferial Days supporting contained or adjacent Festivals. In part this method is used also in the transitional weeks before Christmas and after Epiphany.

through the week of Trinity 23, taking the story from the Creation to the Exile, with a final summary on the Fall of Jerusalem from Jeremiah 35-37 in the week of Trinity 24. A late Easter, however, may curtail the end of this course at any point after Trinity 21.

Then a second series of historical readings, comprising the Return from Exile, and some of the literature of that period, is begun at Evening Prayer after Trinity Sunday. First come Ezra, Haggai, Zechariah, and Nehemiah, in passages arranged to give the actual order of events in a straightforward and intelligible way. Then follow four chapters only of I Maccabees: this narrative is very voluminous and largely given over to the account of military operations of little present interest or religious tone and content, so that a portion of this is sufficient. Then come Daniel, Esther, Micah, Nahum, Habakkuk, and Zephaniah. The balance of the year until Advent Sunday is filled up with the "Writings"—Ecclesiasticus, Job, Ecclesiastes, Deuteronomy, and Wisdom—as was the custom of the Breviary.

Cranmer followed the Breviary in reading the whole book of Isaiah in Advent. This is excessive in quantity, and undesirable in quality, since the book is not a unity in either author or subject. We also begin the book in Advent, reading the basic section of chapters 1-12, together with other messianic and apocalyptic passages particularly appropriate to the twofold theme of this Season. Some further apocalyptic matter is assigned to the week of Epiphany 5. The great passages of the Return from Exile, taken from chapters 40-55, are read in the four weeks after Easter. Between Christmas and Epiphany we place the conclusion of the book, chapters 56-66, with their picture of the restored Jerusalem and its forecast of a universal religion.

We follow the tradition of the Breviary again in taking Jeremiah in Lent, and Lamentations in Holy Week.

The variable season after the Epiphany contains from one to six weeks. We cannot put anything there which cannot be interrupted or omitted without serious loss. This appeared to be a good place for Proverbs. This book contains much valuable matter, but in a form which is both concentrated and disconnected. It has no continuity to be broken if interrupted at any point. Moreover, lacking plan and movement, it makes somewhat fatiguing reading, even in carefully selected excerpts; so that it is actually not desirable that it be imposed entire *every* year.

The same thing applies to the book of Ezekiel, which is very mystical and obscure. Some ingenuity enabled us, as we have said, to derive four weeks of lessons from this book which are worthy to be read on occasion; but, as with the book of Proverbs, perhaps not *every* occasion. As to its subject, it is quite appropriate to the Epiphany season, presenting numerous theophanies and strife-torn visions of a universal religion.

The last two weeks after Epiphany belong to the so-called "Wandering Sundays," which are used both here and as an introduction to the season of Advent; as we have seen, they have an apocalyptic coloring which is suitable to either place in the year. Their Sundays are identical in either place; there is no particular reason why their weekdays have to be.

Thus Proverbs is allowed to run through the week of Epiphany 5; but its place is taken by Obadiah and Malachi in the third week before Advent. On the other hand Deuteronomy is continued up to Advent -2, although as we have said, apocalyptic passages from Isaiah occupy the week of Epiphany 5. On the mornings of Epiphany 6 and Advent -2 alike selections from Lamentations are used. In the evenings, we placed the first half of the book of Wisdom, the second half occurring in the week before Advent, so that the book is read continuously whenever this week "wanders" into that position; which is just three times as often as it does not.

Turning to the New Testament, the chief problem here is the Gospels, which are exceptionally long books. St. Luke, followed immediately by St. Matthew, one read at Morning and one at Evening Prayer, between them fill up the Trinity season completely.

If Trinity-tide is cut short by a late Easter, the latter portions of St. Matthew may be omitted that year; but if so, the Passion of our Lord will have been covered entirely by other Gospels earlier in the year.

St. Mark, the first of the Synoptic Gospels to be written, and St. John, which contains the last gleanings of the subapostolic age on the facts of our Lord's biography, and a profoundly considered interpretation of the exalted spiritual meaning of His person and mission, have been rather ingeniously interwoven in the earlier half of the year, so as to supplement each other almost like a Harmony. St. Mark is begun in the three sure weeks after Advent Sunday at Morning Prayer, and St. John at Epiphany 1 at Evening Prayer. St. Mark is continued from Septuagesima to Ash Wednesday, followed by St. John until Lent 3. This is succeeded by two weeks from St. Mark again, ending with chapter 13. The book is not completed; but the biographical narrative is picked up at the precise chronological point by St. John. The events and discourses of the Passion according to St. John then fall naturally in the mornings of Holy Week, dovetailed, so as to avoid repetitions, with the liturgical Gospels which are taken from this book; and the concluding story of the Risen Life follows in the evenings of Easter Week.

In addition, the first chapter of St. Luke is also assigned to the days between Advent 4 and Christmas, for the same reasons which apportioned it to the Sundays in Advent.

Matter from the rest of the New Testament is allotted according to considerations of length and appropriateness. Thus, I John is read between Christmas and Epiphany, as a magnificent pæan of the love of God shown in the Incarnation of his Son. In the same period we put the first six chapters of the Hebrews, amplifying the reflections on the meaning of the Incarnation so grandly initiated by the liturgical Epistle from the exordium of this book on Christmas Day.

Hebrews, however, is given entire at Morning Prayer between Easter 1 and 5, as a comprehensive summary of the whole meaning of the Atonement wrought by our Lord's life and death. Here also, at Evening Prayer we set Ephesians and I Peter, both of which eloquently set forth the implications of the Easter message: "If ye then be risen with Christ, seek those things which are above."

Ephesians, followed by Philippians and Colossians, is also read at Morning Prayer in Epiphany-tide: a setting which emphasizes the interpretation of all three as the Manifestation of Christ through his Church.

Likewise, I Peter may be read again, being assigned to the weeks of the "Wandering Sundays." When these occur as pre-Advent, I Peter makes a natural connection with II Peter, which, because of its apocalyptic content, is placed in the week before Advent. For the same reason of apocalyptic tone, I and II Thessalonians and Jude are appointed for the weeks of the "Wandering Sundays."

The English Lectionary of 1872 and our Prayer Book of 1892 recognized that the eschatology of the book of Revelation was very congruous with the season of Advent, and inserted it in both Morning and Evening Prayer in the month of December. The edifying sections of this book are slightly too much to go under one service during Advent; and we therefore begin it at Evening Prayer the week before. It looks slightly peculiar in a table to have a book lap over the official beginning of the Church Year, but it works unexceptionally in practice, since, as we have seen, the five weeks before Christmas are actually a liturgical unit. Six selected passages from the Revelation, reciting the glories of the Heavenly City, are also assigned topically to the week of Ascension 1.

The two weeks and a half of Pre-Lent, from Septuagesima to Ash Wednesday, have a militant note dating from their institution at the time of the Lombard invasions of the sixth century, and liturgically are dominated by the valiant figure of St. Paul, salient passages from his Epistles occupying the three Sundays. Although the course-reading of Genesis and St. Mark's Gospel has been permitted to continue during this period at Morning Prayer, at Evening Prayer matter immediately appropriate to the season has been selected, giving

Amos and Hosea as First Lessons, and St. Paul's Epistle to the Galatians for Second Lessons.

For the mornings of the days in Lent, the choice seems to lie between Romans and I Corinthians. These are the only two books of the New Testament capable of exactly filling the space with a single treatment of great themes sufficiently important to counterbalance the Gospel narratives assigned to the evenings. We tried Romans in this place one year, but it worked badly. The argument is too condensed and theological to be followed by ear on the part of the laity—and it is precisely in Lent that any appreciable number of lay people are at all likely to attend Morning Prayer on weekdays. I Corinthians is more attractive, if more unequal. There have had to be some few slight omissions of matters of only local and temporary importance. Even then, in parishes having only a couple of morning services a week, the officiant might do well in some cases to avail himself of the rubrical permission to use the selection for any other day in the same week. But as J. K. Mozley says, this book canvasses "great questions of belief and practice involving permanent issues, as to God's way of salvation in Christ, as to the relation of the Church with the world, as to the Eucharist, and spiritual inspiration, and the Resurrection" with "a remarkably developed Christian theology." Moreover, it is eminently human, and hence very interesting; it is searching, challenging, and destructive of spiritual complacency; and the power of its constructive inspirations carries us at last to those two supreme and unmatched climaxes of the great hymn on Christian Charity, and the marvelous sermon on Immortality.

While the Breviary and indeed a usage as old as St. Augustine read Acts in the Easter season, we believe that we have made a better provision for Easter-tide. The liturgical Epistle for Ascension Day begins the book of Acts; and we considered that the lessons would be in better accord with the Christian Year if we continued it from this point at Evening Prayer. Thus most of the history of the infant Church follows the Feast of Pentecost. The book continues until

Trinity 8, when it is followed by the Epistle to the Romans for four weeks.

At this point the reading of the Epistles in course is transferred to Morning Prayer, where the Gospel according to St. Luke has just been completed, in order to begin St. Matthew at Evening Prayer, for variety at the two services. The remainder of the Trinity season is given to the Epistles not already employed, in this order: II Corinthians, I and II Thessalonians, James; I and II Timothy, Titus, Philemon, II and III John, Colossians, and Philippians. James was inserted before the Pastorals to make sure it would not be omitted in any year. Philippians, Colossians, and I and II Thessalonians were included for the same reason—an early Easter, which would eliminate them from the Epiphany season, would insure that they would find a place here. The scriptural order of Philippians and Colossians was reversed to avoid duplicating the liturgical Epistle of the weeks to which they were assigned.

By these various means it was brought about that the substance of the New Testament is read intact, without serious omissions, in any year, regardless of the eccentric movements of Easter and the consequent variation in length of the particular Seasons. Titus, Philemon, and II and III John may be eliminated with the last nine dates of Easter; and the first part of St. John's Gospel may be abridged by a short Epiphany season. These seem to be the only casualties. On the other hand, Philippians and Colossians may be read twice with eight dates of Easter; I and II Thessalonians and I Peter with sixteen; and Ephesians with twenty-five.

We may also mention here that, in our study of the proper allocation of the books to the Seasons, we became aware of a contingency which never arose under the old calendar system: and that is that the framework of the fixed Holy Days shifts across the pattern of the movable Christian Year for a space of five weeks, in the tract from Septuagesima to Trinity 24; with a consequent possibility of collision of Proper Lessons for the dated days with passages read in course in the ecclesiastical weeks. A calendrical check of the material showed this interference would be a certainty in a few instances; and these we dealt with by providing an alternative Lesson for the Holy Day, with directions to use that substitute when the Day fell in specified weeks of the Christian Year.

In all these ways we have endeavored to present all the passages of Holy Scripture which are best adapted to public reading in a form harmonious with the Christian Seasons. The relative brevity of the individual selections alleviates a considerable burden on those whose duty it is to officiate daily in such places as cathedrals and colleges; and it is hoped that eventually it may have a favorable effect upon the size of the congregations at such services. The added clarity and interest which the selective method gives to the great narratives, and to formidable accumulations of prophetic and proverbial discourses, should prove an incentive to explore the *terra incognita* of many neglected tracts of Scripture.

In these matters we have constantly had in mind not only the requirements of the few American churches and chapels which maintain a daily service, but also the advisability of facilitating and extending the laudable custom of the clergy's following the daily offices throughout the year. This has always been required in England; it is not ordered by any American canon or rubric. But the value to any clergyman of the sort of comprehensive and intimate knowledge of the treasures of Holy Scripture which is the result of their constant perusal in his daily devotions is too obvious to be gainsaid. The custom is certainly increasing; and we hope that our work will further encourage it.

Likewise, we believe that this Lectionary is a most usable guide to the private reading of Scripture on the part of the laity; and we trust that the clergy will not neglect to advocate this means to perfect a devout and instructed Church.

VII

THE USE OF THE PSALTER

1 THE HYMNAL OF THE MOTHER CHURCH

THE PSALTER is the great collection of the religious lyrics of the Hebrew people. It is the expression of a nation which had a racial genius for religion; which first among mankind won its way to a fundamentally ethical and unswervingly monotheistic faith. The best of it is religious poetry which has never been surpassed, and which will never grow old, but will remain as an ever fresh fount of devotional inspiration as long as the world endures.

Fortunately for its destined universal use, the form of this poetry was rhythmical, but not metrical. The form-restrictions of any set metre would have greatly circumscribed its translation into all the languages of the world. Free verse has no such limitations. The Psalms' constant use of a telling antithesis imparts a vigorous rhythm in any language; their varied cadences, where thoughts rhyme instead of words, lose none of their effect in translation.

It was also of great importance that Hebrew is an extraordinarily primitive and limited language, radically lacking in sophisticated and abstract words. For instance, you may look from one end of the Old Testament to the other without finding a mention of God's "omnipotence:"[1] instead, it speaks of his "mighty hand" and his "stretched-out arm." This want of philosophical words, which might have afforded a defective vocabulary for the concepts of theology, is the very stuff of poetry. The simplicity, directness, and concreteness which the limitations of the original tongue impose upon the Psalter, rank it automatically with those classical poems of the primitive state

[1] Even the word which we render "Almighty" is only "Mighty" in Hebrew.

of every language, which never lose their universal appeal. First in the field, they said some things once for all.

2   CHRISTIAN USE OF THE PSALTER

The Christian Church took over this collected Hebrew Hymn Book as the basis of its praises. This was not done quite so directly and instantaneously as seems to have been the case with the Old Testament Lesson, which from the very first was adopted into the Christian service from the use of the Synagogue. The Psalms do not seem to have been sung in the Synagogue; their Christian use therefore must reflect a memory of their employment in the ritual of the Temple, or possibly in private devotion. Our first actual record of their use is in the case of the Gradual Psalm between the Lessons of the Liturgy, in the fourth century; though this may well go considerably back of this time. On the other hand it is not probable that the Psalter was included in the Church's Common Prayers much, if at all, before these were set up as a definite system of stated Hours at this same period.

From the first, however, the language of the Psalter saturated the text of the Church's prayers. It was the chief source for the proper chants which multiplied in the Liturgy. It furnished the model for a host of ecclesiastical Canticles, of which our Prayer Book now retains only the *Gloria in Excelsis,* the *Te Deum,* and the Burial Anthem "Man that is born of woman," but which are more numerous in the Latin rite, and which received enormous expansion in the innumerable Canons and Odes of the Greek Hours of Prayer. In due course the systematic recitation of the Psalter became the chief constituent of the Western Hours. During the Middle Ages, a few hymns in modern metre found their way into the text of the Liturgy and the Hours, but without supplanting the use of the Psalter in the slightest. After the Reformation, metrical paraphrases of the Psalms were the first Protestant hymns—there are still sects which admit the use of no others;—and these paraphrases furnished the model for all later hymns.

3 THE PSALTER IN THE COMMON PRAYERS

At the time of the Reformation, the priests and monks recited the entire Psalter every week, with the Psalms taken in course at Matins and Vespers, and fixed Psalms occupying the other Hours. Such, at least, was the theory; though the course had been so broken into by the multiplied Saints' Days with their Proper Psalms, that Cranmer truly complained that "now of late time a few of them have been daily said (and oft repeated) and the rest utterly omitted."

As in the case of the Lectionary, Cranmer deserted the ecclesiastical reckoning in favor of the secular calendar. The whole Psalter was taken in strict sequence at Morning and Evening Prayer alternately, during the thirty days of the calendar month. These resulting sixty portions contained an average of forty-two verses apiece, exactly three pages of the text of our Prayer Book. No doubt at the time this seemed a very moderate requirement, and a great relief from the burden of the Breviary Offices, as this was only two-thirds the average length of the Psalms at Vespers, and actually only *one sixth* of the appalling series of Psalms at Matins—eighteen pages of them—which set the poor old monks hunkering down on the half-support of their "misericord" seats which took the weight off their feet while they were apparently standing up! The Roman Church waited until 1911 to cut the Psalter at Matins to half its former length (it is still nine of our pages!), and by abolishing Fixed Psalms to even up all other Hours to an average of only half a page longer than Cranmer's portions.

There were some grave disadvantages in Cranmer's new simplicity. There was no principle of appropriateness whatever. Distinctive morning psalms fell in the portions appointed for Evening Prayer, and evening psalms in the morning: every one of the old Compline

Psalms, designed for the hour of retiring, was set for morning use. The Christian Year was all but completely ignored: Proper Psalms were appointed for four festivals only in 1552; 1549 had none. The most incongruous psalms might or must be used on the most inappropriate occasions.

Inevitably subsequent Prayer Books multiplied Proper Psalms for special days increasingly, until our book of 1928 contained twenty-two such assignments, some of them to be used on whole Seasons, or as Commons for all Saints' Days. Moreover, the American books from the first offered a number of Selections of Psalms, which might be substituted *ad libitum* whenever the portion appointed for the day of the month proved impossible by reason of length or incongruity of theme. Our last Prayer Book further allowed the use of "one or more" of the Psalms for a festival, or on other occasions from those for the day of the month, or from the Selections; and also permitted the use of "a section or sections" of psalms which the text of the Psalter divided for that purpose by a blank line, as in the case of some very long psalms, or some containing unreadable passages.

All of this really marked the breakdown and bankruptcy of the ideal of a monthly reading of the entire Psalter. Except for those clergy who conscientiously recited the daily Offices, nothing but a shell of the scheme was left in the Church. For the Sundays, it was all but meaningless. Hence, it was most logical that the latest British and American Prayer Books made a move in the right direction by offering an optional Table of Psalms for the Sundays of the Church Year. No form of this Table was really particularly good, although the British books had later revisions of the original proposal of the Convocation of Canterbury than that which had been adopted, with little or no examination, in our Prayer Book.[2] From Advent to

---

[2] For example the English does not commit the error of the American in preöccupying five Sunday evenings in Lent with the interminable "mark-time march" of the 119th Psalm, with its endless iterations and total lack of plan and movement, which can only be considered a blight on evening congregations which are probably larger then than at any other time in the year.

Trinity, Psalms were chosen topically with some sort of general appropriateness to their Season; after Trinity they were read serially in numerical order. The selections were somewhat shortened, to an average of thirty-four verses at Evening Prayer and twenty-four (out of concession to the fixed *Venite*) at Morning Prayer.

4   THE PSALTER IN THE NEW LECTIONARY

It is perhaps a little remarkable that the editors of all the later Prayer Book Revisions did not at once grasp the real meaning of the foregoing facts. These facts establish beyond contradiction that the multiplication of Proper Psalms had vitiated the usefulness or even the practicability of Cranmer's method of reading the Psalms by the dates of the secular calendar, in exactly the same way as the multiplied Proper Lessons had dealt a death-blow to a lectionary on the same essential basis. The half-way measure of a new Table of Psalms proper to Sundays could only further impair anything that was left of such a plan. In fine, it was not only utterly illogical, it was unworkable, to conform the lessons to the Christian Year reckoning, without doing the same thing for the Psalter.

All of this seems perfectly clear in retrospect; but the painful fact is that these considerations did not occur to us any more than to those previous laborers in the vineyard whom we seem to criticize only to admit our own shortcomings. It was only in the last two years that we gave any attention whatever to the problem of the Psalter; and when we did so, it was not with any idea of the need of a complete reformation of the system, and of conforming the entire plan of reading the Psalter to the Christian Year. We were led into it step by step; and before we got out again, we had been in far deeper waters than we had ever contemplated.

We began with the Sunday Psalms, under an impression that we ought to be able to work out something which would fit our treatment of the Christian Year a little more precisely than that second-hand British table.[3] For the Sundays, we had two or three sets of alternative lessons at each service, carefully coördinated for unity of theme. We conceived that the best solution of the use of the Psalter here would be to select psalms which in turn would harmonize with these pairs.

This proved to be an unexpectedly difficult task, because—formally at least—it was an undertaking to find appropriate hymns for every occasion of the Christian Year in a Catholic Church out of a Unitarian Hymnal. It was made possible by the fact that as poetry, the Psalter is emotional rather than intellectual in its method of expression, it is intuitive and suggestive, and in fine the religion of the heart of man is often more comprehensive than the theology of his head. There is besides a really prophetic element in the Psalter; it voices longings and aspirations which were to find their fulfilment only in the Christian Gospel. Hence this task was capable of being satisfactorily accomplished, at least on a basis of selections of a becoming tone and mood, even if not always of a satisfactory theological statement: and after all, this is about all that is ordinarily to be expected of any hymn.

Then we turned our attention to the Holy Days, on the same basis. It seemed a pity to be always recurring to Psalms 1, 15, and 24 every time there was a Saint's Day. We might have rested content with some sort of "Common of Saints," if the Psalter had contained any adequate expression of what Christians mean by sanctity. But the Saint of the Old Testament is at the most a just man; he is not a divinely inspired, transformed, and enabled man. Many of the Apostles, indeed, are little more than names to us; some of them have nothing but "Commons" even in their liturgical lessons. But there was a real opportunity to align the psalms with the lessons in many cases, and to give a telling further application to such themes as St.

[3] The English, who begin Genesis on Septuagesima, logically place Creation Psalms on that Sunday; which was no reason for our doing so, since we read that narrative at Trinity.

Luke the Physician, the generosity of St. Barnabas, St. Matthew's renunciation of this world's goods, and St. Peter's shepherding of the sheep.

It was only after we had completed this really desirable undertaking that we awoke to the fact that we had simply destroyed the last remaining possibility of rehearsing the Psalter in the monthly cycle. Even the relatively few Proper Psalms in the present Prayer Book caused grave inconvenience in the monthly round, since such psalms might and did occur perhaps the very next day in their place in the Psalter. With our greatly multiplied Propers for every individual festival, this sort of clash would become simply intolerable. The only way out was to set up another system of reading the Psalms in rotation, which would not be subject to this kind of repetition at close intervals.

We therefore drew up a standard list of portions of psalms in order, to be assigned to the pattern of the Christian Year in recurring cycles of from four to seven weeks in length; and then removed from each several cycle the particular psalms which might occur as Propers too close to its place in the course.

The list itself was flexible, and allowed the inclusion of marginal psalms of limited utility in such seasons as they were appropriate, and their exclusion when they were not. Eight psalms were omitted outright.[4] We knew, of course, that probably no two persons would ever agree precisely as to all inclusions or omissions. We had to make some practical compromises, to the best of our judgment. Some psalms were used in part, indicating omitted verses. We could have employed more of the Psalter if our text had bracketed offending verses, as has been done to some extent in the Scottish Prayer Book.

---

[4] Some such action is inevitable, since some of the Imprecatory Psalms voice a justifiable moral indignation in terms of such a primitive personal hatred and vengeance as totally unfit them for Christian use. In addition, Psalm 78 is entirely too long to ask of any congregation; nor can it be successfully divided. It is of course quite open to anyone to read it on the fifteenth day of the month; and similarly with any other omissions.

Psalm 55, for instance, contains some beautiful passages, yet is all but unusable as it stands, and it appears only twice in the year.

The omission of the Proper Psalms from their place in the courses was a somewhat intricate problem. It would be extremely easy to arrange in a merely annual calendar—far more difficult in any system designed to be perpetual, and applicable to any years. As the Fixed Feasts stand fast, while three-fourths of the weeks of the Christian Year move up and down with the five-week swing of Easter, the most we felt able to do was to "blank" the incidence of a Proper Psalm for an additional week on either side of the extreme occurrence of its feast in the pattern of the Movables. Even that inhibited it from use in course for seven weeks. And as these Propers are on the whole outstanding psalms, the result would seem to be a certain impoverishment of the excellence of the courses. This impairment was increased when we took account of the Proper Psalms of the Sundays before and after each week. Eventually this difficulty was surmounted by the happy thought of taking the desirable psalms which had been thus excluded from a cycle, and "spotting" them out of course, at Evening Prayer on Saturdays at points where they did not interfere: thus grading up the value of the cycle, and making an opportune provision for a sort of First Evensong of the Sundays.[5]

[5] Similarly, psalms of a penitential color falling within a given week have been appointed for the Friday, which the Church designates as a Fast Day throughout the year. —It will be noted that Psalm 95 is assigned to the Friday mornings in Lent, in order to give a regular and organic employment to the rubric on page 8, which specifies that this Psalm may be used in place of the *Venite*. The American *Venite* of course is composed of 95:1-7 and 96:9, 13, avoiding the penitential contents and discouraging ending on 95:8-11. The rubric of 1789-1892 indicated that Psalm 95 should be "used in the course of the Psalms, on the nineteenth day of the month," when naturally it would be followed by Psalm 96, to avoid reduplicating the two verses borrowed from the latter. The Prayer Book of 1928 allowed the substitution of Psalm 95 at any time: partly because few churches were following the course by days of the month; partly because one might wish to escape the repetition of the two verses when Psalm 96 occurred in the Table for Sunday; and partly, perhaps, because the Church of England always uses Psalm 95, and there are times, especially in penitential seasons, when the old ending has a superior force of its own. It is still good judgment to use 95 when 96 is to follow. But this will be more easily done, if 95 is to be regularly used for its own sake on the very appropriate occasion of the Friday mornings in Lent.

Each constituent of our Basic Table was studied for as close an approach as possible to a standard liturgical length, and likewise for some congruity of subject, in order to avoid the shocking reversals of theme and mood which appear in a mere serial rotation—even if that involved combining short psalms at some distance from each other in the text of the Psalter.

The overall average length of the portions, both Sundays and weekdays, is a little less than twenty verses; with a little "favoring" of the morning service because of the fixed *Venite* which is there used continuously with the Psalms. This average length is a page and a half; it is some six verses longer than the average of the lessons; and we believe it to be sufficient as an element of a balanced service. One chief reason for the common complaint of visitors as to the tedium of our service, and our excessive "calisthenics," is indubitably because of the inordinate length of standing during the reading of three pages from the Psalter! On the other hand, we did not venture to reduce this part of the service to the dimensions of the other Canticles, for the reason that this is the part where the people's contribution to the performance of public worship is most extensive. We had no wish to minimize or unreasonably curtail this laudable self-activity. On the contrary, we hoped to present it in such due proportion as to make the people's participation really significant, intelligent, and edifying.

Although this adaptation of the Psalter to the framework of the Christian Year was the last portion of our work to be undertaken, it is probable that more time was spent on it than on any other. The system was in continual use in two seminary chapels, with and without music. Three complete revisions of the scheme were put through in 1943 alone. The final result, as adopted by the General Convention, was a plan that had been most thoroughly tested, and by those tests had proved itself adequately responsive to the requirements of the Christian Year.

But however clearly we saw that the old methods had totally

broken down, and that no less radical a reconstruction could hope to survive in the use of the Psalter, together with the now-established new plan of the lessons, we were perfectly aware that we were proposing a complete innovation, which was bound to provoke resistance. Some of this opposition would be pure inertia and lack of understanding; some of it conscientious, on the part of clergy in the habit of saying their daily offices, who could not quite make themselves feel that they had done their whole duty if they did not cover the entire Psalter in the course of the month. We are perfectly confident that the new method will approve itself by the test of continued use. But we did not desire to coerce any man into using it, or to withdraw any reasonable liberties of choice previously enjoyed in the Church. Therefore, we were careful to preserve in a General Rubric the right to use the Psalter by the dates of the month; as well as to continue the permission to use "one or more" of the Psalms appointed on any occasion, *except* the Proper Psalms for a limited list of outstanding festivals. Those ought to be used entire as given.

We also greatly enlarged the Table of Selections of Psalms, in such manner as to give what amounts to a subject-index of the more important and edifying themes of the Psalter. Any of these are also available on any occasion, save the chief festivals named in the rubric.

VIII

THE THEMES OF THE SUNDAY CHOICES

THE FOLLOWING pages attempt to give a brief allusive key to the subjects of the several sets of alternative Psalms and Lessons available on each Sunday of the Christian Year. Sometimes an entry will be an abstract or summary; sometimes it will be a direct quotation embodying the essential point. As we found the latter method more effectual in identifying a passage in our work-tables, we have used it predominantly here. It has the further advantage of identifying unmistakably the common element of liturgical harmony.

For comparison, the liturgical Epistles and Gospels are included. They are printed in italics, and for considerations of space put on opposite pages. Otherwise, Morning Prayer appears on one page and Evening Prayer on the opposite page, as in the printed lectionary.

Most Lessons are keyed with a symbol before the number of the Psalms, to indicate their relation in the pattern of the day. E indicates that they were suggested by the liturgical Epistle; with E^1 and E^2 distinguishing sub-themes, as marked in the summary of the Epistle. G, G^1 and G^2 similarly refer to the Gospel. S is to show that the Lessons reënforce the general teaching of the Season or the occasion, instead of being derived from the liturgical Scriptures. C distinguishes the two Courses in Trinity-tide. In addition, E^a and G^a denote the Epistle and Gospel for the principal service on a Festival (Easter, Whitsunday); E^b and G^b those for an early service.

The notations, *Introd.* or *Cont.* E or G, signify that the preceding entry reënforces the liturgical Epistle or Gospel with further context in sequence with it, before or after. G *plus* shows the text of the Gospel, with additional context. Q points to the *quotation* of the First Lesson in the Second Lesson or the Gospel of the Day.

93

Key	Psalms	First Lesson	Second Lesson

FIRST SUNDAY IN ADVENT

Epistle: Rom. 13:8

Love is the fulfilling of the law. Time to awake; cast off the works of darkness, put on the armour of light. Fulfil not the lusts of the flesh.

Key	Psalms	First Lesson	Second Lesson
G	50	Mal. 3:1-6 & 4:4-6	Luke 1:5-25
	Out of Sion hath God appeared. God shall come with fire to judgment. Offer unto God thanksgiving, rather than sacrifices. To him that ordereth his way aright, will I show the salvation of God.	I will send my messenger, and he shall prepare the way before me. Who may abide the day of his coming? Shall purify the sons of Levi; acceptable sacrifice. Elijah sent before the Day of the Lord.	Annunciation of birth of St. John Baptist. He shall go before him in the spirit and power of Elias; to make ready a people prepared for the Lord.
E	46, 97	*Isa. 28:14-22	Heb. 12:14
	God is our strength. In the midst of Sion.—The Lord is King; fire before him. Sion heard and was glad. Hate the thing that is evil.	Covenant with death vs. Cornerstone in Zion. Consumption determined upon the whole earth.	Follow peace and holiness. Esau. Mount of Covenant vs. heavenly Zion. Our God is a consuming fire.

SECOND SUNDAY IN ADVENT

Epistle: Rom. 15:4-13

[1]*Whatsoever things written aforetime were for our learning.* [2]*Christ a Minister to confirm the promises to our forefathers, mercy to Gentiles. Root of Jesse.*

Key	Psalms	First Lesson	Second Lesson
E[2]	25	Isa. 52:1-10	Luke 1:26-56
	Teach me thy paths. Shall guide the meek in judgment. The secret of the Lord is among them that fear him; will show his covenant.	Awake, O Zion! How beautiful the feet of him that bringeth good tidings. The ends of the earth shall see the salvation of our God.	Annunciation of the birth of Christ; Visitation; Magnificat. (Throne of his father David; as promised to our forefathers.)
E[1]	119:1-16	*Isa. 55	II Tim. 3
	The Word and Law of God.	Come to the waters, Seek ye the Lord; he will abundantly pardon. My Word shall not return unto me void.	Perilous times in the last days. From a child thou hast known the Scriptures: given by inspiration of God.

| Key | Psalms | First Lesson | Second Lesson |

Gospel: Matt. 21:1-13

The Triumphal Entry of our Lord into Jerusalem. The Cleansing of the Temple.

E. G 48, 126

We wait for thy loving-kindness in the midst of thy temple. The bulwarks of Zion.—When the Lord turned again the captivity of Zion.

Isa. 62

Watchmen on the walls of Jerusalem. Behold, thy salvation cometh.

Matt. 25:1-13

The Parable of the Ten Virgins. Watch: for you know not the hour wherein the Son of man cometh.

E 18:1-20

The earth trembled; darkness; the brightness of his presence. Brought into a place of liberty.

Isa. 13:6-13

The day of the Lord cometh. The sun and the stars darkened. The day of his fierce anger.

I Thess. 5:1-11

Times and seasons of the end unknown. Children of light, not darkness. Time to watch. We shall live with him.

Gospel: Luke 21:25-33

The signs of the End. The Son of Man coming in a cloud. This generation shall not pass away. My word shall not pass away.

E^1, *G* 119:89-104

Thy Word endureth for ever in heaven.

Amos 3:1-8

The judgment of the Lord. The Lord revealed his secret unto his servants the prophets. The Lord hath spoken, who can but prophesy?

I Thess. 2:1-13

We were bold to speak the gospel of God. Ye received it not as the word of men, but as the word of God.

E^2 67, 111

Show us the light of thy countenance; that thy way may be known upon earth. —The fear of the Lord is the beginning of wisdom.

Isa. 11:1-10

The Rod of Jesse.

John 5:30-40

These things I say, that ye might be saved. The Father hath borne witness of me. Search the Scriptures: for they testify of me.

| Key | Psalms | First Lesson | Second Lesson |

THIRD SUNDAY IN ADVENT

Epistle: I Cor. 4:1-5
[1] *Ministers of Christ, and stewards of the mysteries of God.*
[2] *Judge nothing before the time, until the Lord come.*

G, E[1] 22:23 & 99
All the ends of the world shall remember themselves and be turned unto the Lord.—The Word given to Moses, Aaron, and Samuel.

Jer. 1:4-10, 17-19
Ordained a prophet to the nations before thy birth. I have put my words in thy mouth. Speak unto them boldly.

Luke 1:57
Birth of St. John Baptist. He shall be called the prophet of the Highest; and go before the Lord to prepare his ways.

G, E[2] 85, 107:1-16
Hast turned our captivity. Righteousness shall direct his going in the way.—Redeemed, gathered, delivered from the wilderness.

*Isa. 35
The wilderness shall rejoice. Strengthen the weak. Highway through the desert. The redeemed shall return.

I Thess. 5:12-23
Esteem those who labor among you. Warn, comfort, support, be patient. Preserved blameless unto the coming of the Lord.

FOURTH SUNDAY IN ADVENT

Epistle: Phil. 4:4-7
Rejoice! The Lord is at hand.

G 80
The Shepherd of Israel.

*Isa. 40:1-11
The voice of one crying in the wilderness. He shall feed his flock.

Luke 3:1-17
The voice of one crying in the wilderness. The preaching of John Baptist.

E, G 77, 110
Thou leddest thy people like sheep.—We are his people and the sheep of his pasture.

Jer. 33:7-16
Captivity shall return. The voice of joy. The Branch of David.

I Thess. 1
Gospel in much assurance. Turn from idols to serve the living God, and wait for his Son from heaven.

Key   *Psalms*   *First Lesson*   *Second Lesson*

THIRD SUNDAY IN ADVENT

Gospel: Matt. 11:2-11
The poor have the Gospel preached unto them. My messenger, to
prepare the way before thee.

G, E¹, S 132, 134
Let thy priests be clothed
with righteousness.—Lift
up your hands in the sanctuary, and praise the Lord.

Nahum 1:3-8, 15
Behold upon the moun-
tains the feet of him that
bringeth good tidings!

I Cor. 9:7-23
Woe is me, if I preach not
the Gospel!

G, E¹, S 30, 130
Thou hast turned my heaviness into joy.—My soul
doth wait for him.

Isa. 26:1-11
Open the gates, that the
righteous nation may enter
in.

Matt. 9:35—10:15
Laborers called to the har-
vest. The calling of the
Twelve.

FOURTH SUNDAY IN ADVENT

Gospel: John 1:19-28
The voice of one crying in the wilderness.

E   33
Rejoice in the Lord, ye
righteous. By the word of
the Lord were the heavens
made.

Isa. 40:12-18, 21-31
The majesty of the Creator.
They that wait upon the
Lord shall renew their
strength.

I Thess. 3:7
Stand fast in the Lord.
Shall perfect and establish
to the Coming of the Lord.

G   102:15 & 146
The nations shall fear thy
Name.—The Lord giveth
sight to the blind.

Isa. 42:1-16
A bruised reed shall he not
break. Light to the Gen-
tiles. To open the blind
eyes, etc.

Matt. 11:11-24
None greater than John.
Contrast with Christ. Un-
repentant cities.

Key	Psalms	First Lesson	Second Lesson

FIRST SUNDAY AFTER CHRISTMAS

Epistle: Gal. 4:1-7
In the fulness to time, God sent his Son. We are no more servants, but sons.

Key	Psalms	First Lesson	Second Lesson
G	145	*Isa. 9:2-7	Luke 2:1-20
	The Lord is loving unto every man, and his mercy is over all his works.	Unto us a child is born.	The Nativity, and the visit of the Shepherds.
E	98, 138	Isa. 49:8-13	Heb. 2
	His mercy and truth are toward the house of Israel. —The Lord hath respect unto the lowly.	Now is the acceptable time, now is the day of salvation.	A little lower than the angels. Children of God.

SECOND SUNDAY AFTER CHRISTMAS

Epistle: Isa. 61:1-3
He hath anointed me to preach good tidings.

Key	Psalms	First Lesson	Second Lesson
S	65, 121	*Micah 4:1-5 & 5:2-4	Luke 2:21-32
	God is praised in Sion.— My help cometh from the Lord.	Many nations shall come to God's House. From Bethlehem a ruler of Israel.	The Presentation in the Temple.
S	89:1-30	Isa. 44:1-8, 21-23	Col. 2:6-17
	The Seed of David. I will make him my firstborn.	I will pour my spirit upon thy seed. Ye are my witnesses. I have redeemed thee.	Walk in Christ. Rooted and built up in him. In him all the fulness of the Godhead bodily.

FIRST SUNDAY AFTER CHRISTMAS

Gospel: Matt. 1:18
Annunciation to Joseph. Birth of Christ. They called his Name Jesus.

E	68 or 27	Isa. 63:7-16	II Pet. 1:1-12

E 68 or 27
The Father of the father-less.—The Lord is my light. When my father and mother forsake me, the Lord taketh me up.

Isa. 63:7-16
The lovingkindness of the Lord. He bare them all the days of old. Thou art our Father.

II Pet. 1:1-12
Partakers of the divine nature. Add to your faith virtue. Make your calling and election sure.

G 8, 113
Out of the mouth of babes. —He humbleth himself to behold the things that are in the earth.

Job 28:12
The fear of the Lord is the beginning of wisdom.

Matt. 11:25
Revealed to babes. Come unto me, all ye that labour.

SECOND SUNDAY AFTER CHRISTMAS

Gospel: Matt. 2:19
The Flight into Egypt, and return to Nazareth.

E 111, 112
The fear of the Lord is the beginning of wisdom.— Blessed is the man that feareth the Lord.

Prov. 9:1-6, 10
The Seven pillars of Wisdom. The knowledge of the holy is understanding.

II Cor. 4:1-6
To give the knowledge of the glory of God in the face of Jesus Christ.

S 132
The Lord hath chosen him for our habitation.

Haggai 2:1-9
In this place will I give peace.

Luke 2:34-40
Simeon and Anna.

Key   Psalms   First Lesson   Second Lesson

FIRST SUNDAY AFTER EPIPHANY

Epistle: Rom. 12:1-5
Our bodies a living sacrifice. Not conformed, but transformed.
Members of one body.

Key	Psalms	First Lesson	Second Lesson
S	72, 97	Isa. 60:1-9	Matt. 2:1-12
All kings shall fall down before him.—There is sprung up a light for the righteous.		The Gentiles shall come to thy light, and kings to the brightness of thy rising.	The visit of the Magi.
G, E	92, 93	*Prov. 8:22-35	Col. 1:9
How glorious are thy works! Thy thoughts are very deep.—Thou art from everlasting.		The Coeternal Wisdom.	The image of the invisible God. The mystery revealed. The Head of the Church.

SECOND SUNDAY AFTER EPIPHANY

Epistle: Rom. 12:6-16a
Differing gifts. Be kindly affectioned with brotherly love.

Key	Psalms	First Lesson	Second Lesson
E, S	118	*Zech. 8:1-8, 20-23	I Cor. 12:12-31a
This is the gate of the Lord: the righteous shall enter into it.		Many nations shall come. We will go with you, for we have heard that God is with you.	Spiritual gifts. The Body and the Members. Baptized into one Body.
G	29, 99	Exod. 34:29	Mark 9:2-13
The voice of the Lord.— He spake unto them from the cloudy pillar.		Moses' face shines.	The Transfiguration.

Key	Psalms	First Lesson	Second Lesson

FIRST SUNDAY AFTER EPIPHANY

Gospel: Luke 2:41
Christ among the Doctors.

G 84, 122
How amiable are thy dwellings!—Lift up your hands in his sanctuary. We will go into the house of the Lord.

I Sam. 1:21
The child Samuel in the Temple.

Matt. 18:1-14
Entering the kingdom of heaven as a little child.

E, S 19, 67
Their sound is gone out into all lands.—Let all the peoples praise thee.

Isa. 49:1-7
Kings shall arise, princes shall see and worship.

I John 1:1-9
The Word of Life manifested; the light of men.

SECOND SUNDAY AFTER EPIPHANY

Gospel: Mark 1:1-11
The Baptism of Jesus.

S 102:15 & 117
The nations shall fear thy Name.—Praise the Lord, all ye nations.

Isa. 45:1-15
I have called thee by name. The clay and the Potter. Gentiles shall come and worship.

Rom. 9:14-26
The Potter and the clay. The calling of the Gentiles.

G, S 62, 127
My soul, wait upon God. He is my strength and salvation.—Except the Lord build the house. Children a heritage and gift of the Lord.

Isa. 54:11
All thy children shall be taught of the Lord.

John 1:35
Behold the Lamb of God! We have found the Christ.

Key	*Psalms*	*First Lesson*	*Second Lesson*

THIRD SUNDAY AFTER EPIPHANY

Epistle: Rom. 12:16b
¹Live peaceably with all men. ²If thine enemy hunger, feed him;
if he thirst, give him drink.

G, E^2　　42, 43
As the hart desireth the waterbrooks.—Send out thy light and thy truth.

*Isa. 41:8-10, 17-20
Drink for the poor and needy.

John 4:1-14
The Woman of Samaria. The Water of Life.

E^1　　·11, 12
The righteous Lord loveth righteousness.—The Lord will root out all evil lips.

Deut. 16:18-20 & 17:8-11
Justice without respect of persons.

James 2:1-13
Faith without respect of persons.

FOURTH SUNDAY AFTER EPIPHANY

Epistle: Rom. 13:1-7
Subjection to the ministers of the State.

G　　66
All the world shall worship thee. God hath heard me.

Isa. 61
The Spirit of the Lord is upon me, to preach good tidings unto the meek. (*Q. in 2d Lesson.*)

Luke 4:16-32·
Christ's preaching at Nazareth. His word was with power.

E　　18:1-20
The brightness of his presence. He brought me into a place of liberty.

*Deut. 4:5-13, 32-40
The Lord spoke from the midst of the fire. The Law: Israel's wisdom in the sight of the nations.

Eph. 2
Preach peace to those far off and nigh. Fellow citizens of the Saints.

Key   *Psalms*   *First Lesson*   *Second Lesson*

THIRD SUNDAY AFTER EPIPHANY

Gospel: John 2:1-11
The Miracle of Cana.

G 27, 134	Isa. 56:1-8	John 2:13 (*Cont. G.*)
To dwell in the house of the Lord.—Lift up your hands in the sanctuary and praise the Lord.	My house shall be a house of prayer for all people.	First cleansing of the Temple.

E, S 103	Isa. 54:1-8	Rom. 14:1—15:3
He satisfieth thy mouth with good things. Merciful goodness of the Lord is on them that fear him.	Lengthen thy cords. Thy seed inherit the Gentiles.	The kingdom of God is not meat and drink, but righteousness and peace.

FOURTH SUNDAY AFTER EPIPHANY

Gospel: Matt. 8:1-13
Healing of leper with a touch, Centurion's servant with a word.

S 145	Isa. 45:20	Rom. 10
I will magnify thee, O God my King. One generation shall praise thy works unto another.	All the ends of the earth shall look unto me and be saved. Unto me every knee shall bow.	Confess Christ and be saved. How shall they hear without a preacher?

G 30, 36:5	Dan. 10:10-19	Mark 6:45
Thou hast turned my heaviness into joy.—Thy mercy reacheth unto the heavens; thy judgments like the great deep.	The power of the divine touch.	He calmed the sea with a word. Those that touched him were made whole.

Key   *Psalms*   *First Lesson*   *Second Lesson*

FIFTH SUNDAY AFTER EPIPHANY

Epistle: Col. 3:12-17
Compassion, charity, peace, joy, thanksgiving.

E 15, 85	Ruth 1:1-17	Col. 3:5-11 (*Introd. to E.*)	
No evil to his neighbor.— Thou art become gracious unto thy land. Righteousness and peace have kissed each other.	Ruth and Naomi.	Put away anger, malice; put on the new man.	

G 112, 113	*Hab. 1:12—2:4, 9-14	Luke 12:35-48	
Blessed is the man that feareth the Lord.—Praise the Lord, ye servants.	Vision for the appointed time. Woe to covetous! The earth shall be full of knowledge of the Lord.	The faithful steward waiting for the return of his Lord.	

SIXTH SUNDAY AFTER EPIPHANY

Epistle: I John 3:1-8
When he shall appear, we shall be like him. The Son of God manifested to destroy the works of the devil.

E, G 75, 138	Isa. 2:6-19	Matt. 25:14-29	
In the appointed time, I shall judge according to right.—Respect unto the lowly.	He shall judge the nations. When he riseth to shake the earth.	The Parable of the Talents.	

E, G 93, 98	*Isa. 66:1-2, 10, 12-16, 18-23	II Thess. 1	
The Lord is King.—With righteousness shall he judge the world.	The Lord will come with fire. New heavens and new earth.	The Lord revealed from heaven with angels to judgment.	

FIFTH SUNDAY AFTER EPIPHANY

Gospel: Matt. 13:24-30
The Parable of the Wheat and the Tares. The harvest is the end of
the world.

G 21, 22:23	Joel 3:9-17	Matt. 13:36-52 (*Cont. G.*)
Their fruit shalt thou root out of the earth.—The ends of the world shall remember themselves and be turned to the Lord.	The harvest is ripe. Multitudes in the valley of decision.	Exposition of the Parable of the Tares. The Hid Treasure, Pearl, Net, and end of the world.
G 7	Amos 5:14-24	Gal. 6:1-10
He shall judge the world in righteousness.	Hate the evil, love the good. The Day of the Lord. Righteousness as a stream.	Bear one another's burdens. Whatsoever a man soweth, that shall he also reap.

SIXTH SUNDAY AFTER EPIPHANY

Gospel: Matt. 24:23-31
The Son of Man shall appear, and gather his elect.

E, G 9	Gen. 19:1-3, 12-17, 24-28	Luke 17:20
He shall judge the world in righteousness.	The destruction of Sodom.	The Kingdom cometh not with observation. As in the days of Noe. Destruction of Sodom.
E, G 76, 96	II Esdras 8:63—9:13	II Pet. 3:1-14, 17-18
Judgment heard from heaven.—For he cometh to judge the earth.	Time of the end unknown. Compensation and retribution.	Time of the end unknown. Look for the Coming. New heavens and new earth.

Key	*Psalms*	*First Lesson*	*Second Lesson*

SEPTUAGESIMA

Epistle: I Cor. 9:24
So run that ye may obtain.

E 20, 121
The Lord strengthen thee out of Zion.—My help cometh from the Lord.

*Joshua 1:1-9
Be strong, and very courageous.

II Tim. 2:1-13
Endure hardness as a Christian soldier.

E 1 & 18:21-35 *or* 1, 125
The righteous man.—The Lord rewarded me after my righteous dealing. 125: They that put their trust in the Lord shall not be moved.

Ezek. 3:4-11
The Word of the Lord to a stubborn people.

Matt. 5:1-16
The Beatitudes. Persecutions.

SEXAGESIMA

Epistle: II Cor. 11:19-31
St. Paul glories in his infirmities.

E 71
Be thou my stronghold: fortitude under persecutions.

*Isa. 50:4-10
I gave my back to the smiters.

II Cor. 12:1-12 (*Cont. E.*)
Glorying in infirmities. My grace is sufficient for thee.

G 33
The eye of the Lord is upon them that fear him.

Isa. 30:8-21
In returning and rest shall be your strength.

Mark 4:26-34
First the blade, then the ear. Reliance on God's providence.

| Key | Psalms | First Lesson | Second Lesson |

SEPTUAGESIMA

Gospel: Matt. 20:1-16
Parable of Labourers in the Vineyard. 11th Hour.

E   144
Blessed be the Lord my strength.

I Macc. 2:49-64
Mattathias' exhortation to valor.

I Tim. 6:11-19
Fight the good fight of faith.

G   80
Thou hast brought a vine out of Egypt.

Isa. 5:1-7
The Song of the Vineyard.

Matt. 21:23-32
The Two Sons in the Vineyard.

SEXAGESIMA

Gospel: Luke 8:4-15
The Parable of the Sower.

G   147
He filleth thee with the flour of wheat.

Eccles. 11:1-6
Sow the seed!

John 4:31-38
Bread that ye know not of. Fields white already to harvest.

E   37:26 & 124
The Lord's defence of the godly.—Our help is in the name of the Lord.

Dan. 3:1-26
The fiery furnace. He will deliver us out of thy hand, O King.

Matt. 10:16-23, 40-42
Brought before kings. He that receiveth a prophet.

| Key | Psalms | First Lesson | Second Lesson |

QUINQUAGESIMA

Epistle: I Cor. 13
Panegyric of Charity.

E   103
As a father pitieth his children, so is the Lord merciful unto them that fear him.

Wisdom 7:7-14
The wise are the friends of God.

John 15:1-17
The Vine and the Branches. Ye are my friends.

G   19, 23
The law of the Lord is an undefiled law.—Thy lovingkindness and mercy shall follow me.

*Deut. 10:12-15, 17—11:1
Love the stranger.

I John 2:1-17
A new commandment, that ye love one another.

FIRST SUNDAY IN LENT

Epistle: II Cor. 6:1-10
Workers together with him. By fastings.

E   50
Not sacrifices, but thanksgiving. Salvation of God shown to him that ordereth his way aright.

*Isa. 58
This is the fast that I have chosen, to succour the afflicted.

Matt. 6:1-18
Alms, prayers, fastings not before men.

G   3, 62
The Lord sustained me.— God is my strength, so that I shall not greatly fall.

Ecclus. 2
If thou come to serve the Lord, prepare thy soul for temptation.

Rom. 7:14
Members warring against the soul. What I would I do not.

| Key | Psalms | *First Lesson* | *Second Lesson* |

QUINQUAGESIMA

Gospel: Luke 18:31
Last Journey to the Passion. Healing of blind man.

E 119:33-48
My delight is in thy commandments.

Lev. 19:1-2, 9-18
Love thy neighbour as thyself.

I John 4
The love of God is love of man.

G, S 139
Thou hast searched me out and known me. Try me, and examine my thoughts.

Isa. 51:1-8
The Lord will comfort Zion. My righteousness is near.

Mark 9:14-32
Dumb spirit. This kind cometh forth by nothing but prayer and fasting. The Last Journey.

FIRST SUNDAY IN LENT

Gospel: Matt. 4:1-11
The Temptation of Jesus in the desert.

G 15, 92
He that leadeth an uncorrupt life.—The righteous shall flourish as the palm.

Jer. 17:5-14
The heart is deceitful. Heal me, O Lord.

I Cor. 10:1-13
With the temptation a way of escape.

E 69:1-19, 30-37
I chastened myself with fasting.

Dan. 9:3-10
Daniel fasts and confesses his sins.

Luke 5:33—6:10
Fast while the Bridegroom is taken away. Corn on Sabbath.

| *Key* | *Psalms* | *First Lesson* | *Second Lesson* |

SECOND SUNDAY IN LENT

Epistle: I Thess. 4:1-8
Abstain from uncleanness.

G   86, 142
Bow down thine ear, and hear me.—I cried unto God with my voice.

*I Kings 8:37-43
God receives even the prayer of the Gentile.

Col. 3:12-17
Mercies, kindness, forbearance, charity, peace, thanksgiving.

E   30, 32
Thou hast brought my soul out of hell.—Blessed is he whose unrighteousness is forgiven.

Ezek. 18:1-4, 25-32
The soul that sinneth, it shall die.

Matt. 5:27-37
Fornication; oaths.

THIRD SUNDAY IN LENT

Epistle: Eph. 5:1-14
Be followers of God, as dear children. Avoid uncleanness, and the works of darkness.

E   25
Show me thy ways, and teach me thy paths.

*Deut. 6:1-9, 20-25
Teach the Commandments to thy children.

I Cor. 3
Fed with milk. God's husbandry, God's building. Defile not the Temple of God.

G   34
My soul shall make her boast in the Lord. Keep thy tongue from evil.

Zech. 1:1-6, 12-17
Turn from your evil ways.

Mark 8:27—9:1
Peter's Confession. Take up thy Cross, and follow me.

Key   Psalms   *First Lesson*   *Second Lesson*

SECOND SUNDAY IN LENT

Gospel: Matt. 15:21-28
Woman of Canaan: Great is thy faith.

E   26, 119:1-16
I will walk innocently.—
Blessed are those that are
undefiled in the way.

II Sam. 12:1-10, 13-14
Nathan's parable rebuking
David for Uriah's wife.

I Cor. 6:9
Flee   fornication.   Your
bodies are temples of the
Holy Ghost.

G   31
Thou heardest the voice of
my prayer when I cried
unto thee.

Ecclus. 51:1-12
The prayer of the son of
Sirach is heard.

Luke 18:1-8
The Importunate Widow.

THIRD SUNDAY IN LENT

Gospel: Luke 11:14-28
Exorcism of the Dumb Spirit. The Empty House.

G   119:113-128 & 143
I hate them that imagine
evil things, but thy law do
I love.—I cried unto the
Lord.

Amos 5:4-15
Seek the Lord, and ye shall
live. Hate the evil, and
love the good.

Gal. 5:16-24
Walk in the Spirit, and fulfil not the lusts of the
flesh. Fruits of the flesh;
and the spirit.

E   27
The Lord is my light and
my salvation.

Prov. 4:7-18
Get wisdom. The path of
the just is as the shining
light.

Luke 11:29-36 (*Cont. G.*)
Sign of the prophet Jonah.
Thy whole body shall be
full of light.

Key   Psalms   *First Lesson*   *Second Lesson*

FOURTH SUNDAY IN LENT

Epistle: Gal. 4:21
Jerusalem which is from above is free, which is the mother of us all.

G   147   Exod. 16:4-15   John 6:27-40 (*Cont. G.*)
God the giver of peace and   The giving of Manna.   Manna vs. Bread from
plenty.   Heaven.

E   18:1-20   *Ezek. 39:21   II Cor. 3:12
He brought me forth into   Liberation from captivity,   Where the Spirit of the
a place of liberty.   outpouring of the Spirit.   Lord is, there is liberty.

FIFTH SUNDAY IN LENT

Epistle: Heb. 9:11-15
Christ the High Priest and the Eternal Sacrifice.

E   51   *Isa. 1:10-20   I Pet. 4:12
Thou desirest no sacrifice.   True sacrifice: cease to do   Consolation in the inno-
The sacrifice of God is a   evil, learn to do well. Sins   cent sufferings of Christ.
troubled spirit.   white as snow.

G   71   Deut. 18:15   Luke 20:9-18
I will go forth in the   A Prophet like unto Moses.   The unfaithful husbandmen
strength of the Lord God.   False prophets.   in the Vineyard.

| Key | Psalms | First Lesson | Second Lesson |

FOURTH SUNDAY IN LENT

Gospel: John 6:1-14
The Feeding of the Five Thousand.

G   116
I will offer the sacrifice of thanksgiving.

Isa. 55
Ho, every one that thirsteth.

John 6:41-51 (*Cont. G.*)
The Eucharist.

E   46, 122
A river, whose streams make glad the City of God. —Pray for the peace of Jerusalem.

II Esdras 2:15-32
Mother, embrace thy children. Stablish their feet.

Rev. 3:1-12
Perseverance. The New Jerusalem coming down from heaven.

FIFTH SUNDAY IN LENT

Gospel: John 8:46-59a
Before Abraham was, I AM.

E   42, 43
Put thy trust in God.—I will go unto the altar of God.

Hosea 6:1-6
The third day he will raise us up. Mercy, not sacrifice.

Heb. 10:1-25
The Heavenly Priesthood of Christ.

G   40:1-16
Lo, I come to fulfil thy will, O God.

Jer. 14:7-21
The Saviour a stranger in the land. Break not thy covenant with us.

John 10:17-38
I can lay down my life and take it again. One with the Father.

Key	*Psalms*	*First Lesson*	*Second Lesson*

SIXTH SUNDAY IN LENT

Epistle: Phil. 2:5-11
He humbled himself unto the death of the Cross.

S 24, 97 The King of Glory shall come in.—The Lord is King. Zion heard of it, and rejoiced.	*Zech. 9:9-12 Thy King cometh unto thee, riding upon an ass.	Mark 11:1-11 The Triumphal Entry into Jerusalem.	
G, E 22 They pierced my hands and my feet.	Isa. 52:13—53:12 Despised and rejected of men.	Matt. 26 The Betrayal and Trial of Jesus.	

EASTER

Epistle A: Col. 3:1-4. Epistle B: I Cor. 5:6-8
A: If ye then be risen with Christ, seek those things which are
above.—B: Christ our Passover is sacrificed for us.

G 93, 111 The Lord is King, and hath put on glorious apparel.—He hath sent redemption unto his people.	*Isa. 25:1-9 He will swallow up death in victory.	Matt. 28:1-10, 16-20 The Empty Tomb; the appearance to the Disciples; the Great Commission.	
E^b 57 The greatness of thy mercy reacheth unto the heavens.	Exod. 12:1-14 The institution of the Passover.	Rev. 14:1-7, 12-13 The Lamb and the Elect. Blessed are the dead who die in the Lord.	

Key	Psalms	First Lesson	Second Lesson

SIXTH SUNDAY IN LENT

Gospel: Matt. 27:1-54
The Passion of our Lord Jesus Christ.

G   130, 138
With the Lord there is plenteous redemption.— The Lord hath respect unto the lowly.

Jer. 8:9-15, 18—9:1
The wise men are ashamed. Is not her King in Zion? O that mine eyes were a fountain of tears.

I Cor. 1:17
The world by wisdom knew not God. The preaching of the Cross.

E, G   77
Consolation in despair.

Isa. 59:1-3, 9-21
The Redeemer shall come to Zion.

John 12:20-36
Except corn fall into the ground and die. I, if I be lifted up, will draw all men unto me.

EASTER

Gospel A: John 20:1-10. Gospel B: Mark 16:1-8
The Empty Tomb.

E^b 98, 114
Victory, salvation.—Redemption from Egypt.

Isa. 51:9-16
The redeemed shall return with everlasting joy.

Luke 24:13-35
Emmaus. Known to them in breaking of bread.

G   118
This is the day which the Lord hath made; we will rejoice in it.

Isa. 12
The Lord is my strength and song, is become my salvation.

John 20:11-18 (*Cont. G.*)
The Appearance to Mary.

Key	Psalms	First Lesson	Second Lesson

FIRST SUNDAY AFTER EASTER

Epistle: I John 5:4-12
Eternal life is in his Son. The Three Witnesses.

E 66		*Wisdom* 2:23—3:9	Rom. 1:1-12
How wonderful art thou in thy works; who holdeth our soul in life.		For God made man to be immortal. The souls of the righteous are in the hand of God.	Declared to be the Son of God by the Resurrection from the dead.
G, E 103		*Isa. 43:1-12	Luke 24:36-49
Praise the Lord . . . who saveth thy life from destruction.		Redeemer, Saviour. Ye are witnesses.	Jesus shows his hands and side. Ye are witnesses.

SECOND SUNDAY AFTER EASTER

Epistle: I Pet. 2:19-25
Example of Christ's sufferings. Returned unto the Shepherd and Bishop of your souls.

G, E 23, 146		*Isa 40:1-11	John 10:1-10 (*Introd. G.*)
The Lord is my Shepherd. —Food for all things living.		Comfort ye my people. Behold your God! He shall feed his flock.	He that entereth in by the door is the Shepherd.
E 34		*Baruch* 4:21-30	Phil. 3:7-16
O taste and see how gracious the Lord is. The Lord delivereth out of troubles.		The Everlasting our Saviour. Suffer patiently.	Know the power of his Resurrection and the fellowship of his sufferings. Press toward the mark.

Key	Psalms	First Lesson	Second Lesson

FIRST SUNDAY AFTER EASTER

Gospel: John 20:19-23
Appearance to the Disciples. Jesus shows his hands and his side.

G	33	Zeph. 3:14	John 20:19 (*G. plus*)
Rejoice in the Lord, ye righteous.		Rejoice, O Jerusalem. The Lord is in the midst of thee.	Gospel of Day, with Appearance to Thomas.

E	30, 121	II Esdras 2:33	Rev. 1:4-18
Thou hast brought my soul out of hell.—The Lord shall keep thy soul.		The reward of the Kingdom. Crowned by the Son of God.	I am he that liveth and was dead; and behold, I am alive for evermore.

SECOND SUNDAY AFTER EASTER

Gospel: John 10:11-16
Christ the Good Shepherd.

G	145	Ezek. 34:11-16, 30-31	John 21:1-19
Thou fillest all things living with plenteousness.		I will feed the flock of my pasture.	Appearance in Galilee. Feed my sheep.

S	16, 100	II Esdras 8:20-30, 46, 51-54	I Cor. 15:12-23
My flesh shall rest in hope. —We are the sheep of his pasture.		Paradise opened. The treasure of immortality.	Now is Christ risen from the dead, and become the firstfruits of them that slept.

Key   Psalms   *First Lesson*   *Second Lesson*

THIRD SUNDAY AFTER EASTER

Epistle: I Pet. 2:11-17
Abstain from fleshly lusts. Follow his steps.

G   36:5 & 138
Plenteousness of thy house. With thee is the well of life.—Lovingkindness of the Lord.

II Sam. 12:15b-23
David mourns for infant son: I shall go to him, but he shall not return to me.

John 14:1-14
In my Father's house are many mansions. I go to prepare a place for you.

S   113, 124
He taketh the simple out of the dust.—Escape from the snare.

*I Sam. 2:1b-10
Song of Hannah. The Lord bringeth down to the grave, and bringeth up.

Acts 2:22-36
This Jesus hath God raised up; and made both Lord and Christ.

FOURTH SUNDAY AFTER EASTER

Epistle: James 1:17-21
Every good gift is from above. The engrafted Word.

S, G   116
I will walk before the Lord in the land of the living.

*Job 19:21-27a
I know that my Redeemer liveth.

John 12:44
The word that I have spoken shall judge you. His commandment is life everlasting.

S   107:1-16
He brought them out of darkness, and out of the shadow of death.

Ezek. 37:1-14
Dry bones. I will put my spirit in you and ye shall live.

Acts 3:1-21
The Prince of Life, whom God hath raised from the dead.

Key   Psalms   *First Lesson*   *Second Lesson*

THIRD SUNDAY AFTER EASTER

Gospel: John 16:16-22
A little while. Bereavement and joy.

Key	Psalms	First Lesson	Second Lesson
G	68:1-20 Thou hast led captivity captive.	Isa. 26:12-16, 19 A woman in travail (*Q. G.*) Thy dead men shall live.	II Cor. 5 A house eternal in the heavens. The ministry of reconciliation.
S	115 The Lord shall bless us. The dead praise not thee, O God. But we will praise the Lord.	*Wisdom* 5:1-6, 14-16 The righteous live for evermore. A glorious kingdom, and a crown.	Luke 20:27-39 Children of the Resurrection. God is the God of the living.

FOURTH SUNDAY AFTER EASTER

Gospel: John 16:5-15
I will go away. I will send the Comforter. Judgment.

Key	Psalms	First Lesson	Second Lesson
S	18:1-20 The snares of death overtook me. He brought me into a place of liberty.	Dan. 12:1-4, 13 Many that sleep shall awake.	I Thess. 4:13 Those that sleep in Jesus shall God bring with him.
E	27 The Lord is my light and my salvation.	Isa. 60:13 The Lord shall be thine everlasting light.	John 8:12-30 I am the light of the world; the light of life.

Key	Psalms	First Lesson	Second Lesson

FIFTH SUNDAY AFTER EASTER

Epistle: James 1:22
Be ye doers, not hearers only. Pure religion.

G 65, 67 Thou blessest the earth, makest it plenteous.—Then shall the earth bring forth her increase.	*Ezek. 34:25 Showers of blessing. Fruitfulness; safety.	Luke 11:1-13 The Lord's Prayer. Importunate friend. Ask, and it shall be given you.
S 118 The right hand of the Lord bringeth mighty things to pass.	II Esdras 14:27-35 After death, the Judgment, when we shall live again.	Acts 4:1-13, 33 With great power gave the Apostles witness of the Resurrection.

SUNDAY AFTER ASCENSION

Epistle: I Pet. 4:7-11
Ministering the Gift. The eternal dominion of Christ.

E 21:1-6 & 24 The King shall rejoice in thy strength.—The King of Glory shall come in.	*Isa. 33:5-6, 17, 20-22 The Lord is exalted, he dwelleth on high. The King in his beauty.	John 17 Christ's High-Priestly Prayer for the Unity of the Church.
E 8, 108:1-5 To crown him with glory and worship.—Set up thyself above the heavens.	Isa. 4:2 Cloud and fire sanctifying the habitations of Zion.	Heb. 4:14—5:10 Our great High Priest passed into the heavens.
E 72 All kings shall fall down before him; all nations shall do him service.	Isa. 65:17 New heavens and new earth. Millennial peace.	Rev. 21:1-14, 21-27 New heaven and new earth. No more sorrow; the former things have passed away.

| Key | Psalms | First Lesson | Second Lesson |

FIFTH SUNDAY AFTER EASTER

Gospel: John 16:23[b]
Whatsoever ye shall ask in my name, I will give it you. Ye shall have peace.

S   147
The providence of God. He maketh peace in thy borders.

Isa. 48:12-21
God the First and Last. The Creator and Redeemer. Peace like a river.

Rev. 5
Worthy is the Lamb that was slain, and hath redeemed us to God by his blood.

G   144
That our garners may be full and plenteous.

Ezek. 36:25
I will put my Spirit within you. Increase of fruits.

Mark 11:22-26
Faith that moves mountains. What ye desire when ye pray, ye shall have.

SUNDAY AFTER ASCENSION

Gospel: John 15:26—16:4[a]
The promise of the Comforter.

G   93, 96
The Lord is King.—Ascribe unto the Lord worship and power.

Wisdom 9
Prayer for wisdom through the Holy Spirit.

Eph. 1
Spiritual blessings in heavenly places through Christ.

G   46, 47
I will be exalted among the nations.—God is gone up; God is the King of all the earth.

Isa. 32:1-4, 15-20
A King shall reign in righteousness, until the Spirit be poured from on high.

John 3:16-21, 31-36[a]
God so loved the world . . . He is above all. God Giveth not the Spirit by measure.

E   97, 110
The Lord is King.—Priest for ever after the order of Melchizedech.

Dan. 7:9-10, 13-14
The Son of Man shall have an everlasting kingdom.

Rev. 22
The throne of God and of the Lamb. Blessed are they that enter the City.

Key *Psalms*	*First Lesson*	*Second Lesson*

WHITSUNDAY

Epistle: Acts 2:1-11
The Day of Pentecost.

E, G 68 *or* 18:1-20	*Wisdom* 1:1-7	John 4:19-26
The God who helpeth us, and poureth his benefits upon us. He bowed the heavens and came down.	The spirit of the Lord filleth the world.	God is a Spirit; they that worship him must worship him in spirit and in truth.

E, G 145	*Joel 2:28	Rom. 8:1-11
The might of thy marvellous acts. The Lord is loving unto every man.	I will pour out my Spirit upon all flesh.	The life-giving Spirit.

TRINITY SUNDAY

Epistle: Rev. 4
Holy, holy, holy, Lord God Almighty.

E 29, 99	*Isa. 6:1-8	I Pet. 1:1-12
Ascribe unto the Lord the honour due unto his Name.—The Lord sitteth between the Cherubim.	Isaiah's vision of God. Holy, holy, holy.	Knowledge of God the Father, sanctification of the Spirit, sprinkling of the blood of Jesus. End of your faith: salvation of your souls.

S, C 33	Gen. 1:1—2:3	John 1:1-18
By the word of the Lord were the heavens made.	The Creation of the world.	In the beginning was the Word. All things were made by him.

WHITSUNDAY

Gospel: John 14:15-31a
The Spirit of truth. I will come unto you.

Key	Psalms	First Lesson	Second Lesson
E, G	104	*Wisdom 7:22—8:1*	I Cor. 2

E, G   104
How manifold are thy works! In wisdom hast thou made them all.

Wisdom 7:22—8:1
Wisdom is the breath of the power of God; he ordereth all things.

I Cor. 2
God hath revealed by his Spirit. Spiritual things spiritually discerned.

E, G   48, 122
We wait for thy loving-kindness in the midst of thy temple.—We will go into the house of the Lord.

Isa. 11:1-9
The sevenfold Gifts of the Spirit.

John 6:53-69
The things whereof I speak are spirit, and life. (The Holy Spirit in the Sacraments.)

TRINITY SUNDAY

Gospel: John 3:1-15
God is with him. Born of the Spirit. The Son of man.

S, G   98, 100
All creation praises God.— Speak good of his Name.

Ecclus. 43:1-12, 27-33
The glory of Creation.

Eph. 4:1-16
One Spirit, one Lord, one God and Father: till we come in the unity of the faith unto a perfect man.

S, G   148, 150
Creation praises God.

Job 38:1-11, 16-18 & 42: 1-6
When I laid the foundation of the earth.

John 1:29-34
The Lamb of God. The Spirit descending. The Son of God.

Key	Psalms	First Lesson	Second Lesson

FIRST SUNDAY AFTER TRINITY

Epistle: I John 4:7
The love of God manifested.

S, G   73
God is loving unto Israel. It is good to stand fast by God.

*Jer. 23:23-32
My word is like a fire, and a hammer that breaketh the rock.

Matt. 7:13-14, 21-29
The house on the rock and the house on the sand.

G   89:1-19
Righteousness and equity are the habitation of thy seat.

Isa. 5:8-12, 18-24
Woe to them that join house to house, that call evil good.

James 5
Woe to the rich who make an evil use of wealth. The prayer of faith.

C   90
Thou turnest man to destruction. Come again, ye children of men.

Gen. 3
The Fall of man.

Rom. 5
Adam and Christ.

SECOND SUNDAY AFTER TRINITY

Epistle: I John 3:13
That we should love one another, as he gave us commandment.

E   15, 19
He that leadeth an uncorrupt life.—The law of the Lord is an undefiled law.

Job 31:13-28
Kindness to the helpless.

I Cor. 13
The Panegyric of Charity.

G   76, 125
Promise to the Lord, and keep it.—Such as turn back unto their own wickedness.

*Deut. 20:1-9
Turning back from the battle.

Luke 9:57
Putting the hand to the plough, and turning back.

C   11, 12
If the foundations be destroyed, what can the righteous do?—The Lord shall root out all deceitful things.

Gen. 6:5-8, 13-22
Wickedness before the Flood.

Matt. 24:32-42
As in the days of Noe.

Key	Psalms	First Lesson	Second Lesson

FIRST SUNDAY AFTER TRINITY

Gospel: Luke 16:19
The Parable of Lazarus and the Rich Man.

E 119:33-48
Make me to go in the path of thy commandments.

Deut. 30:11
The word is very nigh thee. I command thee to love the Lord.

John 13:1-17, 34-35
Jesus washes the Disciples' feet. New commandment: love one another.

G 49
God hath delivered thy soul from the power of the grave.

Job 21:17-33
How oft is the candle of the wicked put out!

Luke 16:19
Lazarus and the Rich Man.

C 85
Righteousness shall direct his going in the way.

I Sam. 1:1-11, 19-20
The birth of Samuel.

Acts 6
The Seven Deacons. The arrest of Stephen.

SECOND SUNDAY AFTER TRINITY

Gospel: Luke 14:16-24
The Great Supper. Guests from byways and hedges.

E 112, 113
A good man is merciful.— The Lord taketh the simple out of the dust.

I Sam. 20:1-7, 12-42
David and Jonathan.

I Pet. 1:17
Love one another with a pure heart fervently.

G 138, 146
Respect to the lowly.—He feedeth the hungry.

II Kings 4:8-17
The Shunammite woman's hospitality to Elijah.

Luke 14:12-24 (*G plus*)
Hospitality to the poor; the Great Supper.

C 147
The Lord's delight is in them that fear him.

I Sam. 3:1-18
The Call of Samuel.

Acts 7:44—8:4
The Martyrdom of Stephen.

Key	Psalms	First Lesson	Second Lesson

THIRD SUNDAY AFTER TRINITY

Epistle: I Pet. 5:5-11
Be clothed with humility.

Key	Psalms	First Lesson	Second Lesson
G	145 The Lord's mercy is over all his works.	*Jer. 31:1-14 He will gather Israel, as a shepherd doth his flock.	Matt. 9:9-13 I am not come to call the righteous, but sinners, to repentance.
E	25 Them that are meek, shall he guide in judgment.	Prov. 16:18-24, 32 Pride goeth before destruction.	Phil. 1:27—2:4 Becoming conversation. Nothing through strife or vainglory.
C	27 The Lord is my light and my salvation.	Gen. 9:1-17 The Covenant of the Rainbow after the Flood.	I Pet. 3:17—4:6 The Flood as a figure of Baptism.

FOURTH SUNDAY AFTER TRINITY

Epistle: Rom. 8:18-23
Present sufferings vs. glory to be revealed. Redemption of all creation. Liberty of the sons of God.

Key	Psalms	First Lesson	Second Lesson
E	91 Whoso dwelleth under the defence of the Most High, shall abide under the shadow of the Almighty.	*Lam. 3:22-33 Uses of adversity: He doth not willingly afflict nor grieve the children of men.	Matt. 10:24-39 Persecutions predicted to Disciples. He that loseth his life for my sake shall find it.
G	75, 82 I will judge according unto right.—How long will ye give wrong judgment?	Deut. 32:1-4, 34-39 The Lord shall judge his people.	Rom. 2:1-16 Wherein thou judgest another, thou condemnest thyself.
C	22:23 & 67 Fear him, ye seed of Israel. All kindreds of nations shall worship before him. —All the ends of the world shall fear him.	Gen. 12:1-9 Abraham leaves Ur for Canaan. In Abraham all nations shall be blessed.	Gal. 3:1-9 Abraham believed God, and it was counted unto him for righteousness.

Key   Psalms   *First Lesson*   *Second Lesson*

THIRD SUNDAY AFTER TRINITY

Gospel: Luke 15:1-10
Parables of the Lost Sheep and Lost Coin.

G   32, 36:5
Blessed is the man whose
unrighteousness   is   forgiven.—Thy mercy reacheth
unto the heavens.

Jer. 23:1-8
I will set up shepherds
who will feed them.

Luke 19:2-10
Zacchæus. The Son of Man
is come to seek and to save
that which was lost.

G   103
The Lord is full of com-
passion and mercy.

Ezek. 34:20-24
I will set up one shepherd
over them.

Luke 15:1-10
The Lost Sheep and Lost
Coin.

C   72
God's eternal Kingdom.

I Sam. 8
The people desire a King.

Acts 8:5-25
Philip preaches the things
concerning the kingdom
of God; Peter and John
visit Samaria.

FOURTH SUNDAY AFTER TRINITY

Gospel: Luke 6:36-42
Be merciful. Judge not. The mote and the beam.

G   51
Wash me thoroughly from
my wickedness, and cleanse
me from my sin.

Isa. 29:9-15
This people honor me with
their lips, but their heart
is far from me. (*Q. 2d L.*)

Matt. 15:1-20
Pharisees: blind leaders of
the blind. Defilement from
within, not without.

G   139
Look well if there be any
wickedness in me, and lead
me in the way everlasting.

Prov. 27:1-6, 10-12
Faithful are the wounds
of a friend.

Luke 6:36-42
Be merciful. Judge not.
The mote and the beam.

C   80
Let thy hand be upon the
man   whom   thou   hast
strengthened.

I Sam. 9:1-10, 18-19,
26—10:1
Saul anointed King over
Israel.

Acts 8:26
Philip and the Ethiopian.

Key	Psalms	First Lesson	Second Lesson

FIFTH SUNDAY AFTER TRINITY

Epistle: I Pet. 3:8-15ᵃ
Compassion; courtesy; refrain thy tongue from evil.

G   62, 63

If riches increase, set not your heart on them.—Thy lovingkindness is better than life.

*Eccles. 2:1-11, 18-23
The vanity of possessions.

Matt. 19:16
The rich young ruler. Renouncing possessions.

E   34

Keep thy tongue from evil.

Prov. 15:1-10, 26
Soft answer. Tongue of the wise.

James 3
The tongue is an unruly member.

C   1, 121

Who hath not walked in the counsel of the ungodly.—He that keepeth Israel shall not sleep.

Gen. 17:1-8
The Covenant with Abraham.

Heb. 11:1-16
By faith Abraham went to the Land of Promise.

SIXTH SUNDAY AFTER TRINITY

Epistle: Rom. 6:3-11
Baptized into his death. Dead unto sin.

G   85

Righteousness and peace have kissed each other.

II Sam. 19:16-23
David's forgiveness of Shimei.

Matt. 5:38
Resist not evil. Love your enemies.

E   16, 111

My flesh shall rest in hope.—The fear of the Lord is the beginning of wisdom.

*Isa. 57:13ᵇ-19
I dwell with him that is of a contrite spirit.

II Tim. 2:7-13
If we be dead with him, we shall also live with him.

C   71

Forsake me not in mine old age.

Gen. 18:1-16
Promise of prosperity to Abraham at Mamre.

Rom. 4:13
Promise to Abraham and his seed through faith.

Key	*Psalms*	*First Lesson*	*Second Lesson*

FIFTH SUNDAY AFTER TRINITY

Gospel: Luke 5:1-11
Call of Peter, James, and John. They forsook all, and followed him.

G 66 Thou hast proved us, and tried us as silver is tried.	Prov. 3:1-7, 11-12 Forget not the Law. Honor the Lord with thy substance. Despise not the chastening of the Lord.	Luke 14:25 Renouncing family. Take up thy cross. Count the cost.	
G 65 Blessed is the man whom thou choosest.	Judges 6:11-23 The call of Gideon.	Luke 5:1-11 Call of Peter. James, and John.	
C 97, 98 The Lord is King.—He hath done marvelous things.	I Sam. 11 The nation accepts Saul as king.	Acts 9:1-20 The conversion of St. Paul.	

SIXTH SUNDAY AFTER TRINITY

Gospel: Matt. 5:20-26
Be reconciled to thy brother. Agree with thine adversary. Anger without cause is murder.

E 57, 130 Under the shadow of thy wings shall be my refuge. —He shall redeem Israel from all his sins.	Exod. 24:1-11, 16-18 The blood of the Covenant.	Heb. 9:18 Boldness to enter into the holiest by the blood of Jesus.	
G 94:1-22 How long shall the ungodly triumph?	Gen. 4:1-16 The murder of Abel.	Matt. 5:20-26 Anger and murder.	
C 104 God's wisdom manifested in Creation.	I Sam. 16:1-13 Samuel anoints David as King. The Lord seeth not as man seeth.	Acts 11:1-18 St. Peter's vision; Christianity opened to the Gentiles. What God hath cleansed call not thou common.	

Seventh Sunday After Trinity

Epistle: Rom. 6:19-23
Made free from sin, ye have your fruit unto holiness.

E   18:1-20
He brought me forth into a place of liberty.

*Hosea 14
I will heal their backslidings.

Rom. 6:12-18 (*Introd. E*).
Free from sin, servants of righteousness.

G   133, 134, 138
Brethren in unity.—Praise the Lord, ye servants.—I will give thanks out of my whole heart.

Ecclus. 6:5-17
Whoso feareth the Lord shall direct his friendship aright.

John 15:12
At the *Agape*: That ye love one another. Ye are my friends.

C   40:1-16
Sacrifice for sin hast thou not required: then said I, Lo, I come.

Gen. 22:1-18
Offering up of Isaac.

Heb. 6
God's oath to Abraham.

Eighth Sunday After Trinity

Epistle: Rom. 8:12-17
As many as are led by the Spirit of God, they are the sons of God.

G, E   119:33-48
Make me to go in the path of thy commandments.

*Ecclus. 1:18-27
If thou desirest wisdom, keep the commandments.

John 7:14-24
If any man will do his will, he shall know of the doctrine.

E   126, 127
When the Lord turned the captivity of Zion.—Except the Lord build the house. Children a heritage.

Zech. 4:1-10
Not by might but by my Spirit. Who hath despised the day of small things?

Gal. 3:24—4:7
No longer under a schoolmaster, but children of God. The spirit of his Son, crying Abba, Father.

C   84
How amiable are thy dwellings.

Gen. 24:1-27
Isaac and Rebekah.

Eph. 5:22
Christ and his Bride the Church.

Key	Psalms	First Lesson	Second Lesson

SEVENTH SUNDAY AFTER TRINITY

Gospel: Mark 8:1-9
The Feeding of the Four Thousand.

E   50
Not sacrifice, but thanksgiving. The heavens shall declare his righteousness, for God is Judge.

Dan. 5:1-9, 13-30
Belshazzar's Feast. God hath numbered thy kingdom and finished it.

Rom. 1:17-21, 28-32
Wrath of God revealed against all unrighteousness.

G   116
I will offer to thee the sacrifice of thanksgiving.

Micah 7:14
Feed thy people with thy staff; pardon their iniquities.

Mark 8:1-21 (*G. plus*)
Feeding of the Four Thousand; the Leaven of the Pharisees.

C   24, 29
The Lord of hosts.—The voice of the Lord is a glorious voice.

I Sam. 17:1-11, 32, 40-50
David slays Goliath.

Acts 11:19
Barnabas and Paul at Antioch.

EIGHTH SUNDAY AFTER TRINITY

Gospel: Matt. 7:15-21
By their fruits ye shall know them.

E   25
Them that are meek shall he guide in judgment.

Ecclus. 6:22
Be willing to hear every godly discourse.

Luke 10:38
Mary hath chosen that good part.

G   92
The righteous shall flourish like the palm. More fruit in their age.

Prov. 11:24
The fruit of the righteous is a tree of life.

Matt. 7:15-21
By their fruits ye shall know them.

C   148, 150
Praise the Lord.

I Sam. 26:1-7, 12-17, 21-25
David spares Saul in the wilderness.

Acts 12:1-17
Peter delivered from prison.

Key	Psalms	First Lesson	Second Lesson

NINTH SUNDAY AFTER TRINITY

Epistle: I Cor. 10:1-13
Our examples, that we should not lust after evil things.

Key	Psalms	First Lesson	Second Lesson
E	115 Futility of idols.	Ezek. 14:1-11 Idols in the heart.	I Thess. 4:1-12 God hath not called us to uncleanness, but unto holiness.
G	103 Who forgiveth all thy sin.	*Wisdom* 11:21—12:2 Thou sparest all, for they are thine, thou lover of souls.	John 8:1-11 The woman taken in adultery.
C	91 He shall give his angels charge over thee.	Gen. 28:10 Jacob's dream of angels; Jacob's vow: tithes.	II Cor. 9 That ye may abound unto every good work.

TENTH SUNDAY AFTER TRINITY

Epistle: I Cor. 12:1-11
Spiritual gifts.

Key	Psalms	First Lesson	Second Lesson
E	145 That thy power, thy glory, and mightiness of thy kingdom, might be known unto men.	*Ecclus.* 1:1-10 All wisdom cometh from the Lord; it is his gift.	John 8:25-36 Ye shall know the truth, and the truth shall make you free. The Son shall make you free indeed.
G	147 Praise the Lord, O Jerusalem.	Jer. 26:1-7, 10-15 The Lord hath sent me to testify against this house and against this city.	Matt. 23:34 O Jerusalem, that killest the prophets!
C	144 Blessed be the Lord my strength.	Gen. 32:22-31 Jacob wrestles with an angel.	II Cor. 4:7 Strength through struggle.

NINTH SUNDAY AFTER TRINITY.

Gospel: Luke 15:11
The Parable of the Prodigal Son.

Key	Psalms	First Lesson	Second Lesson
G	119:9-24 Wherewithal shall a young man cleanse his way? Even by ruling himself after thy word.	Prov. 4:1-4, 20-27 I was my father's son. Keep thy heart with all diligence, for out of it are the issues of life.	Heb. 12:1-13 Whom the Lord loveth, he chasteneth. God dealeth with you as sons.
G	51 Cleanse me from my sin.	Lam. 3:40-58 Let us turn again to the Lord. Thou hast redeemed my life.	Luke 15:11 The Prodigal Son.
C	93, 96 The Lord is King.—Worship the Lord in the beauty of holiness.	I Sam. 31 The death of Saul.	Acts 13:1-3, 14-31, 38, 44-49 Paul and Barnabas commissioned; Paul preaches at Antioch.

TENTH SUNDAY AFTER TRINITY

Gospel: Luke 19:41-47a
The Destruction of Jerusalem foretold.

Key	Psalms	First Lesson	Second Lesson
E	15, 46 He that leadeth an uncorrupt life.—God is our hope and strength.	Isa. 44:1-8, 21-23 I will pour out my Spirit upon thy seed.	Rom. 12:1-9 Spiritual gifts.
G	42, 43 Why art thou so full of heaviness, O my soul? Put thy trust in God.	Lam. 1:1-12 Jerusalem hath sinned, therefore is she removed.	Luke 19:41 The destruction of Jerusalem.
C	47, 48 God reigneth over the nations.—The bulwarks of Zion.	II Sam. 1:17 David's lament over Saul and Jonathan.	Acts 14:8 Paul and Barnabas taken for gods at Lystra; return to Antioch.

Key   Psalms   First Lesson   Second Lesson

ELEVENTH SUNDAY AFTER TRINITY

Epistle: I Cor. 15:1-11
The Resurrection Appearances.

E   124, 125
Our help is in the Name
of the Lord.—They that
put their trust in the Lord.

*Isa. 26:12-16, 19
Thy dead men shall live.

Rom. 8:26
More   than   conquerors
through him that loved us.

G   33
The Lord loveth righteousness and judgment.

Job 5:8-18
God taketh the wise in
their own craftiness, sav-
eth the poor.

Matt. 23:13-31
Scribes and Pharisees, hyp-
ocrites! The outside of
the cup.

C   62, 63
My soul waiteth upon God.
—My soul hangeth upon
thee.

Gen. 37:3-4, 12-35
Joseph sold into Egypt.

James 1:1-15
The trying of your faith
worketh patience.

TWELFTH SUNDAY AFTER TRINITY

Epistle: II Cor. 3:4-9
Our sufficiency is of God. Able ministers of the New Testament.
The ministration of righteousness exceeds in glory.

E   139
Thou hast searched me out
and known me.

*Ecclus. 15:11
God desires righteousness,
gives power to choose and
fulfil it.

Phil. 2:12-18
Work out your own salva-
tion...for it is God that
worketh in you.

G   102:15 & 146
God's power in man's
weakness.—Blessed is he
that hath the God of Jacob
for his help.

Ecclus. 38:1-14
Honor a physician.

Luke 4:31
Casting out unclean spirits.
Healing of Peter's wife's
mother. At eventide.

C   72
Then shall he judge thy
people according unto
right.

Gen. 41:1a, 8, 14-40
Pharaoh's dream. Joseph
appointed Vicegerent.

Col. 3:22—4:6
Whatsoever ye do, do it
heartily, as to the Lord
and not unto men.

Key   Psalms   *First Lesson*   *Second Lesson*

ELEVENTH SUNDAY AFTER TRINITY

Gospel: Luke 18:9-14
The Parable of the Pharisee and the Publican.

G   68 *or* 123, 142   *Ecclus.* 35:10-19   Mark 12:38
The Father of the father-   Give to the Lord cheer-   Beware of the Scribes. The
less, defendeth the cause   fully. The Lord will not   Widow's Mite.
of widows.—The scornful   despise . . . the widow.
reproof of the wealthy.—   Trust not to unrighteous
Thou art my hope.   sacrifices.

G   100, 101   Eccles. 5:1-7   Luke 18:9-14
Go into his gates with   Keep thy foot when thou   The Pharisee and the Pub-
thanksgiving.—I will walk   goest to the house of God.   lican.
in my house with a per-   Pay what thou vowest.
fect heart.

C   30, 121   II Sam. 7:18   Acts 15:1-21
I will magnify thee, O   David's prayer for the   The Council of Jerusalem.
Lord. Thou hast turned my   people.
heaviness into joy.—My
help cometh from the
Lord.

TWELFTH SUNDAY AFTER TRINITY

Gospel: Mark 7:31
Ephphatha. He maketh the deaf to hear, and the dumb to speak.

E   27   *Tobit* 13:1^b-5, 7-11   Rom. 15:14-21
The Lord is my light and   Many nations shall come   Ministering the gospel of
my salvation.   from far in the Name of   God to the Gentiles.
                              the Lord God.

G   32, 126   Isa. 29:18   Mark 7:31
Thou shalt preserve me   In that day shall the deaf   Ephphatha.
from trouble.—Then was   hear the words of the
our heart filled with joy.   book.

C   67, 122   II Sam. 15:1-23   Acts 15:36—16:5, 9-15
Let all the peoples praise   The Rebellion of Absalom.   Mark returns; Paul chooses
thee.—We will go into   Timothy; the call to Mace-
the house of the Lord.   donia.

Key   Psalms   *First Lesson*   *Second Lesson*

THIRTEENTH SUNDAY AFTER TRINITY

Epistle: Gal. 3:16-22
To Abraham and his seed. Promise of faith to them that believe.

G 104 God's bounty to all Creation.	**Ecclus.* 17:1-15 God's care for mankind. Commandment concerning his neighbour.	Mark 3:20-21, 31-35 Whosoever shall do the will of God is my brother, sister, mother.
E 73 It is good for me to put my trust in the Lord God.	Hab. 1:12—2:4, 14 The just shall live by his faith.	Heb. 10:35 The just shall live by faith.
C 118 The right hand of the Lord bringeth mighty things to pass.	Gen. 43:1-5, 11-16, 26-34 Joseph and Benjamin.	Heb. 13:1-21 Let brotherly love continue. The Lord is my helper.

FOURTEENTH SUNDAY AFTER TRINITY

Epistle: 5:16-24
Walk in the Spirit, fulfil not the lust of the flesh. The fruits of the Spirit.

E 19, 24 The fear of the Lord is clean.—He that hath clean hands and a pure heart.	**Micah 6:1-8* Do justly, love mercy, walk humbly with thy God.	Phil. 4:4-13 Whatsoever things are true, just, pure, lovely.
G 65 God is praised in Sion for all his bounties.	I Chron. 29:10-17 Willing offering. All things come of thee.	Luke 17:5-10 (*Introd. G.*) We have done that which was our duty to do.
C 85 Thou hast forgiven the offence of thy people. Righteousness and peace have kissed each other.	Gen. 45:1-15, 25-28 Joseph reveals himself to his brethren.	Rom. 12:9 Brotherly love. Recompense not evil for evil.

Key   *Psalms*   *First Lesson*   *Second Lesson*

THIRTEENTH SUNDAY AFTER TRINITY

Gospel: Luke 10:23-37
Who is my neighbour? Parable of the Good Samaritan.

G	11, 12	Deut. 15:7-15	Matt. 26:6-13
His eyes considered the poor.—Because of the needy and poor.		The poor shall never cease out of the land. Mercy to poor brother.	The Alabaster box. Ye have the poor always with you.
G	112, 113	Deut. 24:10	Luke 10:23-37
A good man is merciful. —God's mercy to the humble.		Kindness to the stranger.	The Good Samaritan.
C	20, 23	II Sam. 18:1, 6-14, 19-33	Acts 16: 16-34
The Lord hear thee in the day of trouble.—The Lord is my shepherd.		The death of Absalom.	Paul and Silas in prison in Philippi.

FOURTEENTH SUNDAY AFTER TRINITY

Gospel: Luke 17:11-19
The Ten Lepers. None found that returned to give glory to God but this stranger.

G	50	Jer. 7:1-11	Luke 13:18-30
Why dost thou preach my laws, whereas thou hast cast my words behind thee?		Ye that enter the gate to worship the Lord: Amend your ways. The Temple of the Lord!	Strait gate. Lord, Lord! Depart, ye that work iniquity. The last shall be first.
G	92	Deut. 8:1-14, 17-20	Luke 17:11-19
It is a good thing to give thanks unto the Lord.		Gratitude for blessings on the land.	Thankfulness.
C	42, 43	I Kings 3:4-15	Acts 17:16
Put thy trust in God.		Solomon's vision, and prayer for wisdom.	Paul preaches at Athens.

Key	Psalms	First Lesson	Second Lesson

FIFTEENTH SUNDAY AFTER TRINITY

Epistle: Gal. 6:11
Glory only in the Cross of Christ. A new creature.

G 49	*Ecclus. 5:1-10	Luke 12:13-21
Some put their trust in their goods.	Set not thy heart upon thy goods. Make no tarrying to turn to the Lord.	Beware of covetousness. This night thy soul shall be required of thee.
E 103	Deut. 7:6-13	Gal. 2:15-20
The Lord is merciful unto them that fear him.	The Lord hath chosen you because he loved you.	Not justified by works. The Son of God, who loved us.
C 1, 15	Exod. 2:1-22	James 4
Blessed is the man who hath not walked in the counsel of the ungodly.— He that leadeth an uncorrupt life.	Birth, upbringing, and flight of Moses.	Causes of contention. God resisteth the proud and giveth grace to the humble.

SIXTEENTH SUNDAY AFTER TRINITY

Epistle: Eph. 3:13-21
That Christ may dwell in your hearts by faith.

G 116	*Isa. 12	John 11:21-44
Thou hast delivered my soul from death.	The Lord hath done excellent things.	The raising of Lazarus.
E 91	Jer. 32:36-42	Rom. 11:25
Because he hath set his love upon me, therefore will I deliver him.	Deliverance; Covenant; my fear in their hearts.	Deliverance; mercy; O the depth of the riches of the wisdom of God!
C 145	Exod. 3:1-15	I Pet. 5:1-11
The Lord's mercy is over all his works. He will hear their cry and will help them.	The Call of Moses.	Feed the flock of God.

Key	Psalms	First Lesson	Second Lesson

FIFTEENTH SUNDAY AFTER TRINITY

Gospel: Matt. 6:24
Be not anxious for your life.

G   26, 128
I will walk innocently.—
Thou shalt eat the labours
of thine hands.

             Eccles. 5:8
The profit of the earth is
for all. The sleep of the
labouring man is sweet.
Vanity of avarice.

           I Tim. 6:1-10
Partakers of the benefit.
Godliness with content-
ment is great gain.

G   34
They that seek the Lord
shall want no manner of
thing that is good.

          Joel 2:21-27
God will provide. Ye shall
eat in plenty and praise
the Name of the Lord.

           Matt. 6:24
Be not anxious for your
life.

C   84
How amiable are thy dwellings!

I Kings 8:22-30, 54-63
Solomon dedicates the Temple.

          Acts 18:1-17
Paul before Gallio.

SIXTEENTH SUNDAY AFTER TRINITY

Gospel: Luke 7:11-17
The Widow's son raised at Nain.

G   90
Teach us to number our
days.

          Ezek. 33:1-9
Set a watchman to warn
the people.

         Matt. 24:37
Watch: ye know not at
what hour the Lord doth
come.

G   142, 146
Thou art my hope . . . in
the land of the living.—
The Lord defendeth the
fatherless and widow.

I Kings 17:8-9, 17-24
Elijah raises the widow's
son.

          Luke 7:11-17
The widow's son raised at
Nain.

C   66
His eyes behold the nations.

       I Kings 12:1-20
The division of the King-
dom.

          Acts 19:21
The riot at Ephesus.

Key	Psalms	First Lesson	Second Lesson

SEVENTEENTH SUNDAY AFTER TRINITY

Epistle: Eph. 4:1-6
Lowliness. The unity of the Spirit.

G, E   25
Them that are meek shall he guide in judgment.

*Jer. 13:15-21
Be not proud.

Mark 10:35-45
Who would be chief of all, let him be the servant of all.

E   10
His mouth is full of cursing, deceit, and fraud.

Ecclus. 8:1-9
Avoid contentious men.

II Tim. 2:19
The servant of the Lord must not strive; patient, meek.

C   107:1-16
Deliverance from the desert, and from prison.

Exod. 5:1-9, 19—6:1
Moses demands release of Israel from Egypt.

Heb. 3
Moses was faithful in all his house.

EIGHTEENTH SUNDAY AFTER TRINITY

Epistle: I Cor. 1:4-8
Enriched in all knowledge.

E, G   48, 112
We wait for thy loving-kindness in the midst of thy temple.—Blessed is the man that feareth the Lord; great delight in his commandments.

Prov. 2:1-9
Hide my commandments with thee. Then shalt thou understand righteousness, judgment, and equity; every good path.

I Tim. 3:14—4:16
The Church the pillar and ground of truth. Faith. Take heed to the doctrine.

E, G   62, 63
My soul waiteth upon God.—My soul thirsteth for thee.

*Amos 8:4-12
Not a famine of bread or thirst for water, but of hearing the words of the Lord.

John 7:37
If any man thirst, let him come unto me. Who is Christ?

C   77:11 & 114
Thou leddest thy people like sheep by the hand of Moses and Aaron.—When Israel came out of Egypt: the sea saw that and fled.

Exod. 14:5-14, 19-21, 24-28, 30
Crossing the Red Sea.

Heb. 11:23-29, 32-40
Faith of Moses and the Elders.

Key	Psalms	First Lesson	Second Lesson

SEVENTEENTH SUNDAY AFTER TRINITY

Gospel: Luke 14:1-11
Chief seats: take the lowest place.

Key	Psalms	First Lesson	Second Lesson
E	36:5 & 130 Let not the foot of pride come against me.—Out of the deep have I called unto thee.	Mal. 2:1-10 Condemnation of corrupt priests. Ye have caused many to stumble.	Luke 13:10-17 The healing of the infirm woman on the Sabbath Day.
G	33 The dependence of Creation upon God.	Ecclus. 10:7-18 Pride is hateful before God and man.	Luke 14:1-11 Chief seats: lowest place.
C	144 Blessed be the Lord my strength.	I Kings 18:1-2, 17-39 Elijah and the priests of Baal.	Acts 20:17 Paul's farewell to the Elders of Ephesus at Miletus.

EIGHTEENTH SUNDAY AFTER TRINITY

Gospel: Matt. 22:34
The Two Commandments; confession of Jesus as Lord.

Key	Psalms	First Lesson	Second Lesson
E, G	147 He showed his word unto Jacob, his statutes and ordinances unto Israel.	Deut. 11:18-21, 26-28, 32 Cleave to the Commandments.	Gal. 1:1-12 No other Gospel than that which we have preached unto you.
G	119:89-104 Lord, what love have I unto thy law!	Deut. 5:1-21 The Decalogue.	Matt. 22:34 The Two Commandments.
C	139 Thou hast searched me out, and known me.	I Kings 19 God appears to Elijah at Horeb; the call of Elisha.	Acts 21:7-19, 27-39 The riot and accusation at Jerusalem.

Key	Psalms	First Lesson	Second Lesson

NINETEENTH SUNDAY AFTER TRINITY

Epistle: Eph. 4:17
Ye have not so learned Christ. Put away former conversation, and all malice.

E　　72
He shall keep the simple folk by their right, defend the poor.

*Job 24:1-17
Wicked injustice.

Titus 2
Sound doctrine: denying worldly lusts, live righteously.

G¹　　34
The Lord delivereth the souls of his servants.

Jer. 30:12-22
I will restore health unto thee.

John 5:1-16
Healing of the paralytic at the pool of Bethesda.

C　　29, 99
The Lord reveals himself in the storm.—Moses and Aaron called upon the Lord. The Law that he gave them.

Exod. 19:1-7, 16-19 & 20:1-3
The giving of the Law upon Sinai.

Rom. 3:1-2, 19-31 ·
To the Jew were committed the oracles of God. The Redemption establishes the Law.

TWENTIETH SUNDAY AFTER TRINITY

Epistle: Eph. 5:15-21
¹Walk circumspectly, as wise, redeeming the time. ²Submit yourselves one to another.

G　　11, 12
The righteous Lord loveth righteousness.—The Lord shall root out all deceitful lips.

Mal. 2:14
The God of Israel hateth putting away. Treachery against the wife of thy youth.

Matt. 19:3-9a, 13-15
Marriage; divorce; children.

E¹　　1, 15
The righteous man.

*Eccles. 9:4-10
Rejoice in thy labour. Whatsoever thy hand findeth to do, do it with thy might.

Eph. 6:1-9
With good will doing service, as to the Lord, and not to men.

C　　115
The folly of idolatry.

Exod. 32:1-6, 15-20, 30-34
The Golden Calf.

I Cor. 10:14-22
Flee from idolatry. The Cup and Table of the Lord.

Key	Psalms	First Lesson	Second Lesson

NINETEENTH SUNDAY AFTER TRINITY

Gospel: Matt. 9:1-8
¹Healing of the Paralytic. ²Thy sins be forgiven thee.

E   80
The unfruitful Vine visited.
Let us live and we shall
call upon thy Name.

Jer. 5:7-19
Disaster will follow un-
faithfulness.

II Cor. 13
The power of the Cross to
bring strength to human
weakness. Examine your-
selves.

G²   103
Who forgiveth all thy sin.

Wisdom 12:12-19
God's power in mercy. Re-
pentance of sins.

Matt. 9:1-8
Thy sins be forgiven thee.

C   19, 46
Keep thy servant from pre-
sumptuous sins.—God is
our hope and strength.

I Kings 21:1-22
Naboth's Vineyard.

Acts 22:24—23:11
Paul before the Sanhedrin.

TWENTIETH SUNDAY AFTER TRINITY

Gospel: Matt. 22:1-14
The Marriage of the King's Son.

E²   145
Thine abundant lovingkindness. The Lord is loving
unto every man.

Jer. 31:31-37
A New Covenant, to write
the law in their hearts.

John 13:31-35
A New Commandment, to
love one another.

G 107:1-9, 33-43 *or* 84
The wilderness blessed by
God.—No good thing shall
he withhold from them
that lead a godly life.

Jer. 2:1-9, 13
The Lord remembers the
love of Israel's espousals
in the wilderness.

Matt. 22:1-14
The Marriage Feast.

C   111, 112
He hath commanded his
covenant for ever.—Blessed
is the man that feareth the
Lord.

II Kings 2:1-15
The translation of Elijah.
His spirit descends upon
Elisha.

Acts 24:10
Paul's defence before Felix.

Key	Psalms	First Lesson	Second Lesson

TWENTY-FIRST SUNDAY AFTER TRINITY

Epistle: Eph. 6:10-20
¹The armour of God: above all, ²the shield of faith.

E^1 76, 121
The God of battles.—My help cometh from the Lord.

*Isa. 59:15^b
The armour of God.

II Cor. 10:1-7, 17-18
The weapons of our warfare are not carnal, but mighty.

G^2 27
The Lord is my light and my salvation.

Baruch 3:14-15, 29-37
God the giver of light and wisdom.

John 9:1-38
The healing of the man born blind.

C   91
Whoso dwelleth under the defence of the Most High, shall abide under the shadow of the Almighty.

Exod. 33:1, 12-23
My presence shall go with thee, and I will give thee rest.

Heb. 4:1-13
There remaineth therefore a rest for the people of God.

TWENTY-SECOND SUNDAY AFTER TRINITY

Epistle: Phil. 1:3-11
He that hath begun a good work in you will perform it until the day of Jesus Christ.

G   32, 43
Blessed is the man whose unrighteousness is forgiven.—Put thy trust in God.

Ecclus. 27:30—28:7
Forgive thy neighbor: so shall thy sins also be forgiven when thou prayest.

Matt. 18:7-20 (*Introd. G.*)
If thy brother trespass against thee, tell him his fault between thee and him alone.

E   147
The Lord doth build up Jerusalem.

Baruch 5
God shall lead Israel with joy with the mercy and righteousness that cometh from him.

I John 2:24
Let that abide, which ye have heard from the beginning. Confidence when he shall appear.

C   71
God's protection from youth to age.

Num. 20:14
Death of Aaron, succession of his son Eleazar.

II Tim. 1:3-14
Stir up the gift of God which is in thee by the imposition of my hands.

Key	*Psalms*	*First Lesson*	*Second Lesson*

TWENTY-FIRST SUNDAY AFTER TRINITY

Gospel: John 4:46[b]
[1]*Healing of the Nobleman's son.* [2]*He believed the word.*

G^2, E^2 25
I have put my trust in thee.

Gen. 15:1-6

Rom. 4:1-8

Abraham believed God, and it was counted unto him for righteousness.

G^1 30, 146
God's mercy to the afflicted.

II Kings 5:1-15[a]
The healing of Naaman.

John 4:46[b]
Healing of the Nobleman's son.

C   118
I called upon the Lord in trouble.

II Kings 6:8-23
Horses and chariots of fire about Elisha.

Acts 25:1-22
Paul before Festus.

TWENTY-SECOND SUNDAY AFTER TRINITY

Gospel: Matt. 18:21
Forgiveness. The Parable of the Great Vassal and the Fellow-Servant.

G   51
Wash me throughly from my wickedness and cleanse me from my sins.

I Kings 8:46-53
God forgives the penitent people.

Luke 7:36
Alabaster box. Two debtors. Her sins, which are many, are forgiven, for she loved much.

G   7
God is a righteous Judge.

Zech. 7:8
Punishment of those who refuse to show compassion.

Matt. 18:21
Forgiveness.

C   65
Blessed is the man whom thou choosest.

II Kings 9:1-6, 10[b]-13, 16-26
The revolution of Jehu.

Acts 26
Paul before Agrippa.

Key	Psalms	First Lesson	Second Lesson

TWENTY-THIRD SUNDAY AFTER TRINITY

Epistle: Phil. 3:17
[1]*Follow those who set good examples.* [2]*Our citizenship is in heaven.*

G, E² 33	Jer. 29:1, 4-14	Titus 3:1-8
Blessed are the people whose God is the Lord.	Seek the peace of the city whither ye are carried away captive.	Be subject to rulers, and ready to every good work.

G, E¹ 8, 138	*Isa. 64	Matt. 23:1-12
O Lord our Governor.— All kings of the earth shall praise thee.	Thou art our Father.	The Scribes and Pharisees sit in Moses' seat. One is your Father, who is in heaven.

C 23, 102:15	Deut. 34	II Tim. 4:1-8
The Valley of the Shadow. —He brought down my strength in my journey and shortened my days.	The death of Moses.	I have finished my course. Henceforth there is laid up for me a crown of righteousness.

TWENTY-FOURTH SUNDAY AFTER TRINITY

Epistle: Col. 1:3-12
[1]*We do not cease to pray for you:* [2]*for perfecting and perseverance: inheritance of the Saints in light.*

E² 66	*Mal. 3:13—4:3	Luke 10:17-24
Thou hast proved us, and tried us, like as silver is tried.	They shall be mine, when I make up my jewels. The Sun of righteousness shall arise.	Return of the Seventy. Rejoice not in the *charismata,* but that your names are written in heaven.

E¹ 20, 28	Ecclus. 36:1-17	I Tim. 2:1-8
Hear us when we call upon thee.—Hear my humble petitions.	Prayer for Zion the Holy City.	Intercessions for all men.

C 136	Joshua 23:1-3, 11-16	Luke 13:1-9
Résumé of Hebrew History.	Joshua's farewell. Take heed that ye love the Lord. Avoid the idolatry of the Gentiles.	The Parable of the Barren Fig Tree.

Key   *Psalms*   *First Lesson*   *Second Lesson*

TWENTY-THIRD SUNDAY AFTER TRINITY

Gospel: Matt. 22:15-21
The Tribute Money. Render unto Caesar.

E^1 19, 67

The heavens declare the glory of God.—That thy way may be known upon earth.

Ezek. 33:30

The word of the Lord is heard as a lovely song; they hear, and do not.

I Cor. 4:8-16

The Apostles spectacles to the world, to angels, and to men. Be ye followers of me.

G   72

All kings shall fall down before him, all nations shall do him service.

Wisdom 6:1-11

Rulers' power is given of the Lord, being ministers of his kingdom.

Matt. 22:15-22

Render unto Cæsar.

C   99, 100

The Lord is King.—We are his people.

II Kings 23:1-4, 11-14, 21-23

Josiah proclaims the Law, destroys idolatry, restores the Passover.

Acts 27:1-20, 27-32, 39-44

The shipwreck at Malta.

TWENTY-FOURTH SUNDAY AFTER TRINITY

Gospel: Matt. 9:18-26
The Ruler's daughter raised. Woman touches Jesus' garment. Thy faith hath made thee whole.

E^2 139

Lead me in the way everlasting.

Deut. 33:1-3, 26-29

All his saints are in thy hand. The eternal God is thy refuge.

Jude 1-4, 17-25

The faith once delivered to the Saints. Unto him who is able to keep you from falling.

G   86

Comfort the soul of thy servant.

II Kings 4:18-37

Elijah raises the widow's son.

Matt. 9:18-26

Raising of the Ruler's daughter.

C   73

It is good for me to hold fast by God.

II Chron. 36:11

The destruction of Jerusalem. The Captivity.

Acts 28:16

Paul arrives at Rome.

Key	*Psalms*	*First Lesson*	*Second Lesson*

THIRD SUNDAY BEFORE ADVENT   *See* FIFTH SUNDAY AFTER EPIPHANY

SECOND SUNDAY BEFORE ADVENT   *See* SIXTH SUNDAY AFTER EPIPHANY

SUNDAY NEXT BEFORE ADVENT

Epistle: Jer. 23:5-8
The Branch of David. A King shall execute judgment in the earth.
Return from exile.

S 39 Lord, let me know mine end.	Jer. 4:23 The whole land shall be desolate.	Matt. 25:31 When the Son of Man shall come: all nations to judgment. "Inasmuch."
G 145 Thou fillest all things living with plenteousness.	*Jer. 3:14-18 My pastors shall feed you with knowledge. All nations shall be gathered to Jerusalem.	I Cor. 11:17-32 The Institution of the Eucharist. Let a man examine himself.

| Key | Psalms | First Lesson | Second Lesson |

THIRD SUNDAY BEFORE ADVENT   See FIFTH SUNDAY AFTER EPIPHANY

SECOND SUNDAY BEFORE ADVENT   See SIXTH SUNDAY AFTER EPIPHANY

SUNDAY NEXT BEFORE ADVENT

Gospel: John 6:5-14
The Feeding of the Five Thousand.

S   90

So teach us to number our days, that we may apply our hearts unto wisdom.

Eccles. 11:9—12:8, 13-14
Youth and age.

Heb. 13:1-21
The God of peace make you perfect unto every good work.

E   103

The Lord executeth righteousness and judgment.

Isa. 25:1-9
He shall swallow up death in victory. We will rejoice in his salvation.

John 5:17-29
Judgment committed unto the Son of Man. The dead shall hear his voice, and live.

IX

ALTERNATIVE EPISTLES AND GOSPELS FOR WEEKDAYS

WE MAY note one further possible by-product of the new Lectionary, which is capable of affording a partial solution of a need which is somewhat acutely felt in some quarters of the Church.

The first rubric on page 90 directs that "the Collect, Epistle, and Gospel, appointed for the Sunday, shall serve all the Week after, where it is not in this Book otherwise ordered." Since our Calendar is very scantily provided with proper services for weekdays,[1] the result is that most of the time the same Epistle and Gospel must be read every day in the week, in churches which have a daily celebration.

The monotony of this procedure is obvious. It is perhaps chiefly responsible for the tendency of many celebrants to follow the Missals of foreign rites—undoubtedly much less for their own sakes, than to secure the spiritual refreshment of a greater variety in the use of liturgical Scriptures. It is likewise distinctly dispiriting to the congregation at a daily service, since there is little inducement to attend day after day a service which is identical in every word. Not only is this a burden in such places as seminary chapels: it is felt as an imposition at such special sessions as summer conferences, by persons who may be making their first acquaintance with a daily celebration,

---

[1] The movable observances which displace the Sunday service during the week are: Ash Wednesday, with the three following days; Ascension, with the two following; Holy Week; the two days after Easter and Whitsunday; and (optionally) the twelve Ember and the three Rogation Days. The Octaves of Christmas and Epiphany supplant the services of the previous Sunday on four to eleven days. There are twenty-five Fixed Festivals, and services also for Independence and Thanksgiving Days. Of Eucharists on these twenty-seven occasions, twenty-one to twenty-four will be celebrated on weekdays.

and find its sameness a discouragement to availing themselves of the opportunity for a more frequent communion.

In view of these facts, it may be of more than academic interest that the new Lectionary contains the materials for two complete sets of alternative Epistles and Gospels for every week of the Christian Year. Each Sunday lists at least two lessons from the Gospels, as well as several lessons capable of being utilized as, or in place of, a liturgical Epistle. Moreover, the underlying plan of the Lectionary was to select these lessons with direct reference to the Epistle and Gospel of the Day, in order to reënforce and develop the liturgical lessons with further treatments of their themes. Therefore it is perfectly practicable to derive from the assignments for Morning and Evening Prayer for each Sunday, two sets of liturgical lessons which are virtually equivalent in content and value to those appointed for that Sunday, and which would be perfectly appropriate to substitute for the Sunday lections on some of the days of the following week.

Furthermore, we have seen that the Epistles and Gospels for the Sundays of the year cover a somewhat limited round, and that we seized the opportunity to apply the corresponding lessons in many cases not only to illustrate, but to supplement the Liturgical Lectionary, with the result that the total provision for the Sundays has been made very fairly comprehensive of all the riches of Holy Scripture. If, therefore, we apply the Sunday lessons to a system of alternatives to the liturgical lessons on weekdays, we shall be doing something more than offering mere substitutes: we shall complement the deficiencies, and extend the adequacy, of the underlying Liturgical Lectionary itself.

Indeed, it appears that this particular application of the Lectionary material may serve to integrate its use in a helpful way. In a lectionary of free choices, it will probably be a long time before any user fully explores and appropriates all that it contains, particularly when few of our churches will use the lessons at more than one Sunday service.

Especially the parishes where Morning Prayer is not the principal morning service seem likely to derive a minimum of benefit from the greatly enriched provisions of the new Lectionary. Yet many of these parishes have a daily celebration: and it might be a real gain to make some of the best of the new material available to them in the form of alternative liturgical lessons for use on weekdays. For example, we have mentioned that practically the whole corpus of the harmonized Gospels has been apportioned to the Sundays, between the lections at the Liturgy and the Offices. A method which would bring the Gospel lessons from the Offices into the liturgical course would give a completeness of coverage of these Words of Life such as no Church has ever had.

In the working out of the following Table, it will be noted that the suggested Epistles and Gospels have been materially shortened from the corresponding lessons of the Sunday, and still more rigidly confined to a single theme. This is necessary, if they are to conform to the existing standards of length and treatment of the liturgical lessons, and if they are not to be felt as a burden in comparison with those for which they are offered as substitutes. Such standards of brevity were followed in the new alternative Epistles and Gospels listed in the English Book of 1928.

In some cases, the weekday Epistle and Gospel are correlated to a liturgical unity of thought, which may develop the theme of either the Epistle or the Gospel of the Sunday. In others, they are allowed to follow the same diverging lines as the liturgical lessons on which they are based.

Though every Sunday service is provided with at least one lesson from the Gospels, in the Trinity Season the assignment of the Gospel for the Day as the second choice at Evening Prayer is allowed in some cases to fulfil this requirement: hence an occasional substitution has had to be made in this period.

While the Second Lessons for the Sunday usually also provide two selections from the rest of the New Testament, available for use as alternative liturgical Epistles, in a few instances the inclusion of an additional lesson from the Gospels makes this impossible, and it has been necessary to assign a lection from the Old Testament as *For the Epistle*. In a few other cases the same procedure has been followed in order to secure a better balance and unity of thought. It will be remembered that the Prophetic Lesson embodied the first use of Scripture at the Liturgy, though in most cases it was subsequently eliminated to shorten the service, save in a few cases where the superior appropriateness of a selection from the Old Testament caused it to replace the Epistle. For such a system of alternative lections as is here suggested, where the aim is expressly to secure variety of treatment of their themes, it is actually advisable to make more of the distinctive passages from the Old Testament available for liturgical use.

In addition to this utilization of the Sunday lessons, I have listed in the Table a complete set of Epistles and Gospels suggested for the three Rogation and the twelve Ember Days, selected for their appropriateness to their respective Seasons.

The employment of the two sets of alternates for each week would naturally be at the discretion of the celebrant. One possible method might be, for example, in a week vacant of proper observances, to use the official Epistle and Gospel on Sunday, Wednesday, and Friday, the traditional Liturgical Days of the ancient Church; then the first alternate on Monday and Thursday, the second on Tuesday and Saturday. Such an alternation would secure a quite reasonable measure of variety, and at the same time would fully bring home the teaching of the week in its various aspects. The occurrence of proper observances during the week, or the requirements of particular congregations, might suggest a different pattern.

It will, however, be understood that there is as yet no authorization for the use of this material. It is presented here to show the possibility of such a project, and to serve as a basis for further study and suggestion, with a hope that it may further future developments in this direction.

Certainly there is a manifest need for a supplement to the Liturgical Lectionary, in order to extend its limited coverage of Holy Scripture, to enrich the relative poverty of the Anglican Calendar, and to vary the monotony of identical services throughout the week. This is shown by the Tables of liturgical lessons for optional use in the English Prayer Book of 1928, as well as by some current experiments along this line by the Youth Department of our National Council. The simplest way to achieve these objectives is to assign previously undesignated passages, in harmony with the Christian Year, for optional use at celebrations on weekdays. I have endeavored to show that this can be done by the liturgical use of material contained in the new Lectionary. The fact that it is thus practicable affords an interesting demonstration of how intimately and faithfully the Lectionary has been adapted to the teaching of the Christian Year.

PROPOSED TABLE
OF ALTERNATIVE EPISTLES AND GOSPELS
FOR WEEKDAYS

Week	Epistle	Gospel
FIRST SUNDAY IN ADVENT	Mal. 3:1-4 & 4:4-6	Luke 1:5-17
	I Thess. 5:1-11	Matt. 25:1-13
SECOND SUNDAY IN ADVENT	I Thess. 2:9-13	John 5:30-40
	Isa. 52:7-10	Luke 1:26-38
THIRD SUNDAY IN ADVENT	Jer. 1:4-10	Luke 1:57-66
	I Thess. 5:14-23	Luke 1:67-79
Ember Wednesday	I Cor. 3:5-11	John 4:31-38
Ember Friday	Isa. 11:1-10	Matt. 12:15, 17-21
Ember Saturday	Isa. 49:1-6	*Luke 4:16-21
FOURTH SUNDAY IN ADVENT	Isa. 40:1-11	Luke 3:2b-6
	Jer. 33:7-9, 14-15	Luke 3:7-9, 15-17
FIRST SUNDAY AFTER CHRISTMAS	Isa. 49:8-13	Luke 2:1-14
	Isa. 9:2-7	Luke 2:15-20
SECOND SUNDAY AFTER CHRISTMAS	II Cor. 4:1-6	Luke 2:21-32
	Col. 2:6-12	Luke 2:34-40
FIRST SUNDAY AFTER EPIPHANY	I John 1:1-7	Matt. 18:1-6, 10
	Isa. 60:1-9	Matt. 2:1-12
SECOND SUNDAY AFTER EPIPHANY	Rom. 9:20-26	John 1:35-42
	I Cor. 12:12-27	Mark 9:2-13
THIRD SUNDAY AFTER EPIPHANY	Rom. 14:10-17	John 4:5-14
	James 2:1-9	John 2:13-17
FOURTH SUNDAY AFTER EPIPHANY	Eph. 2:11-18	Luke 4:23-32
	Rom. 10:1-13	Mark 6:53
FIFTH SUNDAY AFTER EPIPHANY	Col. 3:5-11	Matt. 13:36-43
	Gal. 6:1-10	Luke 12:35-40
SIXTH SUNDAY AFTER EPIPHANY	II Thess. 1:3	Matt. 25:14-29
	II Pet. 3:8-14, 17-18	Luke 17:20-30
SEPTUAGESIMA SUNDAY	II Tim. 2:1-5	Matt. 5:1-12
	I Tim. 6:11-16	Matt. 21:28b-32
SEXAGESIMA SUNDAY	II Cor. 12:1-9	Matt. 10:16-23
	Eccles. 11:1-6	John 4:31-38
QUINQUAGESIMA SUNDAY	I John 2:1-6	Mark 9:25-32
	I John 4:7-15	John 15:9-17
FIRST SUNDAY IN LENT	Isa. 58:1-8	Matt. 6:1-6
	I Cor. 10:1-13	Luke 5:33-38
Ember Wednesday	I Tim. 1:12-17	Matt. 16:24-27

* Prayer Book assignment.

155

Week	Epistle	Gospel
Ember Friday	Eph. 2:13	Matt. 18:10-14
Ember Saturday	Gal. 6:1-10	Matt. 18:15-20
SECOND SUNDAY IN LENT	*Ecclus.* 51:8-12 or James 1:2-7, 16-17 I Cor. 6:9-12, 19-20	Luke 18:1-8 Matt. 5:27-37
THIRD SUNDAY IN LENT	I Cor. 3:16 I Cor. 3:9-15	Luke 11:29-36 Mark 8:31—9:1
FOURTH SUNDAY IN LENT	Exod. 16:4-15 II Cor. 3:12	John 6:31-35 John 6:47-56
FIFTH SUNDAY IN LENT	I Pet. 4:12 Hosea 6:1-6	John 10:17-18, 24-38 Luke 20:9-18
EASTER DAY	Isa. 25:1-9 Isa. 51:9-16	John 20:11-18 Matt. 28:1-10
FIRST SUNDAY AFTER EASTER	Rev. 1:4-8 Rom. 1:1-12	Luke 24:36-48 John 20:24-29
SECOND SUNDAY AFTER EASTER	Isa. 40:1-11 Phil. 3:7-14	John 10:1-10 John 21:1-14
THIRD SUNDAY AFTER EASTER	II Cor. 5:1-10 Acts 2:22-24, 32-36	John 14:1-6 Luke 20:27-38
FOURTH SUNDAY AFTER EASTER	Acts 3:13-21 I Thess. 4:13	John 8:12-16, 26-30 John 12:44
FIFTH SUNDAY AFTER EASTER		
Rogation Monday	*Ezek. 34:25	*Luke 11:5-13
Rogation Tuesday	James 5:16	Mark 11:22-26
Rogation Wednesday	Micah 6:6-8	Matt. 6:5-8
SUNDAY AFTER ASCENSION	Eph. 1:3-14 Eph. 1:15	John 3:16-21 John 17:1-10
WHITSUNDAY	Rom. 8:1-11	John 4:19-26
Ember Wednesday	Tit. 3:4-8	John 3:27-35
Ember Friday	Acts 19:1-8	*Luke 4:16-21
Ember Saturday	Eph. 4:11-16	John 15:1-8
TRINITY SUNDAY	I Pet. 1:1-12 Eph. 4:1-7	John 1:15-18 John 1:29-34
FIRST SUNDAY AFTER TRINITY	Deut. 30:11-16 Job 21:17-22	John 13:16-17, 34-35 Matt. 7:21
SECOND SUNDAY AFTER TRINITY	I Cor. 13 I Pet. 1:17	Luke 9:57 Matt. 24:32-42
THIRD SUNDAY AFTER TRINITY	Phil. 1:27—2:4 Jer. 31:10-14	Luke 19:2-10 Matt. 9:9-13
FOURTH SUNDAY AFTER TRINITY	Lam. 3:22-33 Rom. 2:1-11	Matt. 10:32-39 Matt. 15:1-9
FIFTH SUNDAY AFTER TRINITY	Prov. 3:1-7 James 3:13	Matt. 19:16-26 Luke 14:25-33
SIXTH SUNDAY AFTER TRINITY	II Tim. 2:7-13 Heb. 9:24	Matt. 5:38-42 Matt. 5:43

* Prayer Book assignment.

Week	Epistle	Gospel
SEVENTH SUNDAY AFTER TRINITY	Hosea 14 / Rom. 6:12-18	Mark 8:10-21 / John 15:12-17
EIGHTH SUNDAY AFTER TRINITY	Gal. 3:24 / Gal. 4:1-7	John 7:14-24 / Luke 10:38
NINTH SUNDAY AFTER TRINITY	Heb. 12:1-13 / I Thess. 4:1-8	John 8:1-11 / Matt. 5:27-37
TENTH SUNDAY AFTER TRINITY	Rom. 12:1-9 / II Cor. 4:7	John 8:25-36 / Matt. 23:34
ELEVENTH SUNDAY AFTER TRINITY	Job 5:8-18 / Rom. 8:26	Matt. 23:23-31 / Mark 12:38
TWELFTH SUNDAY AFTER TRINITY	Phil. 2:12-18 / Rom. 15:14-21	Luke 4:31-39 / Luke 4:40-43
THIRTEENTH SUNDAY AFTER TRINITY	Heb. 13:1-8 / Deut. 15:11-15	Mark 3:31 / Matt. 26:6-13
FOURTEENTH SUNDAY AFTER TRINITY	I Chron. 29:10-17 / Phil. 4:8-13	Luke 17:5-10 / Luke 13:24-30
FIFTEENTH SUNDAY AFTER TRINITY	Eccles. 5:10-15 / I Tim. 6:1-10	Luke 12:13-21 / Matt. 10:24-31
SIXTEENTH SUNDAY AFTER TRINITY	Isa. 12 / I Pet. 5:1-4	John 11:21-27 / Matt. 24:42-46
SEVENTEENTH SUNDAY AFTER TRINITY	II Tim. 2:19 / Mal. 2:7-10	Mark 10:42-45 / Luke 13:10-17
EIGHTEENTH SUNDAY AFTER TRINITY	Gal. 1:6-12 / I Tim. 3:14	John 7:37-46 / Mark 6:1-6
NINETEENTH SUNDAY AFTER TRINITY	Tit. 2:11 / II Cor. 13:5-8	John 5:1-9a / Luke 13:1-9
TWENTIETH SUNDAY AFTER TRINITY	Mal. 2:14 / Eph. 6:1-9	Matt. 19:3-9a, 13-15 / John 13:31-35
TWENTY-FIRST SUNDAY AFTER TRINITY	Rom. 4:1-8 / Isa. 59:15b	John 9:1-11 / Mark 11:22-26
TWENTY-SECOND SUNDAY AFTER TRINITY	I John 2:24 / I Kings 8:46-52	Matt. 18:15-20 / Luke 7:36
TWENTY-THIRD SUNDAY AFTER TRINITY	Tit. 3:1-8 / I Cor. 4:9-16	Matt. 23:1-12 / John 17:11-21
TWENTY-FOURTH SUNDAY AFTER TRINITY	Jude 17-25 / I Tim. 2:1-8	Luke 10:17-24 / John 17:15-23
SUNDAY NEXT BEFORE ADVENT	Heb. 13:16-21 / I Cor. 11:23-32	Matt. 25:31-40 / John 5:24-27

AUTUMNAL EMBER DAYS

Ember Wednesday	*Acts 13:44-49	John 3:11-16
Ember Friday	Acts 20:28-32	John 10:11-16
Ember Saturday	Rom. 12:3-9	Matt. 20:25-28

* Prayer Book assignment.

INDEX

Acts of the Apostles, in the Fathers, 31 f., 66, 80; in the Breviary, 36, 80; after Easter, 32, 36, 38, 40, 50, 66, 80; in Anglican Lectionaries, 37 f., 40 f., 44, 50, 80.

Ad libitum use of lessons, 33, 42, 52, 54, 86.

Advent, Gallican origin, 8, 17; dual meaning, 17, 39, 58 ff., 76, 78; Sundays privileged, 21; Isaiah, 37 f., 76; Revelation, 40, 79.

Advent Sunday, *see* Sundays.

Ætheria, 7, 62 n.

Agape, 71 f.

Alleluia, 62.

All Saints, 12, 68.

Alternative lessons and psalms, 30, 41 ff., 45, 50 f., 53, 60, 65, 72 f., 88, 93, 151.

Ambrosian Rite, 30.

Amos, 80.

Andrew, Feast of St., 12, 15 n., 21 ff.; determines Advent Sunday, 17; affected Gospel of Advent -1, 33, 70.

Anniversaries, 11, 32.

Annunciation, 12, 15 n., 21, 23, 30 n. 9.

Apocalyptic, 39, 59, 76 f., 79.

Apocrypha, 37, 67.

Appropriateness, 32, 37, 43, 49, 52, 65, 85, 87 ff., 151.

Armenian Rite, 30 n. 8.

Ascension Day, 6, 8, 15, 66, 68; precedence, 21, 24, 150 n.; Revelation, 40, 79; Acts, 41, 80.

Ash Wednesday, 6, 15, 30 n. 9, 64; precedence, 21, 24, 150 n.

Augustine, St., 31, 80.

Barnabas, Epistle of St., 29.

Barnabas, Feast of St., 12, 88; precedence, 21, 23.

Bartholomew, Feast of St., 12.

Benedictine Use, 36.

Birthdays of the Martyrs, 11.

Breviary, 13; Lessons, 19 n., 33, 35 f., 40, 74 ff., 80; Psalms, 85; influence on liturgical lectionary, 33.

Brown, Ray F., 2.

Calendars, annual, 3, 21, 90.

Canon of Holy Scripture, 26 f., 29 f.

Canterbury, Convocation of, 86.

Canticles, 28, 84, 91.

Cardinal Feasts, 23 n., 24.

Carmelite Use, 69.

Catholic Epistles, 9, 29, 33, 44, 70.

Chapters of Scripture, 36, 48, 54 f., 57, 74.

Charlemagne, 8.

Choice of lessons, *see* Alternative lessons.

Christian Year, system, vii, 4, 6, 13, 15, 19, 31, 38-41, 47, 75, 80 f., 87, 91, 93; origin, 6-10, 22; teaching value, viii, 5, 35, 45, 73, 88, 154.

Christmas, 8, 17 ff., 46, 58, 60.

Christmas Season, 19, 24, 60, 76, 78, 150 n.

Chronicles, 74.

Chrysostom, St., 31.

Circumcision, 11 n. 5, 12, 19.

Civil Year, 4, 13 ff., 19, 31, 37, 85, 87.

Clement, Epistle of St., 29.

Collect of the Day, 22 f.

Colossians, 79, 81.

Commemoration, 22 ff.

Common of Saints, 86, 88.

Common Sundays, 8 f., 32, 60 f., 67, 69.

Compline, 85 f.

Concurrence, 4, 22.

Corinthians, 80 f.

Correlation of lessons, vii, 45, 49, 52 f., 66, 88, 151.

Course-reading, 31 ff., 36, 40, 48, 61, 70, 74 ff., 93.

Cranmer, Abp., 12-15, 34 f., 36 f., 54, 74 ff., 85, 87.

Cultus-meals, 71.

Cyprian, St., 10.

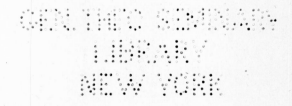